Eye of the Eagle

Luftwaffe Intelligence and the South Wales Ports 1939-1941

Eye of the Eagle

Luftwaffe Intelligence and the South Wales Ports 1939-1941

Nigel A. Robins

Nyddfwch

Copyright © 2025 Nigel A. Robins

All rights reserved.
First Edition 2024
Second Edition 2025

British Library Cataloguing-in Publication Data
A catalogue record for this book is available from the British Library
No part of this book may be used or reproduced in any manner for the purpose of training artificial intelligence technologies or systems,

Nigel A. Robins
Nyddfwch Publishing
16 Voylart Road
Swansea
SA2 7UA
nyddfwch@gmail.com

ISBN: 978-1-7393533-3-9

Acknowledgments

I'd like to acknowledge the help and support of many people over the years, both in my civil service work and academic circles. The many conversations over the years with my friend Dr John Alban have sparked numerous ideas and directions for research. The many museums and archives staff have been so helpful, particularly thanks to the United States National Archives and Records Administration (NARA) staff for my early research and the Royal Engineers Association members who generously helped me understand early bomb disposal activities in Swansea. My friends in Royal Navy intelligence sparked off many lively discussions. The U-boat specialists at the German Maritime Museum in Bremerhaven gave me insight into Bristol Channel minelaying. The errors and omissions that are here are, of course, entirely my own.

Friends at MOD Abbey Wood helped me understand intelligence practices, and the staff I worked with at GCHQ were invaluable in filling in the gaps in my understanding.

So many hours have been spent staring at aerial photographs or looking at the sites on the ground, and I cherish the patience of my wife Alison in accompanying me to docks, factories and U-boats while I waxed lyrical on what they meant (perhaps only to me I suspect).

Technically, many of the images were geo-referenced using QGIS, and I'm sure there will be much more to explore as I spend more time researching the landscapes of the post-industrial areas. Thanks to Rich Burkmar at the Field Studies Council for the help with QGIS tech.

Contents

Introduction

1. Understanding Intelligence and Reconnaissance 1920-1939   5
The German Air Force and Intelligence   6
The Crisis Moment: Munich 1938   10
Munich: For the British   11
Munich: For the Germans   14
Studie Blau (Study Blue) 1938-1939   20
Bombs and Targets   31
Bombs   34

2. The South Wales Ports 1933-1940   41
The Ports as Targets   42
The Ports at War   49
U-boats and the Mine War in the Bristol Channel 1939-1941   56

3. Reconnaissance over the Ports 1940-1941   67

4. Newport   75

5. Cardiff   87

6. Penarth   101

7. Barry   105

8. Port Talbot   117

9. Llandarcy (Swansea)   123

10. Briton Ferry   127

11. Swansea   131

Annexes   147
1. U32 Mining the Scarweather   149
2. The *Zielstammkarte* (Target Master) Document   157
3: Air-dropped magnetic mines   165

Index 167

Introduction

The first version of Eye of the Eagle was published in 1993. At that time, the research was to look at local landscape history, and British government aerial photographs were prohibitively expensive for such research, whereas, with a bit of effort, the Luftwaffe aerial surveys were freely available albeit via the record offices of the USA. As a geographer, my first instinct was to look for photographs and maps that give a first impression of a landscape before experiencing the land by walking. Since those days, a revolution in information sciences has changed so much. British record offices are far easier to engage with, and online and digital sources provide a wealth of resources and historical riches that were undreamed of in the 1990s. Combining the images with appropriate GIS/GPS systems has provided spectacular insights into ancient woodland and post-industrial recovery of land. However, what has not changed is the research and writing techniques that underpin our discipline. This book has been written several times, only to be rewritten when new sources become available or are revealed in the improved access or digitisation of various records. Some of the many images and sources you will see here were rescued from rubbish dumps as organisations sought to 'become digital' in the early 2000s by throwing away 'old' records. Which explains their rather 'worn' looks.

Although the landscape history of the Luftwaffe images remains my primary interest, I became increasingly immersed in why the images were taken, which needs an understanding of the air war over Wales in the earliest part of World War Two. In my early research into the 'whys' of the photographs and the air war, I realised that many books that we've relied on from the 1960s and 1970s were based on poor understanding of sources, assumptions in the face of missing evidence, and the very British notion of avoiding work in the German language, which is the primary source of almost all this work. Many British authors have tended to obscure their reference or source material, sometimes for commercial reasons and sometimes to hide the assumptions made. This is all the more noticeable in intelligence history, which I discuss briefly in the first chapter. If I am not confident about the quality or reliability of a book on the history of the air war, I have neither referred to nor relied on it. This means I have relied heavily on contemporary or near-contemporary reports and assessments made by British or German airmen or intelligence staff, and the reference sections of each chapter have those sources.

The more I sought to understand why the Germans attacked the Welsh ports, the more I realised I needed to understand the nature of military intelligence. My experiences as a Whitehall civil servant helped immensely, as did my occasional work with RAF, Navy, and Army staff on various topics. Being the token 'civilian' on various military projects was immensely useful for insight. I remain incredibly grateful to those military colleagues who patiently answered all my questions as I learned how to do things. Those insights were precious as I worked to understand how intelligence was gathered and the process of converting information into plans for attack and, in turn, assessing the outcomes of attacks. Many of the processes carry on unchanged today, and of course, the strategy of attacking civilians is always with us. I have spent some time explaining the background of intelligence gathering in the early chapters. This is because it mirrored my research approach as I worked to understand the relevance of the images, records or reports I examined.

Over twenty years, I have taught some of the book's subject matter in various University and adult education courses. Chapter Two and the annexes are responses to questions learners have asked me. I knew I was often on the right track when airmen from various air forces also asked me questions about the Luftwaffe's methods of investigation and weapons use.

For me, the star of the show remains the photographs. The port reviews have been a labour of love, and I have visited every location on numerous occasions. It is often a bittersweet experience to see the images of the Welsh ports in their finest hours and how they are today, gloomy, silted up expanses of water or struggling marina-type developments. The GWR ports of South Wales were as much a cultural as an economic phenomenon and have left milestones in our history and indelible traces in the people we are in Glamorgan. If my family weren't working in the Lower Swansea Valley, they were working on ships or in the port. In a rush to nostalgia about coal and the newly reinvented notion of Swansea's 'Copperopolis, it has been easy to forget that the ports of South Wales were ports of the Empire, gateways into Europe and access to the wider world. A true Global Wales.

Although born out of a horrible war against civilians (including the tragic loss of some of my own family in the bombing), the spectacular views of the Welsh industrial landscape that the Luftwaffe recorded are priceless. I regularly use the images in research on post-industrial landscapes, and people will recognise the images in the Cilfái trilogy of history books as part of the collection you see here.

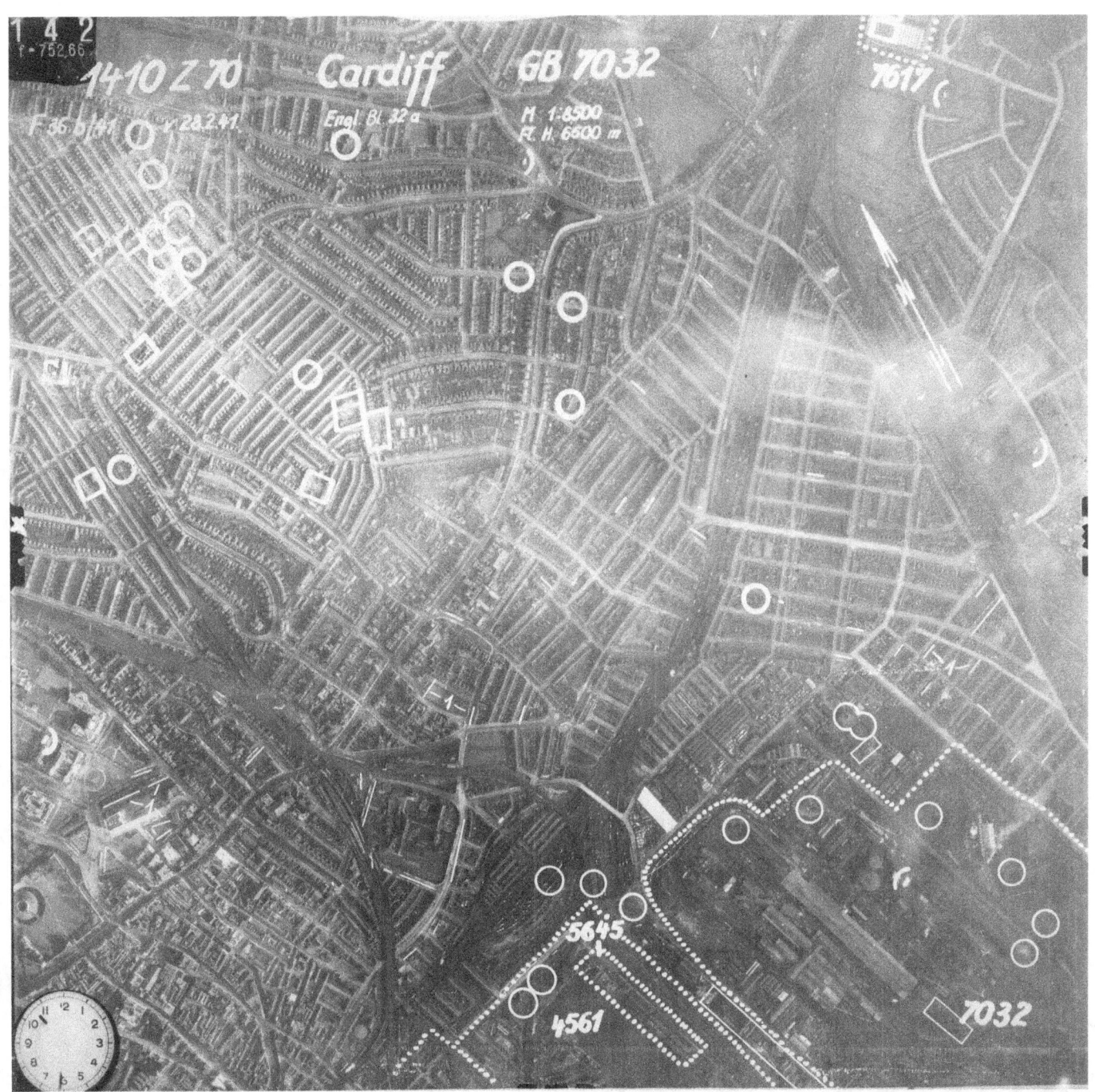

Left: The sand dunes at the mouth of the River Neath in February 1941. The route across the dunes to cross the river at low tide was a medieval route to cross the river at low tide.

Above: Bomb damage assessment in central Cardiff in February 1941.

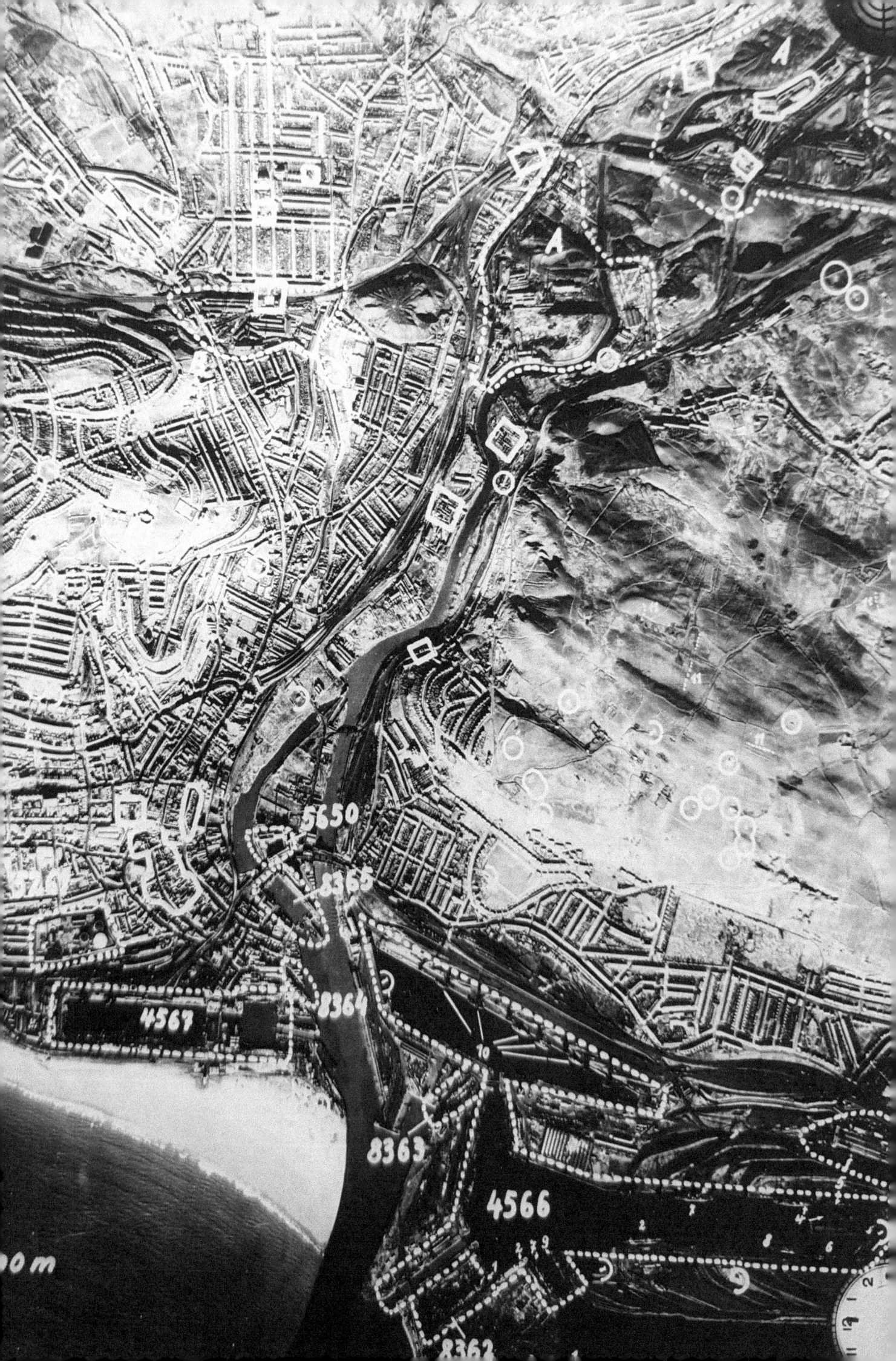

1. Understanding Intelligence and Reconnaissance

The processes of intelligence gathering is complex and complicated. Its history is challenging, and susceptible to assumptions, many of which can be misleading. It is worth some time looking at how the concept of 'military intelligence' was created because so much of what happened in wartime Wales was based on various military and government agencies' actions and knowledge (both certain and uncertain) throughout the 1930s. The clandestine nature of many activities and the lack of authoritative evidence about how information was collected leads to many assumptions that are sometimes unhelpful and sometimes wrong.

Interpreting the history of intelligence sources can be challenging because there are so many misleading sources and fiction (Watkins 2006: 13–14). The existing British and American secondary sources can vary widely in detail, rigour, and quality. The renowned airpower historian James Corum refers to the numerous myths about accuracy, tactics, and intelligence that have grown around studies of the German Air Force (Luftwaffe). He even talks of the struggle to get beyond the clichés that have driven many historians to inaccurate conclusions about the Luftwaffe and their tactics in the early 1940s (Corum 1997: 5–7). Intelligence history is susceptible to a certain amount of 'victory' bias, such as the British intelligence services being credited with quirky genius, often brilliant in their insights, versus the less-able Germans (Caddell 2019). There is a tendency to relate intelligence successes with brilliant flashes of insight. But the truth is often the reverse, with countless hours of routine and mundane work reviewing photographs, maps and other sorts of evidence (or more likely potential evidence) with intense intellectual rigour in the interpretation. The reality of intelligence analysis does not often make for exciting history. Victory bias is often accompanied by what Joseph Caddell describes as 'familiarity bias' where intelligence historians tend to favour their organisations and ways of working and find it hard to accept or understand there are other ways of working to get to the same conclusions.

A good example is the embedded myth that clever British photo interpreters used stereoscopic photography to get 3D views of the ground, whilst their German counterparts did not, meaning that Germans couldn't identify targets adequately (Caddell 2019: 82–84). A similar myth suggests the Luftwaffe did not make strategic investigations as they were only there to support their army, which is also wildly untrue (Corum 1997: 7–9). A recent history of intelligence warns

"It is all too easy for one to assume that the way things are done in one's own community or context represents inherent criteria for the task that must be echoed in every instance. This is perhaps the classic sense of ethnocentrism, but it might more usefully be thought of as the illusion of universality (Davies and Gustafson 2013: 4)."

So, understanding the strategic and geographic target selection processes that operated in the 1930s and eventually ended in death and destruction in Wales is challenging. Understanding the process is, I believe, important now as then because, in over twenty years of researching this subject, I have never discovered a single strategic or tactical benefit for the Germans in expending so much time and resources attacking Swansea, for example. The damage the Luftwaffe inflicted on Swansea was grievous; the effect of the bombing on Swansea's contribution to the British war effort was too small to be

Left: A portion of a Luftwaffe reconnaissance image of Swansea from February 1941. This image was taken in preparation for the three nights of attacks known as the Three Nights' Blitz 19-21 February 1941. Swansea had already been heavily bombed in 17 January but the three nights of raids were going to include larger loads of incendiaries to create firestorm conditions.

Left: Luftwaffe intelligence staff review aerial survey photographs with a variety of magnifying aids including stereoscopic viewers. These officers are in a large room at an airbase but frequently, officers were viewing material in tents and makeshift accommodation on airfields.

measured. I often doubt there was any impact whatsoever beyond the hundreds of ruined lives on the ground or in the air.

The intense effort made by the Luftwaffe in destroying so much of its documentation before final surrender in April 1945 led to a big hole in understanding what exactly happened during the air war and led to an intensive effort by the United States Air Force to reconstitute records and analyse the wartime actions of the Luftwaffe. The project lasted for twenty-seven years, with extensive reports and debriefings of every senior Luftwaffe commander they could find. Most of what we know about the German side of the early air war against Britain derives from these studies and monographs (Shaughnessy 2011). In most cases, the monographs produced under the project (the Karlsruhe Monographs are the closest to primary Luftwaffe sources that many historians can use, particularly for matters of strategy and the politics of the air war against Britain (Shaughnessy 2011: 103–6). In more recent times, we have also had the benefit of wider availability of the impressive research work of the Royal Air Force Air Historical Branch, which is often is often contemporary or near-contemporary with the events of World War Two.

The German Air Force and Intelligence 1920-1939

As aircraft technology accelerated in the early 1900s, the enthusiasm to attack civilians grew among many of the military men of the major European powers. Even before 1914, those men were constructing fanciful ideas about the mental fragility of an enemy's civilian population in the face of aerial bombardment (Biddle 1995: 95–97). The Germans believed the panic on London's streets during the 1938 Munich crisis illustrated the poor moral fibre of British citizens, the senior commanders of the British Royal Air Force held similar views in 1943 about German citizens (Gregory 2011: 253). In all of the bloody conflicts, Geographers would be used to help tell the airmen what to bomb.

The development of reliable aircraft and technology in the early 1900s signalled a change in the perspective of the landscape. Nineteenth-century war could mostly be envisaged and planned through two-dimensional maps and plans. But the new aircraft and cameras could provide a real-time bird's eye view of things. Battlespace changed from horizontal to vertical concepts of space. War became three-dimensional, and new air force departments were there to make sense of it all (Klinke 2020: 454–55).

Attacking civilians, their houses and workplaces became a reality in 1914. The German navy enthusiastically deployed Zeppelin airships against London in response to the British naval blockade of food supplies to Germany. The early Zeppelin target lists for England included electric power stations, not least because, theoretically, they could be readily identified from the air. However, this proved hopelessly optimistic considering the available bomb aiming and bomb fuse systems (Kuehl 1995: 237–38; Robinson 1980: 95). Nevertheless, as early as November 1914, the Zeppelins

> **20** A.R.P.
>
> and also from drums shot for a few hundred yards from trench mortars. How will they be used in air raids?
>
> **HOW AEROPLANES WILL DROP GAS**
>
> An aeroplane can drop gas in two different ways. It can drop a bomb full of a liquefied gas or of a solid which goes up in smoke when heated. Or it can spray mustard liquid from special apparatus on the wings. Suppose a one-ton bomb contains three-quarters of a ton of liquid phosgene. This takes up 6,000 cubic feet when transformed into gas. But one part of phosgene in 20,000 of air will kill a man in five minutes. So a one-ton bomb will poison 120 million cubic feet of air, for example a layer twelve feet high and covering nearly half a square mile. Of course, in practice the concentration would be greater in some places and less in others, and as the gas would rise higher than twelve feet in some places the area of serious danger at any given time would be less than half a square mile. Nevertheless twenty large bombers carrying two or three tons of bombs apiece could render the outside air of a good part of central London, or most of Sheffield, poisonous, so that no one could go out of doors without a gas mask.
>
> If there were any appreciable breeze most of this gas would be blown away in an hour or so, though the drifting gas-cloud might still be dangerous ten miles or more away.
>
> If the same amount of mustard liquid were dropped in bombs the effect would probably be less serious. For the liquid would be concentrated over certain
>
> **THE TECHNIQUE OF MASS MURDER 21**
>
> quite small areas, say 3,000 of them, if twenty bombers dropped 150 twenty-pound bombs each, and all the bombs burst. In this case if the air-raid wardens were efficient, almost everyone could quickly be moved into a gas-free area.
>
> If the mustard liquid could be sprayed evenly, things would be far more serious. All the outside air of a large town would be poisonous for several days. But this would only be possible if the spraying aeroplanes could fly to and fro over the town in formation, and at a height of not more than 300 feet or so. A fine rain of mustard liquid would probably evaporate on its way to the ground, or blow away, if it were let loose several thousand feet up in the air. Spraying from low-flying aeroplanes was possible in Abyssinia because the Abyssinians had no anti-aircraft guns and no defensive aeroplanes. It would probably not be possible in Britain.
>
> Bombs liberating poisonous smokes would let loose an amount of smoke far less than the amount of gas liberated by gas bombs. For it is necessary to heat the chemical which liberates the smoke. This needs a special device which must be solid enough to stand the shock of landing. So a large part of the weight of a smoke bomb must consist of metal, and from the killer's point of view, this metal is wasted.
>
> THE HAMBURG DISASTER. Fantastic nonsense has been talked about the possible effects of gas bombs on a town. For example, Lord Halsbury said that a single gas bomb dropped in Piccadilly Circus would kill everyone between the Thames and Regent's Park. Fortunately, although no gas bombs have been dropped

Above: The fear of terror bombing was very real, particularly as the images of destruction from the Spanish Civil War began to appear in European newspapers. The destruction in Spain was unimaginable in many European governments and the British government was slow to realise the potential impacts on populations, even whilst the RAF was busy planning terror-bombing scenarios for future enemies. The pages here are from a very influential book by J.B.S. Haldane written in 1938 after Haldane had visited Spain to view the carnage for himself. Haldane was concerned that the British population was unprepared and the Government rather blasé about the potential of death and destruction by modern bombing techniques. Although Haldane was concerned with gas and Civil Defence, his counterparts in Germany were more concerned about incendiaries and firestorms.

were lauded as wonderful 'terror weapon' (Tirpitz 1919: 271–72). It took the British a few years to consider the possibilities, but by late 1917 they had established a set of target areas around Cologne, Mannheim and Dusseldorf that were deemed suitable for attack by bombing. If the industries proved difficult to destroy, it was hoped that the ensuing death and destruction would influence the German people to discontinue the war by rioting and political upheavals (Biddle 1995: 92–93; Jones 1973: 130–202). Winston Churchill was a great enthusiast for terror through bombing in the closing months of World War One (Gregory 2011: 3).

Despite dreadful loss of life, and considerable expense, bombing industrial areas was not a decisive issue for any nation in 1918. The one major attempt by the Germans to create a firestorm in Paris in 1918 was aborted at the last moment through personal intervention by the Kaiser, he being unwilling to have his name associated with such barbarous practice (Marquard 1955a: 327). However, the incendiary bomb designed for the Paris attack would be the same one that would create so much havoc and destruction across Swansea and Cardiff in 1941. Despite a lack of use and results, sufficient wartime facts and figures were generated to allow post-war thinkers to draw any conclusions they wanted about intimidation and terror being powerful influencers (Gregory 2011: 251–52).

The 1920s saw a rash of military theories reviewing the new technologies and their application. The Italian theorist Giulio Douhet is often regarded as one of the first to speak openly of the merits of terror bombing civilians, albeit dressed up as attacks on 'housing' or 'areas' or 'capabilities' (Freedman 1994: 228–31). The selection of electricity generation, first identified by the German navy as a desirable target early in 1914, continued to be attractive to air force strategists throughout the 1920s and would feature prominently in the wars to come, even up to current times (Kuehl 1995: 238–39). Douhet's original ideas were repeated and amplified by airpower enthusiasts in other countries throughout the inter-war period, particularly Hugh Trenchard for the British Royal Air Force (RAF) and Dr Robert Knauss in Germany (Biddle 1995: 98–103; Murray 1983: 5–9). For these men, there was no longer any separation between the zone of actual combat and the homes of the civilian population, with the added excitement of using new technologies to deliver the destruction (Maier 2015: 34). In recreating a new offensive German air force in 1933, the Nazi government brought a new sense of focus to the theories of strategic bombing, putting South Wales firmly on the front line of future conflicts.

The development of air attack strategies created new demands for aircraft technology, navigation, bombs, fuses, and target identification and selection. The search for a strategic bombing strategy had begun. The influential German nationalist geographer Karl Haushofer prophesied in 1935 that advances in weapons technology were about to 'bury megacities and nations alike' (Klinke 2020: 454). But the question remained: how do you know what to bomb? One of the most prolific Luftwaffe strategic thinkers was Major Hans-Detlef Herhudt von Rohden, who was a complete convert to the geopolitical theories of Haushofer, particularly the concept of space (Lebensraum) and national security. Developing Haushofer's spatial arguments, von Rohden believed that the Luftwaffe was the nation's first line of defence and that strategic air attack was essential. Von Rohden pioneered the doctrine of 'operational air war', highlighting that the strategic bomber would become the primary weapon of a [future] conflict (von Rohden 1938: 10). It would be too much to say that von Rohden was an exponent of 'terror-bombing' such as Douhet or Knauss. Still, he more cautiously proposed that an air force had to be more than merely an army support service and be capable of attacking ports and industries as these were usually too hard to defend successfully. The destruction of vital factories, or important transport hubs would paralyse an enemy economy and there would be a consequential collapse of morale on the home front. Von Rohden's articles were interesting and popular in the military community, but they were heavy on theory and opinion and light on practical advice. What bombs? On what targets? How many targets? What industries? Which ports? These questions would weigh heavily on the Luftwaffe when they came to attack the Welsh ports.

It quickly became obvious that attacking another nation in a strategic sense, rather than a battlefield attack would require a mass of information, expertise and economic understanding. Most air forces were in the same position. Still, the German doctrine of 'lightning war' (Blitzkrieg) made the issue more challenging for the Luftwaffe, as strategic bombing would take time and resources, rather than a quick resolution. Consequently, the Luftwaffe never fully committed to a strategic bombing force, instead developing a set of aircraft and weapons that hopefully would be sufficiently flexible to do all the jobs that were required (Suchenwirth 1968: 168–71). When the Luftwaffe came to attack the South Wales ports, they had very little guidance on how to destroy the docks and port installations, relying instead on massive improvisation in both aircraft and weapons, often with poor results (Suchenwirth 1968: 169).

Intelligence gathering for a complex industrialised country like Britain or France was far from simple and took a lot of planning and research. Aerial reconnaissance was one of many sources used to understand the intricacies of a country's ability to conduct either defensive or offensive war. Radio stations, factories and industrial complexes, railway junctions, power stations, heavy lift cranes, and council offices were obvious items of interest. Even understanding the shift patterns for critical workers, locations of stockpiles of

Right: There was considerable shock at the extent of urban destruction. This photo of Barcelona was included in a book written in 1938 by John Langdon-Davies. His book entitled ARP included a series of images of bomb victims and the damage in Barcelona. Langdon-Davies described how the bombing raids occurred and the problems faced by civil defence and firemen. The book is still shocking as it describes the effect of high explosives on human bodies and buildings. He describes terror-bombing at its most potent. At the time of its publication in 1938, the British government was inclined to believe that the 'superior' moral fibre of British people would make such alarm unlikely. The panic and mass evacuations that followed the Munich Crisis later that year changed their minds considerably.

crucial resources, and crops in fields and forests were less obvious but equally significant. Specialist teams of geographers, geologists, and engineers of all kinds were quickly assembled to try and make sense of the mass of information received (Rose and Willig 2004: 201–6). By 1935, the evaluation of France alone contained lists of over forty thousand large and medium-sized factories (Nielsen 1955: 45–46; Deichmann 1955: 26–27). Even trying to understand Germany as a baseline for comparison was a challenge for the Luftwaffe intelligence teams; the 1934 Reich Defence Committee listings indicated Germany had some sixty thousand armament factories within the Reich and two hundred and forty thousand other businesses associated with strategic production (Deichmann 1955: 27). As Europe's oldest and most extensive industrial country, Britain would be even harder to comprehend.

A famous adage in the intelligence business is that 'wartime reconnaissance is based on peacetime intelligence' (Nielsen 1955: 7). For the Germans, this meant spending the early 1930s recreating most of what originally existed from their air force of 1918. Whilst the air forces of France and Britain had well-established policies, procedures, and equipment for aerial reconnaissance, the Germans had to start from the beginning. However, they were given a surprisingly good start with the clandestine activities of several entrepreneurial aviators who pioneered aerial activities using the Deutsch Lufthansa organisation, and aerial survey cameras and photography from the famous Carl Zeiss Jena firm (Vogler 2019: 221–25). Being close to the mainland of Europe, some of England's south coast had been photographed as early as 1927, but inspecting the Bristol Channel would require longer-range equipment (Nielsen 1955: 41). Between 1933 and 1936, the German Air Ministry and air force created an intelligence-gathering organisation to collect information on Germany's most dangerous potential enemies, France and Poland. It was only after 1937 that political tensions across Europe increased the likelihood that Britain could be an adversary, and Luftwaffe intelligence gradually made more effort to gather information about the British economy (Nielsen 1955: 32–36).

For decades the American and British film industries have created war films about World War Two that whilst entertaining have been notoriously short on facts. Getting back to facts and accuracy can often be challenging, particularly in the half-light world of intelligence. Reconnaissance and intelligence fit together closely, and people's lives would usually depend on the assumptions and conclusions made.

Swansea and Cardiff were both hammered by German bombing in 1941, the loss of life was awful, the damage terrible, the effect on the ports negligible. We need to understand why.

The Luftwaffe had an incredibly complex and sophisticated reconnaissance organisation. A renewed interest in the bravery and sacrifice of the reconnaissance units and their achievements is now underway with new evaluations of the work of the reconnaissance units emerging (Rabeder and others 2017: 6–21). However, the picture of the corresponding German intelligence services is very different. There were at least twelve major intelligence services in Nazi Germany. Some were run by the air force, others by the army, navy, Nazi Party, government ministries and others. The result was frequent confusion and duplicated effort. The air intelligence networks were some of the worst with at least eight separate intelligence collecting agencies for different countries, signals monitoring, prisoner interrogation and evaluation, and several research offices. All sides had similar organisations but the British and Americans ensured effective command and control of all activities in a structured and measured way. In Germany there was only one man in charge, Adolf Hitler. Some parts of the system worked well enough, for example, signals monitoring and radio traffic analysis was always good (Nielsen 1955: 17–18; Gottschling 1955: 114–21). In other areas, a dire lack of performance caused immense difficulties. For example, German technicians understood most of the British radar service, but evaluation and analysis of the systems and how they were being used by the British RAF was chaotic and dysfunctional (Boog 1997: 55–56). If the importance of the radar stations as a keystone of defence had been appreciated, they would have been relentlessly attacked until destroyed in 1940 (Boog 1986: 124).

The Crisis Moment: Munich 1938

The European crisis that developed from the border dispute between Nazi Germany and Czechoslovakia in

Above: A propaganda photograph from 1939 of young Luftwaffe technicians being shown a small reconnaissance camera. Nazi propaganda relied heavily on the premise that the Germans already knew a lot about its potential enemies because of spying and intelligence activities. It was partially true. 'Secret' bunkers and shadow factories built at Barry and Llandarcy in 1940 had already been identified and mapped even before they were camouflaged.

1938 quickly threatened to plunge the whole continent into war, and Britain would have been compelled to enter any hostilities on the side of France against Germany. By September, tensions were sufficiently high to create air raid false alarms and panic across southern England and parts of Germany. Europe was expected to be unavoidably embroiled in war by October 1938.

Some rapid, last-ditch diplomacy led by Britain and France led to a settlement with Germany at the end of September, essentially giving Hitler everything he demanded in an act of appeasement (Richie 1998: 477–81). France and Britain also got something they wanted, an avoidance of immediate war and a respite of twelve months which the British used well to prepare for the conflict, a point not lost on German intelligence assessors (Schmid 1939: 2). Both the British and German governments drew the same conclusion. War had been averted for now, but it was accepted that a conflict was inevitable. The first actions of both governments were telling: the Germans looked at how to attack Britain, and the British looked at how to defend themselves.

Munich - For the British

Whilst the Germans were busily assembling their intelligence capabilities for attack, the British civil service was starting to re-evaluate the role of the Bristol Channel ports in the future conflict. For an island nation that relied on merchant shipping for survival, the governments of the 1920s had not been particularly diligent in overseeing the British merchant shipping fleet or its ship repair and maintenance resources, and information about imports and how the ports worked was old, seriously outdated or based on vague assumptions (Behrens 1955: 18). At the same time that the Germans were calculating Britain's vulnerability to port attacks from Germany, the British Committee for Imperial Defence was commissioning similar investigations (Nielsen 1955: 60; Behrens 1955: 41). Both sides initially relied on assumptions based on the experiences of World War I, particularly after the 1917 U-boat war in the Atlantic. Still, the advances in aircraft technology in the 1930s quickly invalidated many of those beliefs, particularly modern aircraft's range and load-carrying ability. In the early 1930s, the Bristol Channel was believed to be largely immune to German air attacks because it was protected by the British air defence system, which protected against bombers originating in northern Germany. After evaluating the range and performance of the latest German aircraft, that 'comfortable' assumption had already been abandoned. In the summer of 1936, the British Air Ministry concluded that there was no further sense in thinking of 'safe' and 'dangerous' areas (Behrens 1955: 40–41). The South Wales ports would be significant targets.

The lack of information and knowledge was truly shocking. Clearly, various departments of the British government had no idea about how many ships would be available and how much food and raw materials would be needed should a war break out (Behrens 1955: 22–23). Half-hearted attempts to understand the true nature of British ports and shipping in the early 1930s were, after Munich, replaced by intense efforts to gain the right knowledge. The assumption that someone somewhere must know the handling capacity of the West Coast ports was seen as horribly unfounded in late 1938, as officials admitted nobody knew (Behrens 1955: 44).

The British officials needed somewhere to start as a basis for analysis and planning. Understanding the growing sophistication of bombing aircraft and technology was the start. It came down to one point: aircraft range. Although much was always made of German U-boats and surface raiders, it was air attack on the ports that was quickly identified as the main concern. An attack on a port could destroy dock facilities and ships simultaneously. The biggest worry was not suffering ship casualties on the high seas; it was the risk of losing cargo and ships whilst at port (Behrens 1955: 46).

At the same time in early 1938 that the British were worrying about this, General Felmy of Airfleet Two in northern Germany was being ordered to plan a British air attack strategy (Maier 2015: 44), the Air Ministry, thinking along the same lines, estimated that some 75 per cent of British shipping would have to be diverted from the southern and eastern ports of England into the Bristol Channel and Liverpool (Behrens 1955: 46). Converted into raw tonnage, the GWR ports of Wales

Below: Barrels of Canadian apples in a transit warehouse in Cardiff in the early 1930s. The Welsh ports were importing increasing quantities of food and other commodities as the Great Western Railway sought to replace lost income from the decline of coal exports. Food containers came in all shapes and sizes.

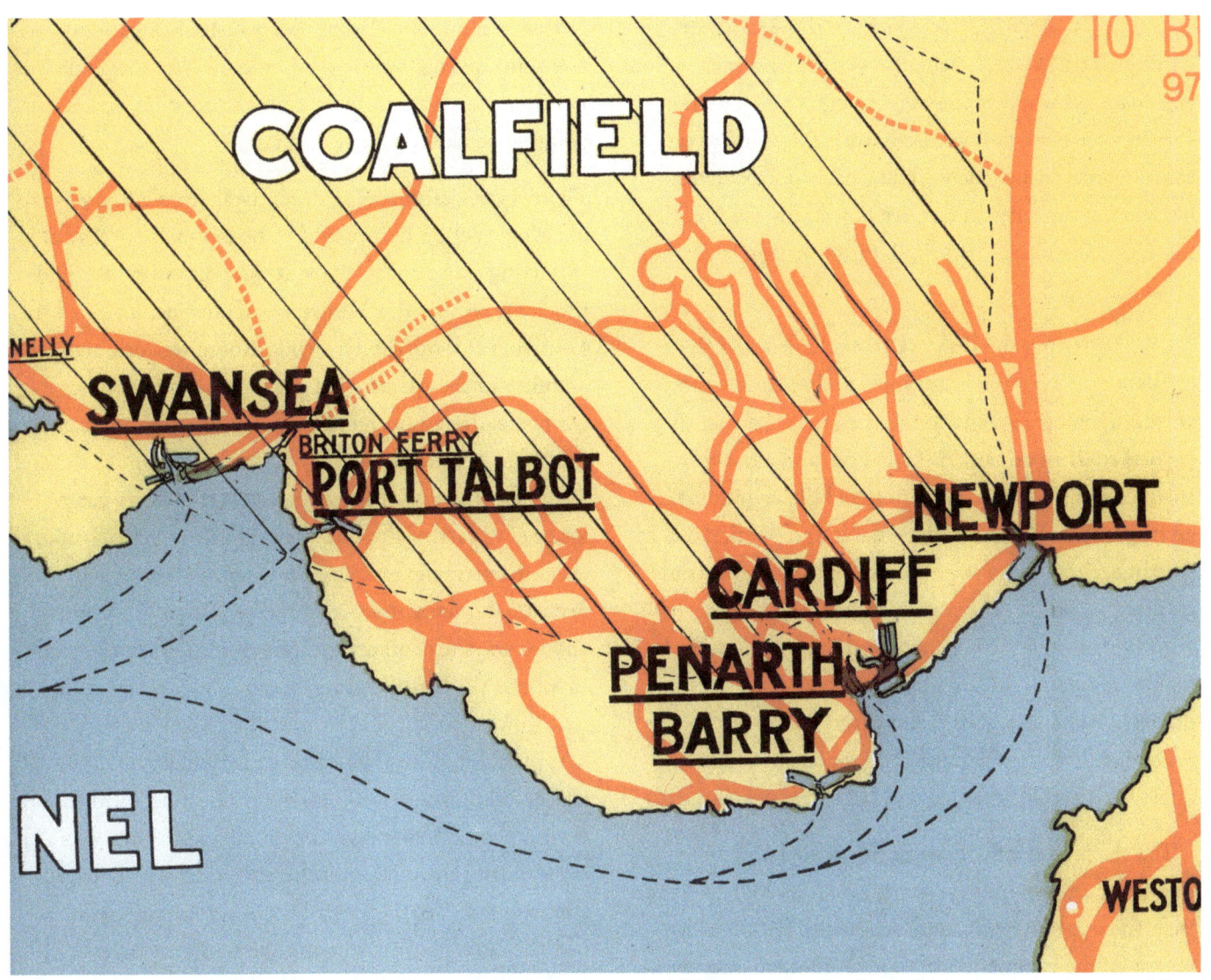

Above: A portion of a Great Western Railway poster from the early 1930s showing the South Wales ports and some of the intensive railway network linking the ports to the coalfields.

might need to handle a volume of tonnage that was eighty per cent higher than normal. Bristol, Cardiff, Barry, and Swansea would have to replace London for food import and storage—a massive commitment.

The notion of shipping diversion was not new. The U-boat wars of 1917-18 also forced the diversion of shipping into the Bristol Channel, thus avoiding risky transit along the English south coast. So, although actual statistics were vague, the notion of diversion was sound. However, the introduction of aerial warfare meant that while in 1916-18, the Bristol Channel ports were considered safe supply and storage areas, the ports in the 1940s would be completely open to air attack. Indeed, they would provide extremely rich targets for bombers, albeit hopefully protected by Midlands air bases and defences (Behrens 1955: 41).

In a move that could be considered prescient, the Committee for Imperial Defence looked at potential shipping problems in 1933. The subcommittee that was created eventually became known as the Headlam Committee, and it had a mission to explore and understand potential port problems. It was a quiet and unassuming start in 1933 for a committee that, despite an uncertain start, eventually contributed to Britain's resilience a decade later and facilitated many of the conditions for victory (Behrens 1955: 43). If the Headlam Committee had an exam question, it would certainly have been, 'How much can the West Coast ports handle?' A question unanswerable in the mid-1930s!

In an almost complete absence of meaningful statistics and analysis of what the West Coast ports actually did, the Headlam Committee staff did what the Germans did: they sought guidebooks, maps, tide tables and trade directories (Appleby 1933). A rough picture of tonnages, cargo types, and rail networks emerged from these open sources. The picture was incomplete and vague because nobody could envisage under what circumstances or conditions the diversions would occur or how big they would be. Assessments were made on how much quay space was available in each dock system, and speculation was made on whether this was enough to deal with a seventy-five per cent increase in traffic. Estimates on railway links and efficiency followed with calculations of carrying capacity. In fact, we now know the German intelligence agencies had similar information from the same sources.

Understanding the Bristol Channel Ports and their challenges in wartime was simply an impossible task, with one simple explanation. In peacetime, a coal ship carried coal, an oil tanker carried oil, and a tramp steamer would carry a cargo of steel billets, grain or anything else. It was understandable and predictable. In wartime, those same ships would carry whatever could be fitted in: an oil tanker with engine parts, a grain ship with fuel in cans and a hundred other mixed goods. In reality, it meant that ships arriving in Cardiff, Swansea, or Barry had a mix of different cargoes not seen in peacetime, which often meant chaos on the unloading quays, as we shall see.

The shock of Munich concentrated government minds on understanding the ports to a far higher degree than the original Headlam Committee. An intensive review of the experiences of 1914-1918 started to reveal insights into ship traffic, wharf and transit space and railways. Moving food alone from the Welsh ports into London and the Midlands would need 16 per cent more railway traffic via the Severn Tunnel and Gloucester. Replacing storage in London would require the ports to hold at least a million tons of commodities in covered storage (Behrens 1955: 47). This would require massive rebuilding of Swansea, Barry, Newport and Cardiff transit warehouses. However, as nobody knew exactly how much to build, very little was built, resulting in open-air storage, which caused severe problems, as we shall see.

The six months after Munich saw a frenzy of activity in the Ministry of Transport as various committees fought to understand statistics, logistics and the experiences of the Great War. One interesting conclusion by January 1939 (and most likely reviewed a year later) was that it was impossible to precisely understand the need for storage and transit space in the ports until the problems emerged. It was too complex a problem to analyse (Behrens 1955: 49). There was another more ominous conclusion: it would be enormously complex and difficult to feed and re-equip Britain for a sustained war with Germany, particularly if the Germans had a large fleet of U-boats, a capable air force, and surface warships. it was going to be close.

However, despite being deceptively simple, there was one single action that proved to be uniquely successful in managing some of the chaos at the ports when the real problems began. The Ministry of Transport invented the Diversion Room. The Diversion Room was originally an office in the Ministry of Transport. The committee members, drawn from experienced dock managers and merchant seamen, met every day at 10.00 a.m. to the end of the war in 1945. Their data was lists of every cargo load being carried by ships coming across the Atlantic, every departmental request on where the cargo was needed, and daily reports on the condition of the ports and railways (e.g. air attack, rail problems, choked with supplies). With all this information, ships nearing the British west coast could be routed to whatever port was best placed to unload as quickly as possible. It was an ad hoc solution that was extremely effective. Whilst nothing could solve the acute problems within the GWR ports during the crisis months, it worked well enough (Behrens 1955: 51). Ironically, and accurately as it turned out, the Nazi government and the senior members of the Luftwaffe were warned in July 1939 that one of the most overwhelming and dangerous capabilities of the British government was an ability to improvise things such as the Diversion Room. Economic experts made the point to emphasise the contrast with the German Nazi economy, which was inflexible and slow to direct and react. The Germans probably thought that was a minor point then, but it would haunt them throughout the conflict (Nielsen 1955: 63).

Munich-For the Germans

As with the British, the Germans saw Munich as a tipping point about Britain as a potential enemy. Adolf Hitler originally perceived Britain as a potential political problem as early as 1935 when he publicly expressed doubts about Britain standing by if Germany launched a campaign in the east to restore old borders in Poland (Maier and others 1991: 41). Even so, as late as 1937, Britain was not regarded as a potential adversary for serious conflict, with only minor consideration in early

Above: Generalleutnant Joseph "Beppo" Schmid with his staff in 1940. Schmid commanded the Luftwaffe's Military Intelligence Branch in the early years of the war. Schmid and his staff frequently produced the intelligence reports of Luftwaffe operations and activities during the attacks in the Battle of Britain and the attacks on the ports. He was a close friend of Hermann Göring which explains why his distinct lack of ability in the role never prevented him from being influential in German intelligence circles. Schmid was responsible for inventing huge numbers of RAF fighter losses that had massive negative effect on Luftwaffe planning as Adolf Galland observed after the war (Galland 1953: 16). Galland also complained that Schmid did nothing to improve the poor organisation of Luftwaffe intelligence services during 1940.

attack or defence planning (Maier and others 1991: 42). Things began to change in November 1937, when Hitler was weighing up alternatives for conflict with Czechoslovakia. In most evaluations, some form of intervention from Britain was thought unavoidable. By early 1938, the concern had developed into a need for a firm defensive plan against British air attack, which for the Luftwaffe usually meant forming an attack plan of their own. The closest Luftwaffe air group to the British mainland was the Second Air Fleet based across northern Germany. The commander, General Helmuth Felmy, was ordered to create a battle plan (Maier and others 1991: 44). It must have been a sobering moment because there was hardly any information about what to attack. Although German intelligence agencies had started to create target information for potential enemies as early as 1935, the emphasis was on countries adjacent to German borders (Nielsen 1955: 41). Information on Britain was mainly Ordnance Survey maps, tide tables, and tourist guides. In fact, very similar to the information the British Ministry of Transport held about the same ports and installations. Based on the evolving Luftwaffe strategic doctrine, General Felmy's staff drew up a list of port installations around London, armaments factories, and army installations on the English south coast. Woefully inadequate.

By April 1938, the lack of knowledge about Britain as a potential enemy was causing concern. The publication of Felmy's attack plan confirmed that there wasn't an attack plan at all. Britain suddenly became a focus of special interest for Luftwaffe planners in seminars and conferences. In an absence of quality information, vague suggestions of attacks on 'import harbours', oil storage and grain silos and cold stores were made (Maier and others 1991: 44). No suggestions of 'how' or 'why' could be made. Felmy confirmed the lack of preparation for any strategic bombing against Britain. He went further, stating that even his preparations for an air offensive across the North Sea were totally inadequate (Murray 1983: 19). The chaotic state of German intelligence

Right: Professor Heinrich Steinmann in a photo from the 1930s. Steinmann flew in the First World War, surviving a number of missions between mid-1917 and the end of the war in November 1918. After the war he returned to education and continued to build up an impressive collection of electrical and engineering qualifications. He also continued his aviation experience with several appointments in military aviation in the Weimar Republic.

A committed Nazi, he joined the National Socialists in 1932 (Nr 1058571). His technical knowledge was immensely valuable to the creation of the early Luftwaffe organisation, and he worked on airbase design and development.

Between 1923 and 1925, he worked as a Geographer specialising in Transport Geography and electricity networks. Steinmann firmly believed that destruction of electricity networks would deal the 'knock out blow' to the important war industries of any enemy, although he was thinking specifically of France and Poland at the time . After 1938, he led the investigation into the Welsh electricity network and is most likely the main instigator for attacks on the Bristol Channel ports. Swansea and Cardiff would have been much more intensively bombed in the Spring of 1941 if Steinmann had been able to promote his strategies with Luftwaffe senior staffr

Steinmann's work for *Studie Blau* on electricity networks was eventually published as a map and a series of power station targets across Wales. The map lower right shows Steinmann's reconstruction of the Welsh main electricity network from 1939. Swansea has two power stations, the original Strand power station from the early part of the century and the larger, modern station at Tir John North. Steinmann's plans for strategic bombing of electricity networks were eventually accepted in early 1943, but the targets were Russian power plants using 'Fritz-X' radio-controlled glide bombs. The planned raids never took place as the military situation in Russia prevented the missions going ahead.

Below is Tir John North from the *Militärgeographische Einzelangabe, the* guidebook on Welsh military targets produced as an output from *Studie Blau* in 1940-41.

The photo opposite (upper right) is the Luftwaffe target image of Tir John (Target No. GB 50 56) from the Luftwaffe *Zielstammkarte* (Target Master Map) from the Luftwaffe target library. (Author's collection).

GB 7, BB 26, Nr. 16: Tir John North Kraftwerk in Swansea (Glamorganshire).
Leistung 120 000 kW, wird auf 240 000 kW ausgebaut. Eines der Hauptwerke für die Stromversorgung von Südwales.

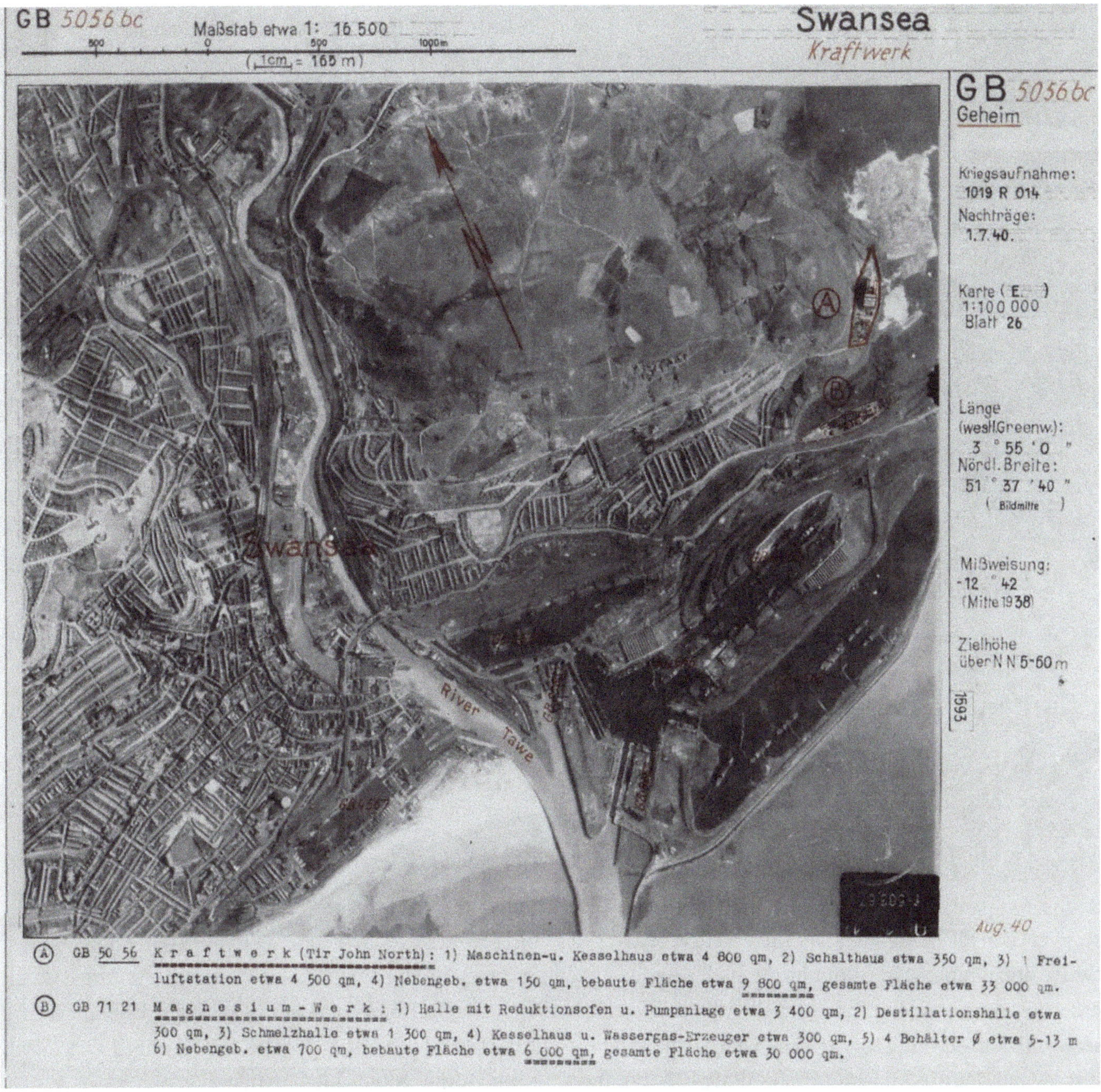

GB 5056 bc
Maßstab etwa 1: 16 500
500 0 500 1000m
(1cm = 165 m)
Swansea
Kraftwerk
GB 5056 bc
Geheim
Kriegsaufnahme:
1019 R 014
Nachträge:
1.7.40.
Karte (E.)
1:100 000
Blatt 26
Länge
(westl.Greenw.):
3 ° 55 ' 0 "
Nördl. Breite:
51 ° 37 ' 40 "
(Bildmitte)
Mißweisung:
-12 ° 42
(Mitte 1938)
Zielhöhe
über N N 5-60 m
1593
N
A
B
Swansea
River Tawe
Aug. 40

Ⓐ GB 50 56 Kraftwerk (Tir John North): 1) Maschinen-u. Kesselhaus etwa 4 800 qm, 2) Schalthaus etwa 350 qm, 3) 1 Freiluftstation etwa 4 500 qm, 4) Nebengeb. etwa 150 qm, bebaute Fläche etwa 9 800 qm, gesamte Fläche etwa 33 000 qm.

Ⓑ GB 71 21 Magnesium-Werk: 1) Halle mit Reduktionsofen u. Pumpanlage etwa 3 400 qm, 2) Destillationshalle etwa 300 qm, 3) Schmelzhalle etwa 1 300 qm, 4) Kesselhaus u. Wassergas-Erzeuger etwa 300 qm, 5) 4 Behälter Ø etwa 5-13 m 6) Nebengeb. etwa 700 qm, bebaute Fläche etwa 6 000 qm, gesamte Fläche etwa 30 000 qm.

EBBW
VALE
LYDNEY
17,5
17,5
LLANELLY
NEATH
SWANSEA
TIR JOHN NORTH
60
UPPER
BCAT
123
NEWPORT
29,2
ARDIFF
35,4
PORTISHEAD
140
BRISTO
34,7
NESTON-SUPER-
MARE
BAT

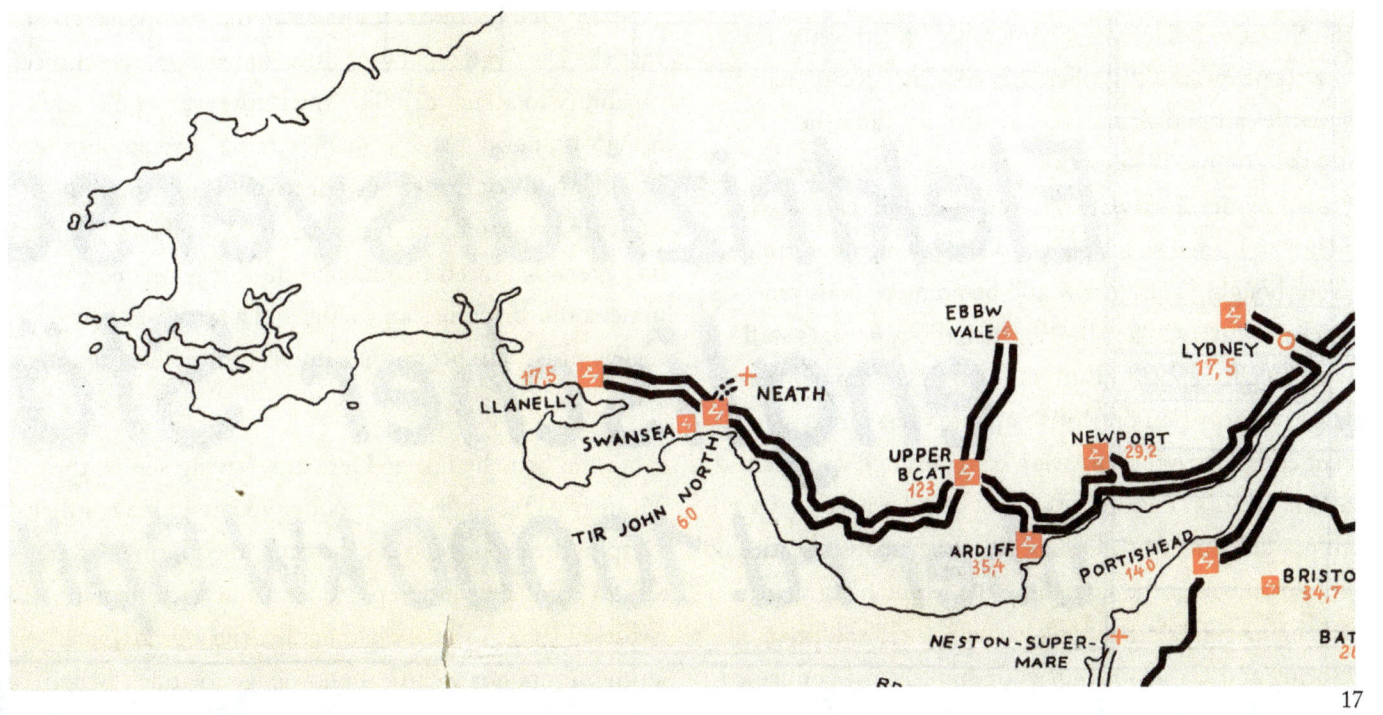

Left: A propaganda photo of Luftwaffe bomber crews at a target conference in 1939. The table is covered in documents from the Military Intelligence packs (*Militärgeographische Angaben* and *Enzelangaben*) and photo packs from the Luftwaffe *Zielstammkarten* (Target Master Maps). There were considerable amounts of information on France and Poland but Britain was not so well covered. The development of bombing attacks on the British Isles from August 1940 meant that the burden of intelligence gathering moved from the Army's military geography unit in Berlin to the long-range reconnaissance groups of the Luftwaffe. This meant that photographic intelligence largely replaced the target maps and geographical details collected in 1938-1940. Photographs were frequently assembled into photo mosaics which provided real-time information on the ground but required much more experienced interpretation of the landscape.

A good example of the challenge facing Luftwaffe planners is shown opposite with a view of Dowlais integrated steelworks (top of the photo) from 28 February 1941. The steelworks is huge and deciding which buildings are crucial to the manufacturing process of steel components requires specialised industrial knowledge. This is why electricity was often targeted as it was easier to understand. Many of the bombs dropped on Cardiff hit Dowlais but rarely resulted in effective damage, and the use of incendiaries or small bombs on such a massive target was pointless. See also the image on page 21.

services didn't help the situation. there were at least twelve organisations, some run by the Nazi party and others by various agencies and armed services. The inter-service rivalry was rife, and agencies weren't allowed to discuss and share information (Boog 1986: 121–25). By May 1938, the German Navy was sufficiently clear on the threat to hold a major conference on Britain as the 'main enemy', but this obviously concentrated on naval activities around Britain's coasts (Maier and others 1991: 46). By August 1938, with tensions escalating on the Czech border, Luftwaffe High Command instructed Felmy to formalise his plan and allocate bomber groups, even though the attacks would be no more than 'pinpricks' (Murray 1983: 18–19). Incredibly, Felmy's staff were able to report to Luftwaffe High Command that target information on British airbases was ninety per cent complete and maps 'were being printed' (Maier and others 1991: 49). Probably an easy task because they were all marked on British Ordnance Survey maps. At the end of September, at the same time the Munich Agreement was being signed, in a frank exchange with Herman Göring and his senior Luftwaffe staff, Felmy confirmed

his aircrews had little training in over-water operations or attacking shipping (at sea or in ports), and there wasn't even an effective meteorology service for the bombers. Attacks on [Britain] were ruled out (Corum 1997: 257). Even Göring couldn't ignore that.

So, by October 1938, it was clear and highly secret that the Luftwaffe had very little knowledge or technical capability to attack Britain. Any future war would rely heavily on naval forces as map exercises throughout the summer had confirmed the effectiveness of dropping mines in estuaries and port areas. by November, Göring had been convinced that a huge effort was needed to understand Britain as an enemy and a target. A new review of Britain began the famous Study Blue (*Studie Blau*).

So, the British and the Germans, having signed the Munich Agreement, were poorly prepared for a conflict. Despite the propaganda at the time, the Germans were almost completely unprepared for a war with Britain (Murray 1983: 18). they had neither the aircraft, ammunition, nor technical knowledge to attack Britain.

They wouldn't have known what to attack. Equally, the British had very little idea how to defend themselves. Admittedly, RAF fighters such as the Hurricane and radar-controlled command structures promised a lot. Still, none of that would matter without understanding the ports and how to import food and supplies into the country. Both sides worked hard to plan what to do next, which involved obtaining as much information and intelligence as possible.

Studie Blau (Study Blue) 1938-1939

The shock of Munich and the blunt assessments of General Felmy about Luftwaffe knowledge and capability forced German intelligence agencies into a different mindset, albeit temporarily. Whereas intelligence assessments on France or Poland reflected ideas of 'knock-out' blows or lightning wars and actually reflected reality and experience in 1939-40, Britain was different and a new approach to understanding the enemy emerged. Study Blue (*Studie Blau*) was a different approach because it was strategic, technical and measured. It was comprehensive and based on the views of economic and industry experts. This is when the Germans began to understand how Britain worked and locally, the significance of the GWR ports.

Study Blue was the document that analysed Britain, identified its strengths and weaknesses and provided the blueprint to attack the British Army, Royal Navy, Royal Air Force, British civilians and everything needed for Britain to defend itself or wage war on Germany.

Study Blue is a `familiar document in intelligence history circles (Boog 1986: 124; Corum 1997: 258; Maier and others 1991: 55). This is all the more interesting because it no longer exists. Only five copies of the document were prepared, and all were destroyed because of what they said about Britain and the likelihood

Left: An over the shoulder view of a bomb aimers training machine from 1940. The staff are learning the layout of a large urban area and how it looks from a preferred bombing altitude. The subject area looks to be a part of London.

The trainees are being taught how effective parachute flares are for illuminating the blacked out streets. Although crews were encouraged to use their electronic devices to control their bomb attacks, many crews preferred to drop their bombs using visual confirmation of the target. This wasn't possible for crews arriving later in the attacks as smoke would frequently obscure the aiming points. The cloudy weather of the winter of 1940-41 also hindered accuracy. Consequently, crews arriving later in air attacks often dropped their bombs on the fires they could see. The British capitalised on this habit by creating hundreds of dummy bomb sites around urban targets which were set alight after the first wave of raids had visited. These sites (codenamed 'Starfish') were effective in Cardiff, Bristol and Portsmouth, and attracted many bombs from aircraft arriving later in the attacks.

The sight of parachute flares drifting down over the ports was often the first sign that bombs were about to fall.

Above Right: The Dowlais steelworks as depicted in the *Militärgeographische Einzelangaben* from 1940. A difficult target to attack which required special bombs of larger size and hardened casings to penetrate concrete walls and floors. Incendiaries were practically pointless against a steelworks. There was also a need to attack at a lower altitude to increase accuracy. The presence of a couple of barrage balloons would frequently discourage crews from flying al lower altitudes.

GB 7, BB 32, Nr. 102: Dowlais Stahlwerke in Cardiff.
Luftbild der Eisen- und Stahlwerke Guest Keen Baldwins Iron & Steel Co. Ltd. (Dowlais), ostwärts vom Bute Dock gelegen. 47 ha Ausdehnung: Stahl- und Walzwerk, eigene Kokerei, 6 SM-Öfen; Erzeugung: 7000 t Koks, 9000 t Roheisen, 10 000 t Rohstahl; Herstellung von Maschinenteilen, Panzerplatten, Flugmotorenteilen. 1939: 6000 Arbeiter.

of success if Germany were to enter a war. It is an interesting story because it shows how vague political desires eventually get translated into lethal military actions. It was true then and remains true today.

There is enough material surviving to reconstruct much of what Study Blue contained. The process of creating the study shows how geography, economics, history, politics and desire for conquest came together in the months before the war began. It also helps to understand why things happened as they did. If the question 'Why' is hard, the answer 'Because' can be even harder. Here's the story.

General Felmy's frank admission that effective air attacks on Britain were impossible as late as September 1938 may have been a shock. The recognition that information and interpretation on the nature of Britain as a potential adversary was non-existent or poor was a big step for the fledgeling German Air Force. The Luftwaffe leadership, including senior Nazi party leaders, realised that the 'unknown unknowns' of Britain needed to be urgently clarified.

In common with all the other European intelligence services at the time, the Germans quickly found themselves swamped with a mass of intelligence, some secretly obtained, but most from open sources such as newspapers, guidebooks and journals. Whilst secret information was often highly prized, open-source information was more valuable for economic warfare. Open-source information could be derived from newspapers, radio broadcasts, tourist guides, postcards and financial journals. Information could be validated and verified quickly by reviewing diverse sources. The British newspapers were considered a rich source of information because of their traditional lack of regard for secrecy or national security. However, the transcripts of debates in the British Parliament, freely available via Hansard, proved equally valuable in providing detailed

Left: Hermann Göring with Hans Jeschonnek who was Luftwaffe Chief of Staff 1939-43. This photo dates from 1939 shortly after Jeschonnek's promotion. This was at the time when Göring was presented with the unpalatable news about how hard it would be for the Luftwaffe to overcome the RAF and British air defences. Even the sycophantic Jeschonnek was unable to dress up the bad news. Jeschonnek was an able staff officer with a lot of experience in air operations. He was not an effective leader and often came into conflict with the more experienced officers such as Albert Kesselring and Hugo Sperrle, who were both highly competent and experienced. Sperrle in particular was highly effective and ruthless in the administration of his bomb group which led the attacks on the Welsh ports. Jeschonnek never really understood the potentials and limitations of airpower. He hero-worshipped Hitler and went along with the ludicrous proposal that all bombers should be dive bombers, thus ensuring that the Luftwaffe would be severely hindered by a lack of heavy bombers. Jeschonnek also believed there was little need for long-term reserves of pilots or resources. He eventually committed suicide in 1943.

Below: A portion of the full telecommunication network of the British Isles as mapped by the German experts as part of *Studie Blau* in 1938 and 1939. This mapping included telephone, telegram and radio networks. Radar installations were also mapped although the full significance of Radar as a vital early warning tool was not fully appreciated by Luftwaffe Radar technicians. The missing link was how the information about distance and direction could be successfully linked to operational air manoeuvres in real-time. In this plan, the importance of telephone hubs in Cardiff and Swansea further highlighted their importance in communications networks (Marked with a 'V;). Merthyr Tydfil and Carmarthen were also important second rank telephone exchanges. The telecommunications link to Ireland and the USA from Weston Super Mare was also mapped.

The locations on this map did not automatically translate into aerial bombing targets as buildings and the installations could be small and not regularly displayed on Ordnance Survey maps. For example, Swansea's telephone hubs in Pier Street and Gower Street were never identified as targets, and both buildings survive to this day.

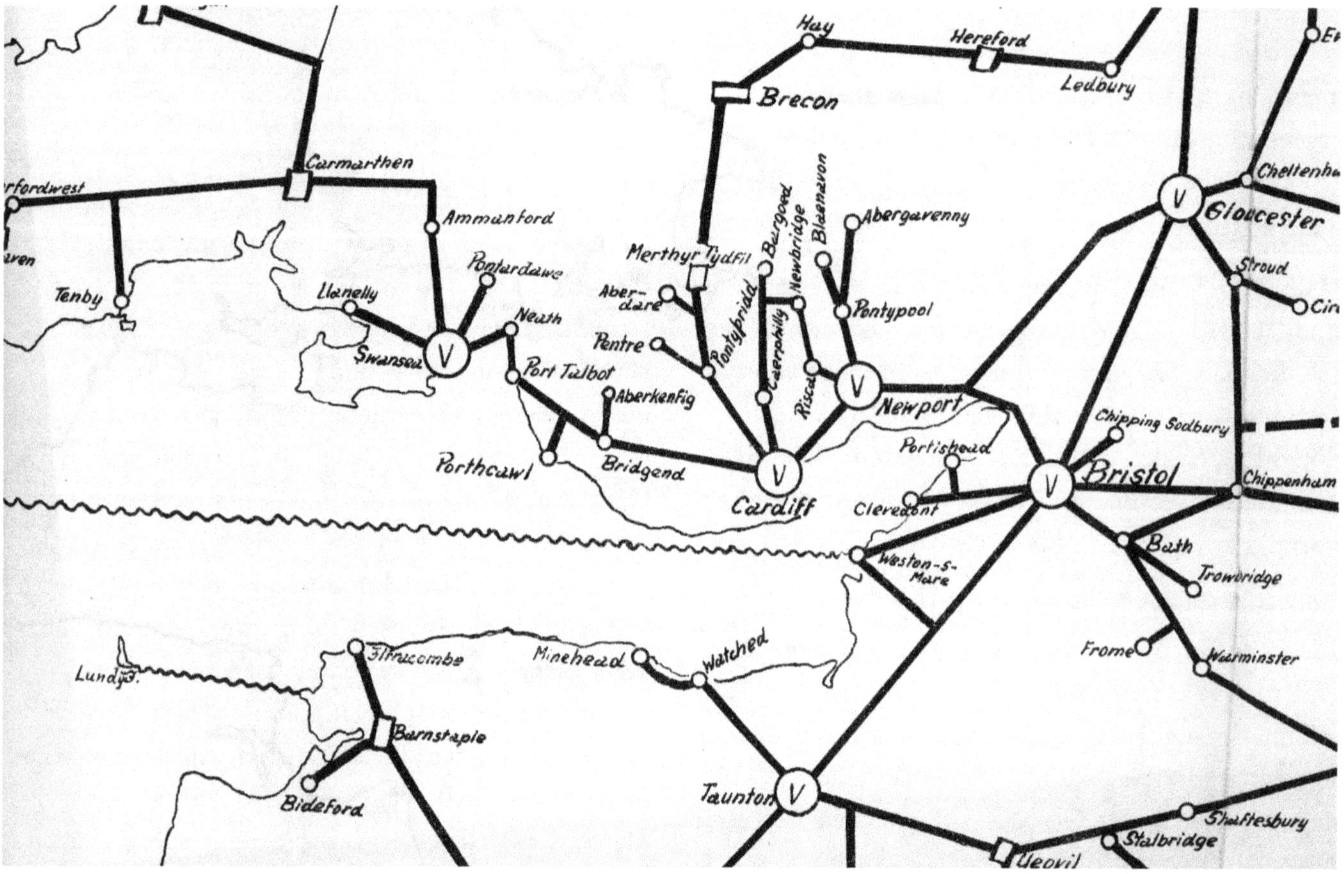

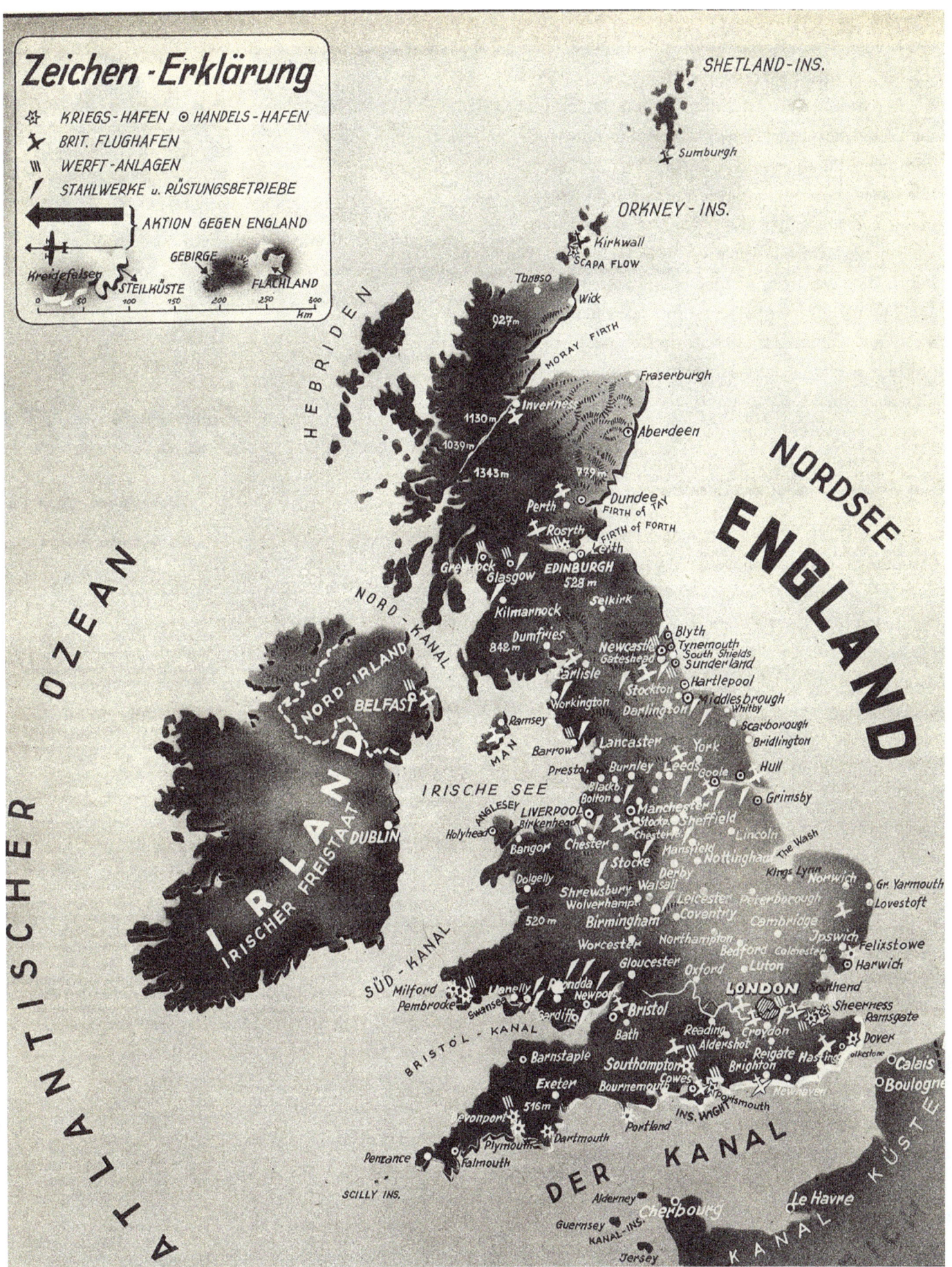

Above: German propaganda made considerable use of maps and illustrations to convey familiarity and high levels of knowledge about the enemy. It was a useful approach as it instilled confidence in German people and fear in enemy populations. This map shows how prominent the Bristol Channel ports were in perception of the general geography of Britain. Port Talbot's steelworks are also here. The Germans equated 'England' with 'Britain, and the concept of Wales and Scotland were not recognised, so 'South Wales' was a region of England. Swansea and Cardiff were recognised as important western ports.

appreciations of economic and industrial issues across 1930s Britain, as MPs openly discussed political matters referring to their own constituencies (Nielsen 1955: 32–35). Swansea and Cardiff's economic importance to the GWR meant that those ports were comprehensively documented in the annual GWR port handbooks and tide tables given out to traders and merchants with intricate details of lock dimensions, crane capacities and storage facilities (Appleby 1933). Such commercial information was freely distributed throughout Europe as a vital part of international commerce and was assiduously collected by all sides; in fact, the Germans probably had too much material to sift and process to understand many of the strategic issues they faced. A famous analysis of intelligence techniques recorded that 'analysis failures, not collection failures, usually cause major intelligence failures (Heuer 1999: 62–63).

Culturally, the work of 'intelligence' was not a prestige role in the German military. Even basics such as foreign-language skills were in short supply as officers chose to develop their careers in other departments in more promising directions (Boog 1986: 122). Managing the quantities of information proved difficult for the military, and specialists in industry, transport, geopolitics, and electricity worked alongside military men in determining vulnerabilities and targets. One expert, Professor Heinrich Steinmann, was of particular significance for Swansea and Cardiff. Steinmann trained as a pilot in 1917 and had an academic career in the 1920s, including several years as a transport geographer in Brunswick. He later specialised in aviation engineering, electric power generation and transport planning. His early Nazi Party membership (number 1058571) and his prominence as an aviation expert meant that by 1935, he was involved with the target selection committees of the Luftwaffe (Nielsen 1955: 41–44). Steinmann led the technical evaluation and selection of targets suitable for attack. It wasn't an easy job, and he spent much of his time trying to overcome the intense rivalry and poor communication between all the groups collecting intelligence. He was likely the primary decision-maker in selecting the GWR ports as suitable targets in the autumn of 1938 (Nielsen 1955: 60,104). His influence is seen in the emphasis on analysing vulnerable railway routes and power stations (Deichmann 1955: 34–36).

By 1935, Professor Steinmann and his team had created a classification system with various military, industrial, communications, and transportation target types. A comprehensive numbering system was designed to match target types to the growing technological advances of Luftwaffe bombing ambitions and capability (Deichmann 1955: 23–26). The relationship between target types and bombing capability was crucial. Industrial targets such as Swansea or Cardiff had some buildings susceptible to fire and, equally, portside buildings and installations were often impervious to fire but vulnerable to blast. Using the wrong bombs and fuses against the diverse types of buildings risked a failure to meet the military objectives. This distinction would be of immense importance for Swansea in the forthcoming attacks. Suitable targets became classified in *Zielstammkarten* (Target Dossiers), with all the necessary information neatly organised and structured in thousands of target files covering military, industrial, communication, and political targets (Nielsen 1955: 44–46).

The question of how all the data and information collected by the various agencies gets translated into action is interesting for geographers. It is the essence of applied geography. There is a strong contrast between how France and Poland were regarded as enemies compared to Britain. France and Poland were considered potential enemies for over twenty years, while the Luftwaffe were only told of the need to view Britain as a potential enemy in 1938 (Murray 1983: 18–19; Corum 1997: 283–84). The intelligence appraisals for Poland were accurate and thoughtful, whereas the assessments

Right: The technical problems of bomb aiming were massive for all air forces. The Luftwaffe began the war with an ambition of pinpoint accuracy for key targets and expected electronic systems to guide their attacks. The Heinkel He 111 aircraft was an interim bomber that carried a light bomb load and had a cramped crew cabin making space for the bomb aimer challenging, as can be seen from this early illustration. The Luftwaffe bomb sight was technically advanced for the 1930s but less effective in the more demanding flying conditions over wartime Britain. The early attacks on the ports were daylight raids and allowed for accurate bombing. This near miss of four bombs at Llandarcy oil storage (opposite) was from a daylight raid in 1940. The switch to night time bombing and the need to bomb from higher altitudes led to more inaccuracy and error. Pinpoint targets such as grain mills, lock gates and warehouses, or ships in the docks were missed but the surrounding streets of the Welsh ports suffered badly from the inaccurate bombs.

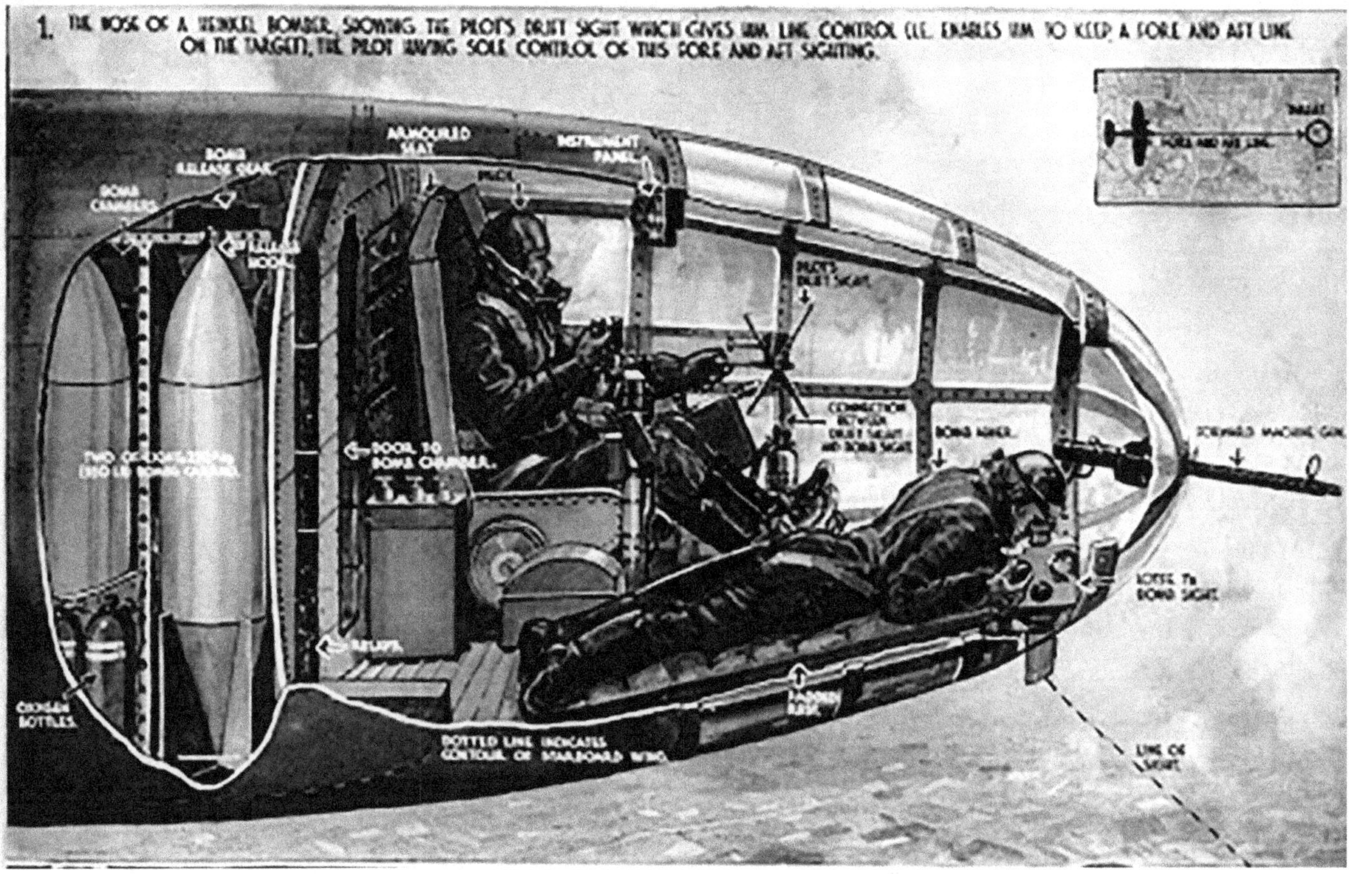
1. THE NOSE OF A HEINKEL BOMBER, SHOWING THE PILOT'S DRIFT SIGHT WHICH GIVES HIM LINE CONTROL (I.E. ENABLES HIM TO KEEP A FORE AND AFT LINE ON THE TARGET), THE PILOT HAVING SOLE CONTROL OF THIS FORE AND AFT SIGHTING.
TARGET
FORE AND AFT LINE
ARMOURED SEAT
INSTRUMENT PANEL
BOMB RELEASE GEAR
PILOT
BOMB CHAMBERS
PILOT'S DRIFT SIGHT
CONNECTION BETWEEN DRIFT SIGHT AND BOMB SIGHT
BOMB AIMER
FORWARD MACHINE GUN
DOOR TO BOMB CHAMBER
OXYGEN BOTTLES
DOTTED LINE INDICATES CONTOUR OF STARBOARD WING
LINE OF SIGHT

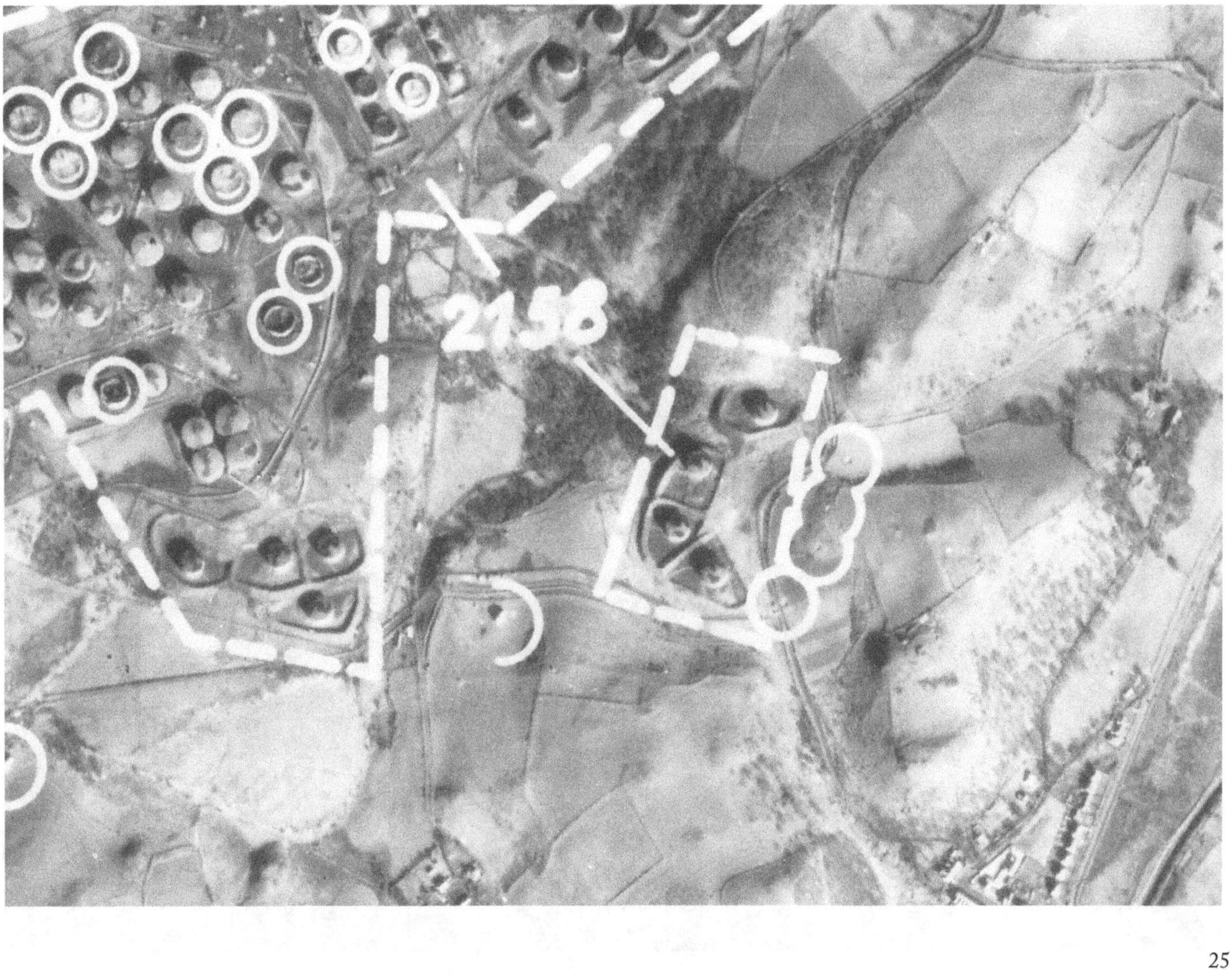
2158

for Britain were significantly poorer. The rapid success of the military campaigns against France and Poland convinced the military and the Nazi Government that they had things right.

In the 1950s, some of the authors of *Studie Blau* reconstructed critical parts of the report from memory. The reconstructed details suggest the Study was an analytical masterpiece, reflecting the talents of the academic and military experts involved (Nielsen 1955). *Studie Blau* (Study Blue) examined not just Britain but its more expansive empire and the support it could expect across the world. We know the sources they used, and they were classics of open-source intelligence, covering libraries, parliamentary debates and official histories of World War 1. The Luftwaffe radio intercept services provided vast amounts of data on how the RAF operated because the radio discipline of the RAF was notoriously lax (Gottschling 1955). Special affection was held for the British press for providing massive quantities of military and economic information in their newspapers with no regard to security or national interest. This situation is quite different from that of the French media, for example, which was always diligent in its self-censorship.

(Nielsen 1955: 59) Open-source intelligence was the key; the traditional espionage services of Admiral Wilhelm Canaris apparently had very little to offer (Nielsen 1955: 64).

Studie Blau contradicts many commonly held views of the early part of the Battle for Britain. For example, the British radar defences were well-known, and their presence was frequently betrayed by poor radio discipline. The study described how radar networks were being expanded along the west and east coasts and were constantly upgrading, although the German analysts failed to recognise the detailed control capabilities of new technology (Galland 1953: 13). The British 'shadow-industry' policies of redistributing key factories to the fringes of Britain and the hoarding and stockpiling of raw materials were also described. The *Graf Zeppelin* airship even flew several aerial survey missions over England's North Sea coast, collecting extensive radio signals intelligence (Nielsen 1955: 65,127).

As air force commander, Göring commissioned Study Blue in November 1938. Finding a collection of experts to create the report couldn't have been easy. Felmy and his team from Air Fleet Two were an obvious

Below: Pit props stacked on the yards north of Swansea's King's Dock in 1932. Swansea had a vigorous mining timber import industry and local Glamorgan forests were completely inadequate in providing mining timber for the coal industry. This timber came from Norway, northern Russia and the Baltic. The Luftwaffe calculated that over sixty five percent of Welsh timber came from these areas. The Luftwaffe strategists had access to this picture and it is highly likely that this picture alone led to the Luftwaffe creating an attack plan for the future bombing Swansea by November 1939. concluding Swansea was a vital link in imports of mining timber.

Above: Unloading grain via a grain elevator at Cardiff's Queen Alexandra Dock in the early 1930s. Cardiff's grain and flour processing facilities became a priority target in the *Studie Blau* investigations. Attacks on grain mills and silos was a specific Mission of the Luftwaffe bombing units (Mission Seven). Which meant that crews were trained to understand the layout of mills at Swansea and Cardiff and the ferro-concrete storage silos which were the most important targets.

starting point, and other participants the of the precious summer's intelligence conferences were also quickly involved. Naval staff had already war-gamed the role of a mine war against ports (Maier and others 1991: 46). Senior Luftwaffe intelligence had even thought of strategic, quick wins by targeting oil storage, grain silos and cold stores, but with no idea how this could be achieved (Maier and others 1991: 45). December and January must have been intense months as a study group was assembled. The military men were obviously first priority. The first choice was Hans Jeschonnek, a senior air commander and friend of Göring. He was an intelligent and able senior officer but fatally infected with blind faith in the powers of Adolf Hitler, which would contribute to his eventual suicide in 1943. A small group of experienced officers followed, almost all experienced in military aviation from the Great War. Most notable was Erhard Milch, who became prominent in the overall running of the air force. The military men were easy to find, and the technical experts were harder. The role of Heinrich Steinmann was mentioned previously, and a number of university professors with experience in geography and politics joined him. They were joined by senior leaders from industry, to address the lack of skills and understanding of modern industrial production and manufacture methods. Experts from the arms manufacturers added that there is a need to understand the nature of bombs and fuses. Economics graduates from the Counter-intelligence branch of the armed forces High Command gave the expertise of the economics of war. These were the central groups of analysts. Political spin was added by inputs from the Luftwaffe foreign specialists and air attaches from the German embassy in London (Nielsen 1955: 49).

Between February and June 1939, this diverse group met to analyse Britain. Junior staff wrote reports and appraisals, which were discussed and graded by the senior team members (Nielsen 1955: 47–48). The topographic and military geography branch of the army prepared maps. Topographic maps were derived from British Ordnance Survey sheets, usually redrawn at metric scales. Thematic maps were created from the reports of the 1931 British Census to provide population, radio stations, railways, and electricity networks. Expert panels met once or twice a week and held conferences and workshops discussing how Britain worked as a nation.

The range of sources used gives a good indication of

	Deep Water Area	Normal Depth of Water	Dimensions		Quayage	Entrance Lock		Average Depth on Outer Cill	
			Length	Width		Length	Width	H.W. O.S.T.	H.W. O.N.T.
	Acs.	*Feet.*	*Feet.*	*Feet.*	*Feet.*	*Feet.*	*Feet.*	*Feet.*	*Feet.*
CARDIFF.									
QueenAlexandra Dock ..	52	37	2,550	800	9,315	850	90	40	30
Roath Dock ..	33	33½	2,400	600	9,885			40	30Q.A.
						600	80	36	26 R.
Roath Basin ..	13	Tidal	1,000	550		350	80	36	26
East Dock ..	44	25	1,000	by 300		220	49	32	22
			3,300	by 500	9,480				
East Basin ..	2½	Tidal	380	250		220	55	32	22
West Dock ..	19	19 & 13	4,000	200	8,950	152	36	29	19
West Basin ..	1½	Tidal	300	200		—	45	29	19
Two Passenger Pontoons ..	—	HWOST 28¾	—	—	4 boats 260 ft. long can berth.	—	—	—	—
Entrance Channel ..		HWONT 18¾							
Totals ..	165	—	—	—	37,630	—	—	—	—
SWANSEA.									
King's Dock ..	71	about 29	4,200	400	13,971				
Queen's Dock	150	,, 29	3,200	350	3,650	875	90	40	32½
Prince of Wales Dock ..	28	,, 23	3,221	500	7,164				
North Basin ..	2½	Tidal	500	220	1,441	—	58	32	24½
South Dock ..	13	about 21	1,538	360	6,310	370	58	34	26½
South Basin ..	5½	,, 21	380	440					
River Tawe ..	—	—	—	—	1,735	—	—	—	—
Totals ..	270	—	—	—	34,271	—	—	—	—

Left: The nature of commerce and maritime trade means that essential technical information is always freely available for commercial operators, this is the central tenet of open-source intelligence. Here is the technical detail of the entrance locks for Swansea and Cardiff from a 1933 tide table. From this it is a relatively simple matter to calculate the number and calibre of bombs necessary to destroy the locks. The Luftwaffe had the bomb technology, accuracy, and training to destroy the lock systems. However, they never had the strategic planning or leadership skills to conduct a strategic war against Britain. We have senior officers such as 'Beppo' Schmid and Hans Jeschonnek to thank for the poor performance of the Luftwaffe during the air attacks on Wales. If Spanish Civil War veterans such as Hugo Sperrle and Wolfram von Richthofen were in charge, Swansea and Cardiff would have been devastated in exactly the same attacks as the RAF used against German cities after 1943.

the depth of the investigation. Open-source intelligence from company records or Ordnance Survey maps was simple to obtain. Libraries in European universities were packed with information. The histories and documents from the Great War, supplemented with biographical writings and travelogues, were also used (Nielsen 1955: 32). The British Parliament proved of immense worth, and minutes of debates and Hansard were considered especially valuable. The German radio intercept services constructed the complete RAF order of battle and operations procedures by intercepting radio traffic from aircraft and airfields, where staff were notoriously lax at following any security procedures (Nielsen 1955: 16).

It is in the scope of the final report that we see the immense task that was unfolding. In the 1930s, based on the experiences of the Great War, Britain still had command and control of the immense resources of the British Empire. This needed to be explained in detail, particularly as German armed forces would come into contact with soldiers and airmen from many nations in their combat roles. The structure and relationship between England and her empire were difficult to understand for many Europeans.

Further sections deal with people, government and constitutional arrangements. The German experiment with democracy had largely failed with the demise of the Weimar Republic. Many German politicians found it hard to comprehend how democratic processes worked. Equally, the unwritten constitution and Cabinet government of Britain were hard to understand when viewed from the stark dictatorship of Nazi Germany. It was assumed British society would collapse in the face of some German bombing, although even Göring didn't believe that (Suchenwirth 1969: 250). Organisations such as Home Guards or Civil Defence were of interest. The relationships between county councils, police forces, and any civil defence were important in estimating the levels of control of the population if air attacks created civil unrest. British experts were considering the same issue (Zuckerman 1978: 101–3).

Naturally, much of Study Blue was taken up with the British economy because that was what was misunderstood. Reports were written on industrial control of resources with coal and iron ore stockpiles, and a big effort was made to understand important supply chains, such as how the British made carburettors. Where were the main factories? Eventually, studies covered the power, gas and water industries (power stations, electricity substations, gas and pipelines, reservoirs and drinking water, and drainage and sewerage). The British chemical industry was huge and covered coal mines, coking plants, explosives, artificial silk, petroleum, and industrial gases. The metal industries were seen as the lifeblood of a war effort, from basic iron making to high-quality steel. Aircraft landing gear were particularly complex and technical products and were singled out for identification. Machine tools were considered vital on both sides. Shipyards and ship repair were vital components for a war against the ports, and the GWR ports would feature highly in the appraisals. Professor Steinmann's unit produced a mass of information about transportation and communication. Railways, roads and bridges were covered. The ports also

The Luftwaffe had a wide range of weapons available to drop on urban areas in the early years of the war. Lock gates, coal mines, and food storage all had buildings with varying levels of resilience and required different tactics to destroy them. The ports were susceptible to damage in some aspects such as power stations or cranes but generally quite hardy in the face of attack. Larger bombs over five hundred kilogrammes in weight with hardened steel noses were need for the power stations and lock gates. The Luftwaffe was always short of these types of bombs. However, the real terror weapon was the incendiary bomb shown right. This one kilogramme bomb (the 'Elektron') was dropped in thousands on the Welsh ports but it was only ever effective in destroying houses and shops. Creating a firestorm to kill civilians was eventually developed by the RAF and perfected by the US Army Air Forces. The Luftwaffe were experimenting in firestorm tactics in late-1940 and the raid on Swansea in February 1941 shows the early firestorm approach with early arrival of incendiary bombing followed up by high explosive bombs to kill firemen and civil defence staff. The damage to Swansea (shown below) was typical of intensive firestorms which could not be extinguished because firemen were killed and their pumps destroyed. Burning buildings collapse and obliterate the streets with rubble.

The RAF intensively investigated these early Luftwaffe raids and based their own strategic campaign against Germany on the nature of these early raids.

came under this category, and whilst naval bases were obvious targets, Steinmann emphasised the importance of commercial ports such as those in the Bristol Channel. Communications covered telephone and telegraph exchanges, cables and radio stations. A series of network maps were produced to show Britain's power and telephone distribution networks.

Agricultural production was also considered important. Food supply was a strategic service and warehouses, cold stores, mills and grain silos were all listed, again ensuring the GWR ports were prominent. The possibility of attacking crops in fields was passed to the explosives experts who created a specific bomb and incendiary strategy for that instance (Deichmann 1955: 234–35).

The reports, information and assessments were categorised into Steinmann's target classification system, which enables some structured categorisation and prioritisation and possibly understanding for senior staff. The classification system will be examined later.

After a few months of conferences, enough was known to start drawing conclusions from all the information. We know a few of them because they kept emerging in other sources that survived the massive document destruction of 1945.

- Britain was a strong and stable country. This conclusion echoes the collapse of Imperial Germany in 1918, which was considered unimaginable in 1914. The collapse and the German Revolution have been comprehensively discussed in one of the best recent histories of the Great War, which re-establishes the German experience of the conflict as a central tenet (Leonhard 2020: 2–19). Moreover, the British Government was seen as capable of adapting and improvising in response to changing political or economic circumstances. The 'spiritual strength' of the British people meant that Britain could not be defeated by air attack alone.

- The Royal Navy was extremely strong and capable. Although hammered with spending cuts throughout the 1920s, the Navy was still a global force linking Britain with its Empire. An extremely tough adversary.

- The Royal Air Force was rapidly re-equipping and may be as strong as the German Air Force by the end of 1940.

- Britain's air defences are constantly being upgraded, and radar developments are fast. The RAF will use radar as an effective tool for national defence.

- The British army is small and ineffective but is being modernised rapidly. However, it can only operate in close cooperation with the French armed forces.

- A strategic air campaign against the complex British economy may not be enough to guarantee victory.

- Stockpiling of strategic industrial resources has already begun across England. Some of these stockpiles are aluminium, copper, tin, molybdenum and chromium.

- Dispersal programmes for key industries away from the South-East of England have already begun. In the Bristol Channel, this meant establishing shadow factories at Swansea, increased storage for oil and lubricants at Llandarcy, and new dock storage facilities at Barry. (All of which would be confirmed by reconnaissance flights after the fall of France in May 1940).

- The weakest points of Britain's economy are reliance on imports into west coast ports and the vulnerability of overseas communications and trade routes from the Mediterranean and across the Atlantic.

Although *Studie Blau* had considerable detail, it had a simple set of conclusions. A successful war against Britain had three prerequisites:, the defeat of the RAF, the destruction of the British aircraft industry, and the neutralisation of the British Royal Navy. Britain's weakest points were dependence on ports and overseas communications and that those ports were vulnerable to air attack. Swansea and Cardiff are featured highly because of their flexible general cargo capacity and oil handling facilities.

From these three priorities, the primary mission of the Luftwaffe could emerge: destroy air power, neutralise all naval and commercial port facilities (the 'breathing organs of the economy') and destroy British shipping. The Luftwaffe would need a powerful air force; even then, no time estimate for success could be set. Writing after the war, Luftwaffe General Albert Kesselring recalled the impact of the study on senior air staff. He acknowledged the input of scientists and economists and the worth of the Study in providing a basis for the "air battle against

Left: A Luftwaffe SC-250 (two hundred and fifty kilogramme) bomb from 1940. Although the Luftwaffe preferred the smaller fifty kilogramme bomb for many missions,v the trend for bigger bombs was seen in many air forces. Swansea was frequently attacked with this kind of bomb. However, not is all as it seems. This bomb is created from welded sheets of steel (you can see the weld seams) which makes it extremely poor quality and is likely to break up on impact with a solid object such as a wall. The explosive contents would frequently spill before the detonator could operate leading to a much smaller explosion. The explosive filling of this bomb was also sub-standard, meaning the explosive yield was half of what could be expected from higher-quality bombs. The bomb has two fuse pockets for different types of fuse to allow for better prospects of effective detonation. Luftwaffe Chief of Staff General Jeschonnek halted quality bomb production after May 1940 in the belief that Britain would surrender. This meant that The Luftwaffe used poor quality bombs to attack the Welsh ports. Swansea was frequently a target for poor-quality bombs resulting in large numbers of unexploded bombs across the Borough. It is likely that up to forty percent of the bombs dropped on Swansea failed to explode,although, of course all had to be treated very carefully by the bomb disposal teams, and some exploded in a delayed fashion. The shortage of bombs resulted in the Luftwaffe being forced to drop expensive magnetic mines as 'land mines' across the ports in 1941.

Britain". He also believed the Study provided enough detail for planning the invasion of the British Isles (Kesselring 1955: 67).

Studie Blau was presented to Herman Göring at a secret conference on the island of Sylt in June 1939. The sensitivity of the contents meant that only five copies were produced. Göring knew he could not present these conclusions to Adolf Hitler and ordered the report destroyed. No copies survived because the report honestly reported the Germans' extreme difficulty overcoming a determined Britain. Ironically, Studie Blau may have been the best intelligence document the Nazi intelligence services ever produced (Nielsen 1955: 221).

Bombs and Targets

By April 1939, Professor Steinmann and his technical, economic, and military colleagues had the challenge of combining the masses of information in Study Blue with the Luftwaffe doctrine of lightning war and pinpoint accuracy. The state of technology in 1939 meant that although the Luftwaffe had a principle of pinpoint accuracy, they did not have a sufficiently accurate bomb sight to deliver that ambition (Suchenwirth 1959: 28). This shortfall was made worse because of the German lack of a 4-engine bomber similar to an American Boeing B-17 or a British Stirling, meaning that the smaller German bombers had to have the highest accuracy levels possible to deliver their smaller bombloads effectively.

After the war, two senior Luftwaffe officers at the front line of operations lamented that Germany failed to develop a four-engine strategic bomber for attacks (Koller 1956: 14; Galland 1953: 8). The debate continued into the 1990s with later air power analysts suggesting that the Germans' two-engine bombers were sufficiently accurate to attack Britain, provided they were protected from RAF fighters (Corum 1997: 282). Nevertheless, the Heinkel and Junkers bombers used by the Germans were to inflict dreadful death and destruction on the South Wales ports.

Regardless of the propaganda newsreels of the time, the Luftwaffe continuously operated on a limited budget and a lifelong shortage of resources, forcing creative use of available resources at all times. This meant that air attacks had to be meticulously planned and have clear strategic outcomes. When planning was lacking, as was often the case because of the inherent chaos of the Nazi leadership, the raids never achieved their goals. As an air force, the Luftwaffe was always subject to political interference, frequently from politicians and Nazi party apparatchiks with no comprehension of the advanced technical nature of the war in the air. This problem was frequently seen in the inconsistency of German attacks on the ports. There was no centralised control of targeting or grand strategy in the air attacks (Koller 1956: 5). This lack of a centralised strategy even confused the RAF bombing analysts as they tracked the often strange tracks and targets of individual units flying across Britain (Air Historical Branch Not dated: 47). The result was a great deal of almost random death and destruction. The air raids on Britain were always made with limited numbers of planes and bombs with a tight squeeze on resources. Equally, the lack of a sufficiently accurate bomb sight would cause considerable difficulties for the coming bombing campaign, particularly as the Luftwaffe General Staff renewed their 'technical' insistence on pinpoint bombing shortly before the war began (Suchenwirth 1959: 31).

Understanding targeting in the early part of World War II is an appreciation of several constraints. Significant factors included the capabilities of the attacking aircraft (flight range and bombload), the distance to the target (navigation and fuel loads), the nature of the target (industrial, commercial, naval, or military), and the political and military objectives of the attack. Technologies changed fast, and of course, aided by the unpleasant fact that after the fall of France in the summer of 1940, the Germans could use French airbases and airfields to attack the west coast and the Bristol Channel by flying across Cornwall and Devon directly into the Bristol Channel.

German intelligence staff recognised their information complexity problem as early as 1935 while collecting target information on France and Poland. Their solution was a set of numbered categories covering all aspects of any likely targets they would find. The system was comprehensive and allowed for further expansion as the military situation changed (Deichmann 1955: 3–17). The system is described in Annex Two. The complexities of the British military and industrial economy were distilled into the many target categories. Installations relating to armed forces were always a top priority, with airfields, command posts, radar sites, and fuel supplies keenly investigated and listed. More interesting from a geographical view was the assessment of industry. Power, gas and water supply were prioritised, with electricity supplies attracting particular attention. Chemical industries were important because of explosives and gas manufacture, both for poison and industrial), and paper, rayon and textiles. Some industries were considered to produce 'keystone' products, such as coking plants (essential for iron and steel) or complex technical processes such as engine carburettor production. Transport was also critical, covering rail, roads, bridges and tunnels. Steinmann's experience as a transport geographer influenced the search for complex road and rail interchanges for 'interdiction' attacks intended to delay and disrupt vehicle movement. Eventually, over sixty types of target categories worth attacking were identified with a range of identification and significance criteria. (Deichmann 1955: 49–288) The hard part would be sorting the thousands of potential targets into sixty or more target categories.

Combining the information in targets with the technical capabilities of the Luftwaffe to attack such targets was a complex process. An attack on a target had to be packaged into a 'mission' that conformed to the capability of the air force in the prosecution of war against another country. A great deal of reliance was placed on the writings of the Prussian military theorist General Karl von Clausewitz, particularly in his views of the application of force and the need for clarity of purpose (Clausewitz 1989: 1). Despite Clausewitz basing his views on the outcomes of the Napoleonic Wars of the early 1800s, his views are still studied in modern military circles. For the Germans, the creation of the Luftwaffe in 1933 presented a massive problem of creating a modern organisation and then working out what it should be capable of. The Germans were not alone. The British and Americans were also reviewing what to do about strategic air bombing (Biddle 1995; Zuckerman 1978: 140–45). For the Germans, the debates about technical advances, political aims, military realities and costs, ended in a set of definitions for the German air services that would deliver unprecedented successes in the early part of the war and equally contribute to the complete destruction of Nazi Germany in 1945.

For the Luftwaffe, there was a list of priority targets that were considered crucial to a nation's will to defend itself:

- Manufacturing industries.
- Food supplies and food supply sources.
- Import activities, facilities, and installations.
- Electricity supplies.
- Rail and road routes.
- Military reserves.
- Centres of government and administration.

The German senior air staff initially rejected the concept of attacking the civilian population unless it was in direct retaliation for terror attacks on its own population (Schmid 1939: 2). An altruistic motive for this restraint is unlikely. It is more about the technical difficulties of attacking population targets and assessing their successes. However, the realities of air attacks on Warsaw in 1939 and Rotterdam in 1940 revealed that whenever thought convenient, the adoption of terror bombing to achieve a quick capitulation of defences was completely acceptable to Göring, even going so far as to overrule his senior generals (AHB6 1954).

In summary, German air commanders did not believe an air force alone could force an enemy's capitulation. it needed to work alongside other armed services and strategies (Deichmann 1955: 6–9). The debates that raged between air force generals and other military and political figures would have profound consequences for the German air war against Britain as the Luftwaffe was designed with a particular set of capabilities in mind (Corum 1997: 124–45; Murray 1983: 3–13).

As a service, the Luftwaffe was designed to have the capability in aircraft and bombs to undertake nine types of 'missions.' To undertake these nine types of missions, specific types of aircraft were procured, bombs and fuses designed, aircrew trained, and replenishment and support services put into place. Luftwaffe units attacking Britain would be assigned missions from the type list. Any deviation from the mission-type list, for example, to attack unorthodox or misunderstood targets, required more improvisation and a higher risk of failure. The mission-type management structure dictated the order of battle of the Luftwaffe in its aircraft types and numbers and the types of bombs to be used (Deichmann 1955: 12–17). For the Welsh ports, the most important missions were:

- Mission Type Five: Combat action against enemy resources (manufacturing, oil, electricity, coal stocks.
- Mission Type Six: Action to prevent enemy import traffic (shipping in ports or in shipping lanes, port facilities, lock gates).
- Mission Type Seven: Disruption of enemy food supplies (grain storage, oil, electricity, cold stores, canning and food preservation plants) .

Swansea and Cardiff were frequently attacked under Mission Type Seven rules.

Understanding how the Luftwaffe, in its operations, used geographical information needs an appreciation of how the Luftwaffe was designed in the late 1930s. It used modern management techniques for its resources and staff, a situation that was unique at the time. The concept of Lightning War (Blitzkrieg) required flexibility and adaptability for all the armed forces. This presented a considerable technical challenge for operating complicated aircraft at or near the front line, often supporting army or navy operations. With little or no notice, the Luftwaffe was expected to be flexible enough to switch between battlefield support, strategic bombing, and naval support. Many of the units that attacked Swansea and Cardiff operated from basic airfields in France with limited facilities for maintenance and support. This was when the RAF could not even move fighter aircraft between operational British airbases without considerable preparation and notice. (Hinsley 1979: 470–71) For such flexibility to be delivered across occupied France, each German airfield had to be largely self-sufficient in information, bombs and spare parts.

The most significant issue is munitions. Luftwaffe forward air bases in France were usually supplied with 'bomb packages' rather than the traditional munitions dumps of other air forces. The bomb manufacturer assembled a package based on war experience and feedback from the front-line units. The packages would contain a mix of fragmentation, mine, and incendiary bombs delivered in a fixed ratio related to the types of anticipated targets. Advanced electrical fuses allowed fully fused bombs to be moved safely between manufacturers and airfields (Deichmann and Marquard 1955: 85–87). Whilst not perfect, the package system offered flexibility and adaptability that was incredibly advanced. The process relied on one crucial pre-requisite…it needed first-class knowledge of the intended target, and aircraft could not be loaded with bombs until the target had been designated (Deichmann 1955: 11–14). This was the link to the effective use of the available intelligence material. As late as the early 1980s, the official British histories rather snottily characterised this process as improvisation. Still, the integration of manufacturing, logistics, and planning was exceptional, making the early-war Luftwaffe a formidable enemy (Hinsley 1979: 166).

Each Luftwaffe airfield kept a map library of information on the potential targets based on the master data in the entire target library held at the Luftwaffe General Staff headquarters. The basic product contained in the local airfield map libraries was a *Zielstammkarte* (Target Master Document) with various maps and a recent aerial photograph of the target with a mass of supplemental information in a red overprint. The marginal information was sufficient for each aircraft to plot a course to the target, understand its significance, and recognise the essential structures for the attack.

The GWR ports were fully represented in the Luftwaffe Target Dossiers, with approximately sixty-four port facilities identified and some of the most significant metal works and manufacturers that were considered important. Food storage is also prominent, and the important role Swansea/Llandarcy had in oil imports and processing.

- Newport: c. 13 Targets.
- Cardiff: c. 20 Targets.
- Penarth: At least 1 Target.
- Barry: c. 3 Targets.
- Port Talbot: c. 3 Targets.
- Briton Ferry: At least 1 Target.
- Swansea/Llandarcy: c. 20 Targets.
- Llanelly: At least 1 Target.
- Burry Port: At least 1 Target.

Other targets around the ports were inland factories, power stations, water supply, and any military installations such as barracks or airfields. These have not been included in the assessment here unless they are directly related to the ports.

Bombing

The attacking aircraft obviously dropped all kinds of explosive articles on the ports. Bombs are the most poorly understood, terrifying, destructive, and confusing artefacts of air war. Unexploded bombs still pose a very real fatal threat today and regular surveys of the Welsh ports are essential to assess the potential of builders and developers digging up unexploded bombs. Some areas around the Welsh ports carry a substantial risk of unexploded bombs still existing below streets, roads and fields.

The technical development of bombs as weapons of war began in the fifteenth century. Still, it was the arrival of aircraft in World War One that really pushed the technical development of an explosive device that could be dropped from the air, kill people and destroy buildings effectively. Target intelligence gives a guide about what to attack; the aircraft is the vehicle used, and it is the bomb that brings about the result. A bomb should be of sufficient size to destroy or damage the target, but no bigger; this is why in conventional terms, accurate bombs and missiles are usually smaller. Bombs can be of different types depending on the type of target. High-explosive bombs provide a blast effect, armour-piercing bombs can be used to attack buildings and vehicles or ships with heavy protection, and incendiary bombs create fires and are often used when high-explosive would have limited effect. Combinations of these types of bombs depended on the target's general nature, such as docks, houses, factories, or railways. Finally, fragmentation bombs create a combination of blast and metal shrapnel and splinters, often creating grievous injuries to people. In a series of landmark studies, the famous scientist Solly Zuckerman studied the dreadful effects on the human body of German bombs in 1940 (Zuckerman 1978: 122–30). To explode correctly, a bomb needs a fuse. The detonation of a bomb at the right time is more important than the actual size of the bomb. Fuses could detonate on impact, detonate after a short delay, or detonate after

Above: Luftwaffe bomber crews reviewing a model of East London whilst they discuss flight routes across the urban area. The officer in the centre is holding a *Zielstammkarte* book of the target photos which shows the targets outlined in red on individual photos. Bomber crews were equally at home bombing battlefield targets or urban areas.

a long delay. Delayed action fuses could disrupt life and prevent recovery after an air raid. This could extend the effect of an air raid over days as bomb disposal teams fought to defuse bombs before they exploded. This was the case at Cardiff in July 1940 (Jappy 2001: 29–31).

An exploding bomb has a number of potential effects on the area around it. The explosion's pressure or the penetration of explosive fragments into the target can inflict tremendous damage. The explosion produces a flame, a shock wave, excess pressure, and finally a sub-pressure. The shock-waves and the pressure can also be reflected off other structures, increasing the effect (Marquard 1955b: 11–19). Very often, if the bomb had penetrated a target before exploding, the force of the exploding gases could be more destructive than the original detonation (Marquard 1955a: 61).

One of the biggest threats in the ports was fire. The Germans developed a very effective incendiary bomb in 1915 (the Elektron). However, it was never used in the Great War in planned firestorm attacks on Paris and London. But in 1938 it was ready for use again. Many targets, including the GWR ports, were, in parts, very susceptible to fire (Collier 1957: 273). The cramped commercial centre of Swansea and its South dock were an easy target, and the large residential areas of Cardiff were also of concern. The centre of Swansea was destroyed by a firestorm over three nights in February 1941. Although the raid on Swansea was not considered a heavy raid because of the comparatively low tonnage of bombs dropped, the impact of incendiaries was immense and extremely effective in their destruction (Collier 1957: 275, 281, 506; Alban 1994: 10–11). Regardless of the tonnages of bombs dropped, in February 1941, Swansea suffered a major raid through the numbers of incendiaries dropped and the resulting firestorm and the consequent death and destruction.

Despite appearing to have a simple shape, a bomb is designed to quite exacting standards. The shape must be aerodynamic to prevent tumbling in flight and allow for accuracy. The bomb may spin in flight, and those spin speeds may be up to three thousand revolutions per minute. This can put immense stress on the structure of the bomb and its fuses. When the bomb finally hits a target, it must be at a precise angle to allow it to impact or penetrate a building or vessel and detonate at exactly the right time. The bomb often has a thicker point or nose cone to allow it to hit a target without it breaking up and spilling its contents before they have a chance to explode. Finally, the bomb has to be released from the aircraft at an exact height to allow the bomb to fall out of the aircraft, settle on its aerodynamic trajectory and fall at the correct speed onto the target. If too high, the bomb may tumble and fragment. If too low, the bomb may not assume its correct falling angle and break up. The science of bombs and bombing was (and remains) intensely technical. The initial research for the bomb designs that would ultimately be used against Britain began in secret testing in Sweden in the late 1920s as part of clandestine actions to recreate the German armed forces (Marquard 1955a: 31–33). The technical story is complex and repeated in all the warring powers' air forces, but it often comes down to two crucial things. The first was the ability of the fuse to detonate the bomb at exactly the right time. The second was the ability of the bomb to remain in one piece once it had come into contact with the target. This was to allow the fuse detonator time to explode the main charge. If a German bomb hit a roof or a wall at the wrong angle, it could (and often did) shatter into pieces, making the whole effort of getting the bomb there useless (Marquard 1955a: 113). Consequently, the actual construction of the bomb was of crucial importance, whether it was one tube of thick steel or welded from several parts of thinner or weaker materials. This will matter when we come to examine the bombing of the Welsh ports.

There were many types of bombs. By 1943, the British believed they had identified approximately 17 types of German bombs being dropped on Britain or in action in the Mediterranean (Civil Defence Training Pamphlet (2nd Edition) 1943: 1–24). However, we now know that at that date, there were over forty types of bombs available for use against Britain, showing the need for variation of size, build, and makeup to attack British targets successfully (Marquard 1955b: III). Despite such large variations in the types of bombs, the Luftwaffe only dropped a limited number of bomb sizes on the Welsh ports. In terms of weight, these were 50kg, 250kg, and 500kg. Exceptionally, larger bombs of 1000kg could be dropped by German units equipped with special aircraft on unusual or significant targets. There was also a range of incendiary bombs, but in 1940-41, the mainstay of fire attacks against the Welsh ports was the *Elektron* incendiary discussed earlier.

The Germans also used aerial mines as blast bombs. These weapons were designed as anti-shipping weapons to be dropped in certain areas of estuaries and shipping channels. The weapons had an automatic or emergency fuse that detonated if the bomb landed on dry land to prevent bomb disposal officers from finding out the secrets of the magnetic and acoustic detonators. The Bristol Channel mine war will be discussed later.

References

AHB6. 1954. German Bombing of Warsaw and Rotterdam (AHB6 Air Ministry)

Air Historical Branch. Not dated. The Air Defence of Great Britain: Night Air Defence. June , 1940-December, 1941, The Second World War Campaign Narratives (London: Air Ministry)

Alban, J.R. 1994. The Three Nights' Blitz: Select Contemporary Reports Relating to Swansea's Air Raids of February 1941, Studies in Swansea's History, 3 (Swansea: City of Swansea)

Appleby, H.N. (ed.). 1933. Great Western Ports (Cardiff: H. N. Appleby)

Behrens, C.B.A. 1955. Merchant Shipping and the Demands of War (London: HMSO)

Biddle, Tami Davis. 1995. 'British and American Approaches to Strategic Bombing: Their Origins and Implementation in the World War II Combined Bomber Offensive', in Airpower: Theory and Practice (London: Frank Cass), pp. 91–144

Boog, Horst. 1986. 'German Air Intelligence in World War II', Aerospace Historian, 33.2: 121–29

———. 1997. 'A Luftwaffe View of the Intelligence War', Air Intelligence Symposium Bracknell Paper No. 7: 52–61

Caddell, Joseph. 2019. 'Seeing Things Differently: Contrasting Narratives of British and German Photographic Intelligence during the Second World War', Intelligence & National Security, 34.1: 79–84

Civil Defence Training Pamphlet (2nd Edition) (ed.). 1943. 'Objects Dropped From The Air' (HMSO)

Clausewitz, Carl von. 1989. On War (Princeton, NJ: Princeton University Press)

Collier, Basil. 1957. The Defence of the United Kingdom (London: HMSO)

Corum, James S. 1997. The Luftwaffe: Creating the Operational Air War, 1918-1940 (Lawrence, Kansas: University Press of Kansas)

Davies, Philip H. J., and Kristian C. Gustafson (eds.). 2013. Intelligence Elsewhere: Spies and Espionage Outside the Anglosphere (Washington: Georgetown University Press)

Deichmann, Paul. 1955. The System of Target Selection Applied by the German Air Force in World War II (Maxwell Air Force Base, Alabama: USAF Historical Division)

Deichmann, Paul, and Ernst R. Marquard. 1955. Luftwaffe Methods in the Selection of Offensive Weapons (Maxwell Air Force Base, Alabama: Aerospace Studies Institute)

Freedman, Lawrence (ed.). 1994. War (Oxford: Oxford University Press)

Galland, Adolf. 1953. The Battle of Britain (London: AHB6 Air Ministry)

Gottschling, Kurt. 1955. The Radio Intercept Service of the German Air Force (Berlin-Charlottenburg: Aerospace Studies Institute, Maxwell Air Force Base, Alabama)

Gregory, Derek. 2011. '"Doors into Nowhere": Dead Cities and the Natural History of Destruction', in Cultural Memories: The Geographical Point of View (New York: Springer), pp. 249–83

Heuer, Richards J. 1999. Psychology of Intelligence Analysis (Washington: Central Intelligence Agency)

Hinsley, F.H. 1979. British Intelligence in the Second World War, 6 vols (London: HMSO), I

Jappy, M.J. 2001. Danger UXB: The Remarkable Story of the Disposal of Unexploded Bombs during the Second World War (London: Macmillan)

Jones, Neville. 1973. The Origins of Strategic Bombing (London: Kimber)

Kesselring, Albert. 1955. Gedanken zum Zweiten Weltkrieg (Bonn: Athenäum-Verlag)

Klinke, Ian. 2020. 'Geography at War', in The SAGE Handbook of Historical Geography, 2 vols (London: SAGE), II, pp. 449–65

Koller, Karl. 1956. German Air Force Policy During the 2nd World War (London: AHB6 Air Ministry)

Kuehl, Daniel T. 1995. 'Airpower vs. Electricity: Electric Power as a Target For Strategic Air Operations', in Airpower: Theory and Practice (London: Frank Cass), pp. 237–66

Leonhard, Jorn. 2020. Pandora's Box: A History of the First World War (Cambridge, Massachusetts: Harvard University Press)

Maier, Klaus A. 2015. 'Total War and Operational Air Warfare', in Germany and the Second World War Volume II Germany's Initial Conquests in Europe, Germany and the Second World War, 10 vols (Oxford: Oxford University Press), II

Maier, Klaus A, Horst Rohde, Bernd Stegemann, and Hans Umbreit. 1991. Germany and the Second World War (Oxford: Oxford University Press)

Marquard, Ernst R. 1955a. The Planning and Development of Bombs for the German Air Force 1925-1945 (Maxwell Air Force Base, Alabama)

———. 1955b. The Selection of Bombs and Fuses for Air Attacks (Maxwell Air Force Base, Alabama: Aerospace Studies Institute), p. 178

Murray, Williamson. 1983. Strategy for Defeat: The Luftwaffe 1933-1945 (Maxwell AFB: Airpower Research Institute)

Nielsen, Andreas L. 1955. The Collection and Evaluation of Intelligence for the German Air Force High Command, p. 225

Rabeder, Harald, Stefan Ommert, and Alois Schlee. 2017. Der Adler Mit Dem Fernrohr : Mit Der 2. Staffel Der Fernaufklarungsgruppe (F)/123 Uber Frankreich, Grossbritannien, Nord Afrika Und Dem Mittlemeer (Wurzburg: Verlagshaus Wurzburg GmbH & Co. KG, Wurzburg)

Richie, Alexandra. 1998. Faust's Metropolis: A History of Berlin (London: Harper Collins)

Robinson, Douglas H. 1980. The Zeppelin in Combat: A History of the German Naval Airship Division 1912-1918 (Seattle, WA: University of Washington Press)

von Rohden, Hans-Detlef Herhudt. 1938. Vom Luftkriege: Gedanken über Führung und Einsatz moderner Luftwaffen (Berlin: e.s. Mittler und Sohn)

Rose, Edward P. F., and Dierk Willig. 2004. 'German Military Geologists and Geographers in World War II', in Studies in Military Geography and Geology (Dordrecht: Springer)

Schmid, Joseph ('Beppo'). 1939. Proposal for the Conduct of Air Warfare against Britain (Berlin: German Air Force Operations Staff (Intelligence))

Shaughnessy, Ryan. 2011. No Sense in Dwelling in the Past?: The Fate of the US Air Force's German Air Force Monograph Project, 1952-69: (Fort Belvoir, VA: Defense Technical Information Center) <https://doi.org/10.21236/ADA544432>

Suchenwirth, Richard. 1959. Historical Turning Points in the German Air Force War Effort, USAF Historical Studies: No. 189 (Maxwell AFB: USAF Historical Division), p. 157

———. 1968. The Development of the German Air Force 1919-1939, USAF Historical Studies (Maxwell AFB: Aerospace Studies Institute)

———. 1969. Command and Leadership in the German Air Force (Valmy)

Tirpitz, Alfred von. 1919. My Memoirs, 2 vols (New York: Dodd Mead), II

Vogler, Philipp. 2019. Die Deutsche Militarische Luftbildaufklarung: Von Deb Anfangen Bis 1945 (Karlsruhe: Karlsruhe Institut fur Technologie (KIT))

Watkins, Gwen. 2006. Cracking the Luftwaffe Codes: The Secrets of Bletchley Park (London: Greenhill Books)

Zuckerman, Solly. 1978. From Apes to Warlords 1904-46 (London: Hamish Hamilton)

Opposite: In similar style to the map on page 23, this one shows the ports, relative significance and the extents of the important industrial regions. The comparative size and importance of London is extremely well illustrated and is an accurate depiction of the significance of London over the other British ports. The Germans knew that preventing London from acting as the major food port for Britain would put severe stress on the western ports. The Bristol Channel ports accounted for about twelve percent of war imports. The most important ports were the Clyde and Liverpool.

2. The South Wales Ports 1933-1940

By the 1930s, the South Wales ports were facing several challenges. The economic dominance of coal was starting to lose its traditional grip on Welsh trade. Although coal was still vital for the nation, the rise of oil and petroleum products as alternative energy sources were slowly beginning to challenge the primacy of Welsh coal. In the early 1920s, many industries were keen to replace solid fuel with more flexible oil-based products for power-raising and industrial processes. The financial gamble of introducing oil refining into South Wales in the early 1920s was a big leap into a new world (Payton-Smith 1971: 190–93).

Coal exports peaked shortly before World War One, with over 41,000,000 tons shipped from South Wales, and the war encouraged more imports of general cargoes into the Bristol Channel as the German navy's U-boat offensive intensified after 1917. The post-war boom in trade lasted into the mid-1920s until the global economic collapse of the 1930s brought shutdown and some collapse across the coalfield. By 1931, the tonnage of Welsh coal exported had almost halved to about 21,000,000 tons. Nevertheless, the war years 1914-1918 demonstrated that general cargo could be handled through South Wales, providing rail transport to the Midlands and Southeast England could be maintained and improved. By the early 1930s, the main South Wales ports had passed into the ownership of the Great Western Railway Company (GWR), giving the essential integration of port, transit, and delivery needed to ensure successful operation.

If there was one constant theme in early GWR ownership of the ports, it was 'faith in the future'. The GWR needed to modernise port facilities with improved ship handling machines, new hydraulic and electric cargo handling, communications and railway marshalling yards, coal handling methods and new fuels. All these areas were subject to rapid changes in technology, putting immense pressure on financial planning and investments.

Without the ports, the Welsh coal, iron and steel industries would not work, and increasingly, throughout the 1930s, the importance of food imports and general commodities could only grow. Everybody knew this on some level in Wales: the workers, the businessmen, the entrepreneurs, the port managers, the government and the Germans.

Not every port in the Bristol Channel was a GWR port. Many small ports and inlets, often with remarkable medieval or even earlier history, didn't feature on the grand Industrial Welsh landscape of the nineteenth century. The Welsh ports in the Bristol Channel were the central part of the GWR network, these being from East to West: Newport, Cardiff, Penarth, Barry, Port Talbot, Briton Ferry, and Swansea/Llandarcy. By 1939, the twelve German intelligence services believed they knew a lot about these ports. The German navy understood the Bristol Channel as thoroughly as any local mariner and senior naval staff understood the role of the Bristol Channel in the First World War and the nature of shipping and trade, often because they had fought in the Channel themselves. The German Air Force had similar knowledge, although nowhere near the level of detail enjoyed by the navy. It was a remarkable quirk of the Nazi government that the various intelligence services were never allowed to discuss and share what they knew among themselves, which, luckily for the British, meant that, when it really mattered, the German armed forces were never fully in command of the correct information to attack South Wales (Boog 1986: 127–29).

As mentioned previously, the Germans had considerable challenges in effectively managing the conduct of its armed forces. The difficulties of translating information into action (and that action being effective) was a constant problem. The in-depth research of Study Blue provided Luftwaffe intelligence with a sobering picture of the complexity of Britain as an enemy. The conclusion presented in the Study was suitably pessimistic in its prediction of a victorious outcome for Germany. For *Reichsmarschall* Göring, that was sufficient for him to hide the report from his leader, Adolf Hitler. However, the information collected by the expert intelligence teams could not be disposed of. The notion of attacking the Welsh ports by air emerged in early November 1939. Barely two months into the war, the Germans temporarily postponed military action against France. This left the possibility of beginning an air war against Britain from air bases in northern Germany. A proposal for conducting an air warfare campaign was drafted using the information collected by Study Blue. The document carried an initial justification, acknowledging that Britain was Germany's 'most dangerous of all possible enemies'. The proposal confirmed that air action needed to be against three types of targets: ports, the British merchant Fleet, and the British Navy. Amongst the ports to be attacked, Bristol/Avonmouth was the significant local target (Schmid 1939: 4). Later that day, a further document was issued with a more detailed plan in a characteristic sign of the confused nature of the command structure. This second document (the 'plan for air warfare') mentions Cardiff and Swansea for the first time. Cardiff was identified as significant for grain mills and silos, cold storage and coal supply for France. Swansea's justification was the Llandarcy oil refineries and storage, grain mills and silos and timber stocks (pitwood and mining timber was a massive import into the eastern docks). These November 1939 references to Cardiff and Swansea are the first official indications that both ports were in the top five targets in Britain (German Air Historical Branch (8th Abteilung) 1939: 4). By the end of that November, the target status of both ports was formalised in a War Directive authorising air war against Britain's war economy (Alban 1994: 6–7).

It is interesting here to look at the German Navy's view of the role of the ports, which has survived in entries in the war diaries of the naval operations staff. The German Navy was increasingly apprehensive of its proposed role in any invasion of Britain. The Luftwaffe may have had doubts over the RAF's quality, but the German Navy knew they were going up against the most dangerous and capable navy in the world. On 6 June 1940, as planning for the next phase of war intensified in the German High Command, the senior naval staff sought to impress upon Göring that trade and imports were still (even always) the sensitive spot to attack. The navy had likely heard of the Luftwaffe's intent to attack southern English naval bases as a next phase of air attack. The navy men disagreed with the strategy, asking Göring to accept that only the south-western docks and harbours were likely to matter ('War Diary of German Naval Staff (Operations Division)' 1940a: 48–50). In what was a sign of anxiety over the Luftwaffe now being passed the mine laying task, the Navy also pointed out that mining heavily defended naval bases will be challenging as they will have strong anti-aircraft cover and abundant mine clearance equipment. The war diary entry concludes by saying that the navy would be best supported in its war on British trade by heavy bombing and mining attacks on Liverpool and the Bristol Channel. Göring accepted the argument but only in part, and haphazard uncoordinated air attacks continued throughout 1940.

The Ports as Targets

The packaged German intelligence information on the GWR ports was a combination of the research from *Studie Blau* (Study Blue), some early aerial photography collected between 1939-40, and a massive amount of mapping and cartographic work by the Topography and Military Geography Branch of the German Army. After August 1939, further work was completed by the German Army's Mapping and Survey Branch in Berlin (*Generalstab des Heeres Abteilung für Kriegskarten und Vermessungswesen*) (O'Neill 1968: 233–36). The available information (to support bombing missions) was supplemented by aerial reconnaissance conducted by specialised long-range reconnaissance units of the air force, which is discussed in a separate chapter.

The information was packaged into two types of information packs for distribution and use by various

---

Opposite: The folder and contents of the *Militärgeographische Angaben*. The full folders with their maps and guides are relatively rare as most were destroyed at the end of the war. Although it refers to 'England' prominently on the cover, the portfolio does cover Wales and Scotland. London had its own *Angaben*. This is an invasion copy of the *Angaben* from 1940, although the German General Staff kept working on revised maps and contents well into 1941 and even after the invasion of Russia in June 1941.

GB 7, BB 32, Nr. 86: Roath Dock in Cardiff (Glamorganshire).
Roath Dock (a 3) mit Großmühle, Bute East Dock (a 4), Bute West Dock (a 5), großes Stahlwerk (b).

Above: An oblique view of Cardiff's Roath Dock and Dowlais Steelworks from the photo handbook of the *Militärgeographische Einzelangaben*. This photo was taken before the war began as part of the clandestine photographing of potential targets in 1938. The ferro concrete building of the grain mills can be seen at the bottom of the photograph. Lighter coloured buildings tended to appear larger in black and white photos because of the extra light they reflect.

Opposite: The folder of the *Militärgeographische Einzelangaben* and some of the maps it contains. These folders have survived more often because they were numerous at Luftwaffe airbases. The maps in the *Einzelangaben* were meant to be useful for both army and air force. These maps are often misinterpreted as 'target' maps but they record details of military or community significance rather than bombing targets. This *Einzelangaben* is Nr 7 covering South (*Süd*) Wales although as always the cover refers to 'England'. However, the handbook does actually have a *Walisisch für deutsche Soldaten* (Welsh for German Soldiers) section which is a Welsh wordlist of the kinds of phrases an invading soldier would need. You will see extracts from the map portfolio throughout the book.

army and air force units. The first was a general thematic information pack (the *Militärgeographische Angaben* or 'the Military Geographical Details', often shortened to Mil.-Geo.). This was a thick bundle of maps covering England and Wales at the 1:100,000 scale, covering railways, roads, electricity, population, main roads and terrain. The bundle also included handbooks detailing every city and town the German military was likely to encounter. The handbook also contained an essential German-English dictionary. There was even a small German-Welsh wordlist (Generalstab des Heeres 1940: 234). The *Mil.-Geo. Angaben* also contained a booklet of street maps of each significant town (Generalstab des Heeres Abteilung für Kriegskarten und Vermessungswesen 1940).

The second type of pack was more detailed, with larger scale maps covering important military detail. This second type (known as the *Militärgeographische (Mil.-Geo.) Einzelangaben* or 'the particulars') was a thinner pack based on German maps of Britain at a scale of 1:250,000. The South Wales area (Sheet 7) was one of 12 packs covering the regions of England and Wales (Generalstab des Heeres 1941). Where the *Angaben* is full of broadly thematic maps describing the geography

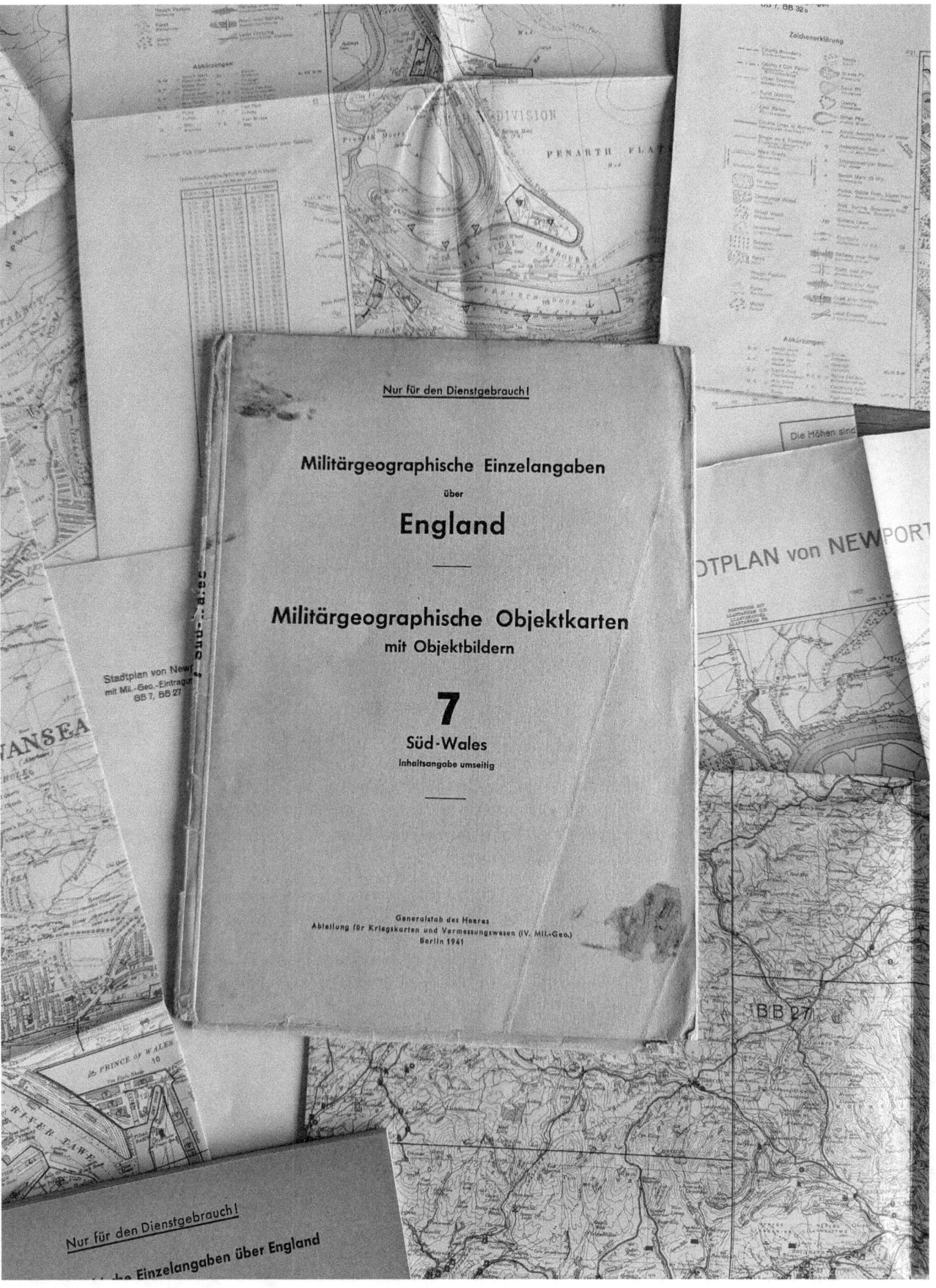

Above and Opposite: The two main parts of a Luftwaffe *Zielstammkarte (L)* (Target Master Map (L(uftwaffe)) are shown here. This is how the Luftwaffe categorised and evaluated targets for attack. Maps were used for navigation and photographs for target identification. These documents were stored in libraries at each bomber airbase and were readily available for the bomber crews to use for navigation and the technical crews to plan their bomb packages for the attacking aircraft. This target map is of an interesting part of the coastline between Swansea and Briton Ferry. A full description of the Luftwaffe Target Master document is included in the Annexes.

We would often call this area Jersey Marine and today some of it includes a new estate of University buildings and a water treatment works. As you'd expect the area has totally changed in its character from the industrial phase of the 1940s.

The main target element of this Master is Target GB 10 226, which was identified as a *Privat--Flugplatz* (small airfield) with a length of eight hundred metres and a function as an emergency landing strip, so it is a useful landing ground. At the time this document was written, the Germans were using parachute—and glider-borne troops, and landing spaces were identified throughout the country. The British Army recognised this fact, which encouraged obstructions and anti-glider defences on any attractive landing ground.

The target photo also highlights the many industrial installations in the area. At the extreme left is the eastern tip of Swansea's Queen's Dock (oil terminal), so any infrastructure related to oil supply will be identified. In this example, Oil infrastructure is numbered with the prefix '21', so the Anglo-Persian storage and pumping facility is GB 21 56, and the Llandarcy Oil Storage is numbered 2158. The Magnesium Works is marked GB 71 21 (important for explosives and pyrotechnics). The wagon and locomotive repair works are also identified in detail and marked 'G'.

The ideal approach to low-level bombing of Llandarcy was from the coastal side and the anti-aircraft and barrage balloon sites to interfere with such attacks are also identified and marked with 'H'.

| GB 10 226 bc | Swansea | Karte 1 : 100 000 |
| N. f. D. | Flugplatz | Engl. Bl. 26 b |

Bild Nr. F 316/41/015 v. 15.1.41. **Geogr. Lage:** 3° 57' W, 51° 37' 24" N, **Höhe ü. d. M.** 5 m **Stand:** II. 47.

Maßstab etwa 1 : 15 000 [1 cm = 150 m]   Lfl. Kdo. 3

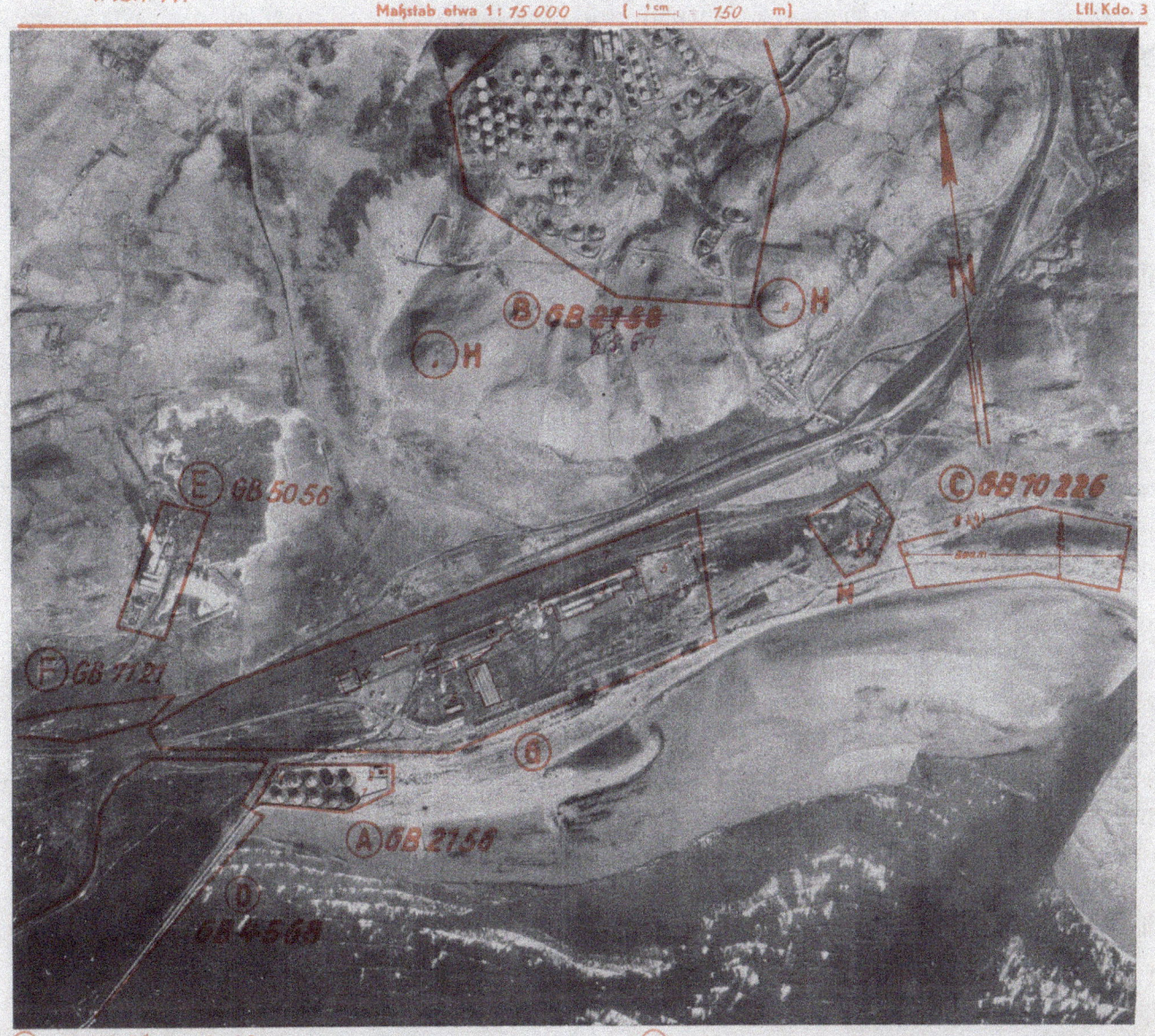

- (A) GB 21 56 Tanklager
  1) 9 Behälter etwa 9 700 qm
  2) Betriebsgebäude etwa 600 qm
     bebaute Fläche etwa 10 300 qm
     Gesamtfläche etwa 67 800 qm
- (B) GB 45 57 Tanklager
- (C) GB 10 226 Flugplatz 230 x 800 m
     keine Gebäulichkeiten, Rollfeld unbrauchbar
- (D) GB 45 68 Hafenanlage
- (E) GB 50 56 Grosskraftwerk
- (F) GB 71 21 Magnesiumwerk
- (G) GB Eisenbahnanlage mit Reparaturwerk
  3) Werkstättenhallen etwa 56 400 qm
  4) Lokomotivschuppen etwa 4 500 qm
  5) Ballonaufstiegstelle
  6) Nebengebäude etwa 2 500 qm
  7) Verschiebeanlagen
     bebaute Fläche etwa 63 400 qm
     Gesamtfläche etwa 845 000 qm
- (H) Flakstellungen
  8) Geschützstellungen
  9) Unterkünfte

of England and Wales, the Einzelangaben is a more practical set of maps used by army and air force men to prepare their attacks. The pack is underpinned with a top-quality topographical base map at 1:250 000 scales in five colours with a German language overprint of strategic, tactical, and economic features in red and purple. Important urban areas were covered in townplans (stadtpläne) at a 1:10 000 scale. These were sufficiently large-scale to act as tactical combat maps should the need arise. For South Wales, Newport, Cardiff, Aberavon-Port Talbot, and Swansea were depicted at this larger scale. In red or purple, these maps had overprints of tactical, industrial, energy, transport and political features. They are often misinterpreted as 'target' maps, but the Luftwaffe never used them for this.

Flight maps for England and Wales were produced separately by the Luftwaffe. These were often produced on the same lines as the Army 1:100,000 map, although they had five colours and red or magenta overprints.

The *Angaben* and the *Einzelangaben* map packs provided the basic information for the Luftwaffe Target Dossiers, which were the files that packaged all vital information for each target individually. The Target Dossiers were maintained by intelligence staff at a map library at or near each airfield. This ensured immediate access to target information when needed (Nielsen 1955: 44–51). The most common parts of the Dossiers that have survived are the *Zielstammkarten* or 'Target Master Cards' and the associated map extracts and aerial recognition photographs if they were available. The surviving GWR ports' targeting information is included in about sixty surviving target dossiers, maps, and explanatory notes.

The basic *Zielstammkarte* was a master record of seven sections covering sufficient target information to enable navigation to the target, an appreciation of the significance, and other important information. In these documents, we see the use of the individual numbers assigned to each specific target. The numbering format was the prefix 'GB' for *Grossbrittanien*' followed by four or five numbers. The numbers denoted two things; the first was the nature of the target. for example, ship repair is numbered '83', and gasworks are numbered '52'. The second element of the number was an individual identifier. So, Crindau Gasworks in Newport is Target (*Ziel*) GB 5256, and GB 8363 is Prince of Wales Dry Dock in Swansea.

The preprinted template was amended and circulated freely with relevant map extracts. The structure of a *Zielstammkarte* gives an insight into the type of air war the Luftwaffe wanted to fight over Britain. Amongst the essential flight and target information on longitude, latitude and map references, there is space for some other information on the precise nature of the target. Study Blue had already highlighted the need to understand basic working patterns and industrial workers' housing alongside some sociological information on the politics and local administration. The *Zielstammkarten* show us how this information (where known) translated into functional military information. Section 3c allows comment on the fire risk of target areas, and Section 3f goes further, prompting a workforce breakdown into men, women, nationality, political views and the quality of their housing, suggesting that should it be necessary, a degree of war against the population could be provided for. The individual port entries give some more details. One important point to bear In mind when looking at the target notes below is to appreciate the incredible amount of change that has taken place in the urban fabric of the GWR ports since 1945. Until the 1960s, most wartime features were still recognisable in Welsh towns. Still, dereliction and demolition transformed many areas and redevelopment since the 1990s has removed many landmark buildings and transformed the industrial landscapes. The once-thriving port areas of Newport, Cardiff and Barry have almost disappeared, leaving behind desolate expanses of water in the unused and deteriorating docklands. The defining characteristic of the early twentieth-century Welsh ports was that people worked near where they lived and vice versa. The mix of residential, industrial and port buildings was incredibly complex. Newport's dock area has changed beyond all recognition, with many streets surrounding the busy dock quarter hollowed out or wholly destroyed. Barry Docks is in the process of redevelopment but still retains an atmosphere of loss and dereliction. Should it ever happen, much of Swansea's Royal docks await their turn in redevelopment. In the German records of the GWR ports, we see the last of the best years of the Welsh ports when they were the centre of urban life, excitement and global travel and trade.

Above: Electric cranes at Newport discharging general cargo at the No. 5 Transit Shed, south side of Alexandra South Dock. Electric cranes were fast and efficient at unloading. These cranes were newly installed in the early 1930s with improved concrete flooring in the transit sheds to facilitate wheeled traffic.

The Ports at War

The outcome of the switch to wartime working would be that millions of tons of goods and commodities of all kinds would be diverted to Cardiff, Swansea, and Barry. Even though the GWR had invested heavily in the 1930s to make these ports more responsive to commercial needs, there were going to be problems in goods handling.

A vital component in the port management process was the transit shed. These were where goods were laid out and sorted before despatch on railway systems dedicated to the quick and efficient distribution of goods to the surrounding towns and cities. The dedication of the GWR ports to the Welsh coal and steel industries meant that most of the facilities were designed to export coal and import ore, iron, steel and timber (Behrens 1955: 148–49). The 1930s additions of grain mills, cold storage, and food imports were substantial investments that attracted the attention of the Study Blue researchers.

There are three primary tasks that a port undertakes: first, the discharge of a ship; second, the handling and sorting of goods on quays and wharves; and finally, the despatch of goods to markets or storage areas. With regard to discharge, machines designed to deal with unloading specific materials such as grain or minerals could rarely be used for other commodities. Moreover, before the container revolution of the 1960s, general cargo came in various packages of all shapes and sizes: bags of sugar, sacks of flour, carboys of chemicals, hogsheads of tobacco, crates of fruit or bales of cotton and wool. All of these goods required different skills and techniques in unloading and distribution.

The merchant ships of the 1930s usually had their own cranes and derricks, which were able to unload the ship quite quickly, but only if the ship was carrying a cargo she was designed for, which was often not the case in wartime. It was always desirable to use the dockside cranes if the port was so equipped. In the inter-war period, there was a common dockside saying, 'The ship can always beat the quay,' which reflected the relative speed with which a ship could be unloaded and the somewhat slower nature of how goods were sorted for transit after that (Behrens 1955: 30). The heavy-lift cranes of Cardiff and Swansea became front-line equipment as only they could be used to unload new types of American and Canadian lorry (Behrens 1955: 150). Cargo sorting was often an extremely complicated process for many goods that needed careful processing, which entailed large transit warehouses holding the

Above: The Cardiff grain mills at Queen Alexandra dock in late November 1940 and opposite the wider area on 3 January 1941. Although the Dowlais works were considered important, it was the grain mills that were considered vital to Britain's war effort. The Norwegian ores that supplied Dowlais were cut off at the Fall of Norway and the contingency measure was importing increased quantities of steel products from America, boosting the economic prospects of the American steel industries. The increase in shipping massive quantities of steel billets from America caused a lot of damage to merchant ships making the Atlantic crossing and the arrival of a convoy always meant queues for ship repair at the Mountstuart shipyards. The 1940 image shows a lot of imported goods being stacked in the open air and being protected by a barrage

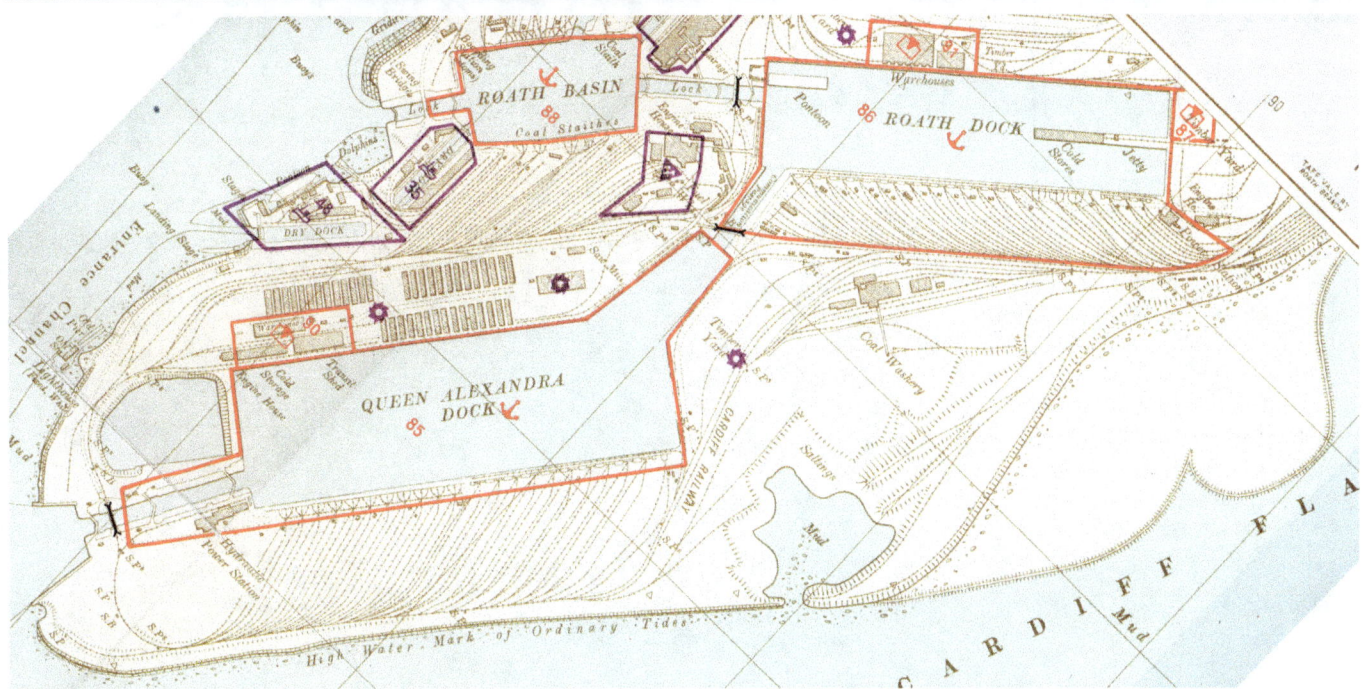

balloon. The winter of 1940 saw the beginning of the Welsh ports crisis when Cardiff and Swansea ran out of space in their transit sheds and a shortage of locomotives and wagons meant that the ports could not be cleared of goods. The grain wharves can be seen as busy in both images as Britain relied on American and Canadian grain. Above is the German *Stadtplan* for Cardiff which shows the significant docks and buildings as strategic assets, although, the edition of the map was too early to include the newly built grain mills which were completed in the 1930s. The red triangles on the map show the Germans were aware of the transit sheds that were used to store goods.

goods. Although the South Wales ports were equipped with transit warehouses, they were often inadequate in dealing with the vast amount of goods handled (Behrens 1955: 149). In both Cardiff and Swansea, Luftwaffe aerial reconnaissance photographs show large quantities of material stacked and sorted in the open air because the transit sheds were full of material. Congestion on the quays was one of the biggest problems the South Wales ports faced in the war.

In the crisis period of the winter of 1940-41, there was great concern that merchant ships arriving at Swansea, Cardiff, and Barry were waiting for days and even weeks for available quay space. Simply put, had the congestion at Swansea, Cardiff Barry and the other western ports lasted into 1941 in any substantial measure, Britain would have lost the war because it could not feed its population and maintain and re-equip its armed forces (Behrens 1955: 154).

In addition to being severely challenged about unloading and sorting, the ports also faced problems with distributing goods. London and Liverpool had developed superb rail networks (and increasingly, in the 1930s, road networks) to distribute goods to markets or storage as needed. The South Wales ports relied heavily on railways to distribute goods inland and into England. The marshalling yards, junctions and working routines, whilst superbly geared to the coal trade, proved extremely difficult to adapt to wartime requirements. It fell to the railway companies to clear the ports of all incoming goods and to keep them clear so that ships could be unloaded quickly and returned to outgoing convoys (Behrens 1955: 154). Eventually, the rail industry could not cope, and in early 1941, a tremendous increase in road haulage encouraged the development of the British lorry industry (Savage 1957: 479).

In the winter of 1940, the speed at which a ship could be discharged and cleared from the port became crucial, particularly as German U-boat operations improved in skill and results. It was quickly acknowledged that Cardiff, Barry and Swansea needed immediate improvements to their railway systems to enable them to rail supplies away from the ports. Between July 1940 and January 1941, £117,000 was spent on additional sidings at the Welsh ports, and another £257,090 was committed to line improvements between Newport and Severn Tunnel Junction (Savage 1957: 647–48). It soon became apparent that the Severn Tunnel was the critical element in clearing the Welsh ports, for coal had to be shipped to England in massive quantities, and general cargoes also needed to move south and east. Of course, the other side of the equation was that laden wagons would ultimately have to return empty, thus compounding the traffic problems. The only solution was to use the tunnel to maximum capacity all day and every day, including Sunday, traditionally a day for track and tunnel maintenance. This was eventually done in early 1941 and did go some way towards alleviating the situation.

In addition to the sheer numbers of wagons that needed to be moved, there was also the problem of the nature of the goods being received. The massive increase in frozen meat coming into Cardiff and Swansea soon resulted in an acute shortage of refrigerated and insulated wagons, which prevented the ships' unloading and increased congestion at the ports. While all these problems were central to Britain's war effort, none proved insurmountable, and, given time, solutions were found to most of the difficulties.

However, the challenge to the Welsh ports did not end there. The fall of France in May 1940 changed the strategic map of the war almost completely. France was

---

Previous pages: South Wales as depicted on the German 1:250 000 *Militärgeographische Objektkarte*. This is from the August 1941 edition which shows that background preparations for an invasion were still happening after the invasion of the Soviet Union in June 1941. The quality of this map easily exceeds the normal mapping standards from Britain's Ordnance Survey at the time.

Opposite above: Railway sleepers stacked at Newport Docks. If coal was the export, timber for the coal and rail industries was certainly a main import. Britain consumed thousands of tons of timber and any threat to the timber trade was a serious strategic threat. Cardiff, Barry and Swansea had large storage spaces for mining and railway timber.

Opposite lower: The Cardiff Mountstuart Shipyards on 28 February 1941. The repair docks are full of merchantmen either being repaired after Atlantic journeys or being treated with magnetic mine countermeasures. The convoy system meant that many cargo vessels had to carry goods and materials that they weren't designed and equipped to handle. Cargoes would shift in the holds in heavy seas and cause internal damage to the ships.

an ally, not only in the military sense but also in the way of raw materials. The implication of the German victory was much more profound than the government had imagined. Whilst the Battle of Britain raged overhead, the consequences of Britain's isolation emerged item by sinister item: Britain's traditional sources of iron ore were from France, Spain and French North Africa. With the German occupation of the French Atlantic coast, Britain had lost access to over six million tons of iron ore a year. The Dowlais works in Cardiff had been rebuilt in the 1930s specifically to take advantage of high-quality Spanish and Norwegian iron ore supplies, and a shortage of the appropriate quality iron ore would severely jeopardise its effective contribution to the war effort. Alternative supplies were eventually received from Sierra Leone and South Africa. Other supply sources were lost: Flax, nickel, bauxite, zinc, hemp, and chrome ore, all of which were lost in significant quantities. New sources of supply had to be sought in Africa, the Far East and the Americas. The implications for the British merchant fleet were ominous. Many vessels had to travel farther afield carrying cargoes which, if not unfamiliar, were unsuitable or even dangerous as many ships had never been designed to carry bulk cargoes in the variety and quantity now required. Ships returning to Britain were heavily laden with these much-needed goods and raw materials, and they had to run the gauntlet of the U-boats. If this was not daunting enough, the North Atlantic in winter took its toll on heavily laden ships crossing some of the roughest seas in the world.

The above result is that many ships arrived at the Welsh ports in a dilapidated state, often severely damaged by shifting loads in their holds. Whilst the quays of the Welsh ports filled with goods, the repair yards filled with many of the ships that had carried them. By January 1941, thirteen per cent of Britain's merchant fleet was tied up, awaiting repair. The number of ships laid up and awaiting repair posed a more significant threat than the U-boat menace. Ships queued up at Cardiff, Barry and Swansea for attention. Ship repair facilities are always featured amongst Luftwaffe target lists. The dry docks were also used extensively for fitting ships with degaussing apparatus to protect against magnetic mines.

This was particularly important in the Bristol Channel because the physical characteristics of the approach channels to Swansea and Cardiff were particularly suited to the magnetic mines laid by the Germans. The Bristol Channel featured prominently in the mine war. With an eye on the strategic implications, the German Naval High Command attempted to use U-boats to disrupt the Welsh timber import trade, which had close links with the northern ports of the Soviet Union. Equally, the iron ore traffic from Narvik to South Wales was also considered worthy of disruption. Although the U-boat command always remained sceptical of the value of this trade, it preferred to concentrate on the high-value convoy trade of the North Atlantic. The conflict of opinion highlights the different views evident in the German Navy's command on how an effective trade war could be waged against Britain. The Germans' lack of clear focus was to have disastrous consequences for their effective prosecution of the North Atlantic trade war.

U-boats and the Mine War

For the German navy, mines had proved their worth in disrupting British coastal trade in the First World War. Technical advances in the early 1930s ensured they would become an even more effective weapon in the coming conflict. The basic contact mines of the early 1900s had become much more sophisticated with various developments in explosives and fuses and methods of delivering them to their target areas. Chief among the developments was the magnetic mine.

The first magnetic mines were developed by the Royal Navy and laid off the Belgian coast in August and September 1918. They were not considered a success; many detonated soon after being laid, and further British interest in developing the weapon waned with the armistice in November 1918. However, the 1920s saw some progress in developing a moored magnetic mine for defensive purposes.

German interest in magnetic mines dates back to the earliest days of rearmament in 1932. The German

Right: A 1940 British information sheet issued to army and naval staff on the characteristics of the German Navy TMB magnetic mine. This type of mine was laid in Swansea Bay by U-boats in 1939 by U28 and U32. The U32 war diary describing the Scarweather mission in December is in the Annexes.

Mine Type GS (GN)

General

1. Ground, influence mine, laid by submarine. Magnetic needle, acoustic or magnetic-acoustic firing.
2. German designation, "TMB".
3. Offensive mine, for use against surface craft.

Description

1. Case

Shape	Cylindrical, with hemispherical ends. Deflecting fin on tail door.
Color	Black or buff
Material	Aluminum.
Diameter	21"
Length	
Overall	7'7 1/2"
Case	6'6"
Tail door	13 1/2"
Charge	1221 lbs. cast Hexanite.
Total weight in air	1540 lbs.

2. External fittings

Positioning lug	On top center line, 3'9 1/2" abaft the nose.
Hydrostatic clock	6" diam., on top center line, 5' 6 1/2" abaft the nose, secured by keep ring.
Booster release mechanism	4" diam., on top center line, 4'5" abaft the nose, secured by keep ring.
80-day clock cover plate	8" diam., on top center line, 3'2" abaft the nose, secured by keep ring.
Detonator cover plate	4 3/4" diam., 180° from top center line, 4'6 1/2" abaft the nose, secured by keep ring.
Filling holes	Two; one, 5" diam., threaded to nose; one, 6" diam., 90° from top center line, 4' 6 1/2" abaft the nose; secured by four screws.
Safety bar clamp	On top center line at after end.

3. Mine Type GN differs from Mine Type GS as follows:

    (a) Its German designation is, "TMC".

    (b) It is 11'1 1/2" long overall, carries a charge of 2000 lbs. and weights 2300 lbs.

    (c) It is fitted with extra filling holes due to the larger charge although all essential fittings are positioned identically measured from the tail.

Operation

1. When the mine is launched, a spring-loaded safety bar is released from the top center line of the case, thereby unlocking the hydrostatic clock and booster release mechanism. Water pressure depresses the clock spindle and operates the booster release mechanism, respectively, at a depth of 15 ft., starting the clock and allowing the booster to house over the detonator. The clock runs off its delay setting and the firing unit begins its arming cycle.

2. See Table #1 for possible firing units fitted.

3. The only self-disarming device is the 80-day clock which may be fitted to sterilize the mine at the end of its set period by shorting out the battery.

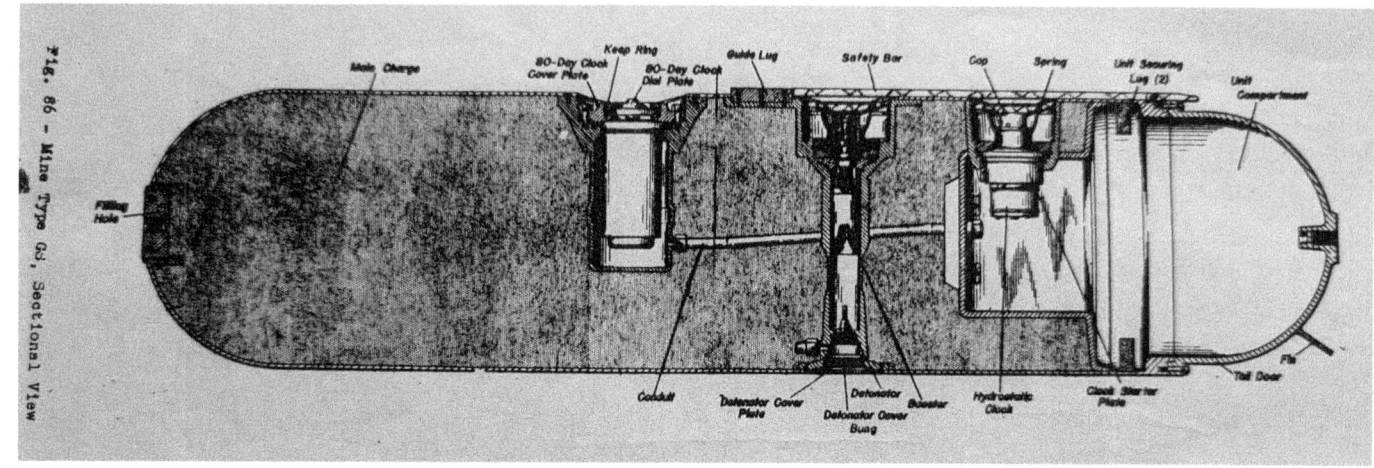

Above: A British bomb disposal diagram of the anatomy of the U-boat launched magnetic ground mine from 1940. These mines were laid successfully near the Scarweather Lightship in December 1939 by U32.

Navy worked closely with Rheinmetall-Borsig, which was also heavily engaged in developing a series of electromechanical bomb fuses for the German Air Force. An effective magnetic mine presented challenging technical problems, and a satisfactory solution was not achieved until late 1936. The German Navy planned to lay their magnetic mines by surface craft and U-boats, building on their experiences of the 1914-1918 war, when covert mine laying proved very successful in disrupting patterns of commerce for both sides.

By 1939, the German navy possessed a highly effective magnetic ground mine, which, unlike conventional moored contact mines, could be laid very accurately in shipping lanes and approaches to ports and which did not have an effective set of countermeasures. The British were unaware that Rheinmetall had solved the technical problems of an effective magnetic fuse. The German naval staff were confident that the mine would be highly effective in a trade war with a maritime power. Furthermore, effective countermeasures would take a long time to develop. In early 1939, there was considerable debate in the U-boat command over how to use this new weapon effectively.

U-boat command realised that the mine weapon could only be used effectively in specific circumstances. The mine would only be effective in depths of 25 to 30 metres (i.e. coastal waters). It was best suited to narrow approach channels and high-activity areas, presumably subject to intense anti-submarine patrols. The submarine-launched mines could be laid accurately and quickly with the minimum exposure by the U-boat. It was also believed that winter nights were the best time to lay mines as bad weather and poor visibility would often prejudice attacks by torpedo and mine laying, thus providing the best value for U-boat sorties. Most submarine-laid mines were fitted with an 80-day clock fuse. At the end of this period, the mine rendered itself inert, thus enabling subsequent U-boats to enter mined areas for further missions. One further element of effective mine laying was a detailed understanding of the nature of coastal traffic. To that end, interviews with German merchant crews were supplemented by careful observation by U-boat captains, particularly during the opening months of hostilities ('War Diary of German Naval Staff (Operations Division)' 1940b: 138). However, both navies were intimately familiar with each other's shipping and trade patterns due to the 1914-1918 war.

The specific requirements of the magnetic mine and the pattern of shipping activity in the Bristol Channel made it an obvious choice for mine operations in the closing months of 1939. Accordingly, several U-boats were given missions to lay mines and operate with torpedoes in the Channel. U28, U29, U32 and U33, each carrying 12 mines and six torpedoes, were despatched to mine Swansea, Milford Haven and The Foreland in September and December (Hessler 1989: 12). The magnetic mine used for these early operations was the TMB mine (Admiralty designation 'Type GS'). This mine contained five hundred kilogrammes of explosive in a cylindrical case just over seven feet in length. Although Type VII U-boats could theoretically carry thirty three TMB mines, carrying a small number of torpedoes was always considered prudent. Thus, a mix of twelve mines and six torpedoes is a typical mission load. Operational experience with the TMB mine revealed that it was ineffective at depths greater than twenty five metres, which put greater pressure on U-boat commanders to place them in the correct position and at the correct depth. It is possible that the loss of U33 in the Firth of Clyde in February 1940 was due to the need for the boat to move as close as possible to the mouth of the Clyde to lay her mines at the required depth and hence being caught in shallow water by an anti-submarine patrol.

The campaigns in the Bristol Channel were supplemented by many other mine-laying operations around the East Coast of Britain, resulting in severe disruptions in coastal traffic. The net result of the campaign was to increase the importance of West Coast ports in the reception of North Atlantic convoys, which was precisely what the U-boat command had anticipated. The mines were beginning to take a worrying toll on coastal ships. However, because of the covert way in which they were laid and the near impossibility of being able to detect them, many mine detonations were attributed to torpedo attacks. The result was many supposed U-boat sightings around the coast, even though the number of boats involved at any one time was minimal.

Clandestine magnetic mine laying was a success by the onset of winter 1939. At a senior staff conference in November to review the mine war, naval officers Dönitz and Raeder considered future strategies. They decided minefields would be laid at as many vital points as possible. The intention being to cause general disruption to shipping traffic. Secondly, narrow access channels were to be given special attention, with many minefields to deny them to the enemy for a long time.

Experience with the TMB mine highlighted the necessity of laying the weapon at the appropriate depth. The 25-metre depth limitation was causing problems for the crews. The Mines Inspectorate were in the process of developing a larger weapon with a charge of 2000 pounds. This could be laid at greater depths, allowing for more operational flexibility. This new mine, the TMC (Admiralty designation 'Type GS'), was expected to be ready by December 1939.

The Bristol Channel was confirmed as a perfect environment for mine laying. U-boat command realised that with the virtual closure of the North Sea ports, Liverpool, Swansea, Barry, Cardiff, Newport, and Bristol would be vital for importing food and war supplies. The ports would undoubtedly have experienced far heavier mine-laying attacks but for the shortage of suitable U-boats. The first U boat to lay mines in the Bristol Channel was U32, busy near the Scarweather Lightship on 17 September 1939 (Fricke 1939: 79). See Annex One. The merchant ship Loch Goil struck one of the U32 mines on 6 October. The ship was severely damaged and run aground in Swansea Bay before being taken into Swansea Docks for repairs ('War Diary of German Naval Staff (Operations Division)' 1939a: 44). The German navy command believed the disruption to shipping was huge. A report of eleven freighters being damaged and beached between Swansea and Pembroke between 16 and 21 October was evidence of the impact a set of magnetic mines could have ('War Diary of German Naval Staff (Operations Division)' 1939a: 161). In November, a further Bristol Channel mining mission was given to U33 ('War Diary of German Naval Staff (Operations Division)' 1939b: 34). Perhaps most famously, U28 and U29 were both in the Bristol Channel in early November, with U28 specifically dropping twelve TMB mines at Swansea. The weather was poor at the time, and it took some time before U28 could complete its mission ('War Diary of German Naval Staff (Operations Division)' 1939b: 54, 110, 128, 151). U28 was later seen loitering off Ilfracombe, monitoring ship traffic with eleven patrol vessels in pursuit. U28's mines caused some disruption, and German radio monitoring picked up radio reports of Swansea being shut to shipping for the rest of November. That month also saw the realisation that Barry was of strategic interest as observations and radio monitoring confirmed Barry as a 'port of embarkation' in moving supplies to France ('War Diary of German Naval Staff (Operations Division)' 1939b: 28).

The German Navy was also directed to spend more time looking at the contribution of the GWR ports to the war economy. In a naval conference held at the end of November, Barry was added to the list alongside Cardiff and Swansea, which are important coal export ports for the French industry ('War Diary of German Naval Staff (Operations Division)' 1939c: 1–2). By January 1940, the gradual deterioration of relationships between the warring powers meant changes in the rules for unrestricted submarine warfare in the Bristol Channel. This meant that the Bristol Channel and, eventually, the Irish Sea became more dangerous (Hessler 1989: 40–43). Later in January, U28 mines claimed their most famous victim, the SS Protesilaus, which was blown in half. Protesilaus eventually became a propaganda curiosity as Luftwaffe reconnaissance staff watched from the air the

Der halbierte Britendampfer

Deutschen Aufklärern entgeht nichts

Noch vor den letzten großen Angriffen der deutschen Luftwaffe auf Swansea hatte einen großen britischen Frachtdampfer im Bristolkanal sein Schicksal erreicht. Schwer angeschlagen konnte das Schiff sich gerade noch ins flache Wasser der Küstennähe retten, wo es unter der Einwirkung von Wind und Wellen gänzlich auseinanderbrach. Die Briten können es sich nicht leisten, so viele Tonnen wertvollen Eisens, wie sie ein moderner Dampfer darstellt, brachliegen zu lassen. Wenn der Dampfer nicht mehr als solcher zu verwenden ist, dann muß wenigstens das Eisen als Schrott geborgen werden. Ihre Versuche, den Dampfer zu bergen, gelangen nur zum Teil. Während das Achterschiff allen Bemühungen widerstand, konnte die vordere Hälfte des Schiffes abgeschleppt werden. Sie wurde in Swansea, einem Hafen am nördlichen Ufer des Bristolkanals, ins Trockendock gebracht. Auf dem unteren Bild ist das Vorderschiff, durch einen Pfeil gekennzeichnet, deutlich im trockengepumpten Dock zu sehen. Die beiden Aufnahmen, eine Meisterleistung deutscher Fernaufklärung, beweisen wieder einmal, unter welch genauer Beobachtung alle Vorgänge auf der britischen Insel liegen. Aufnahmen: Luftwaffe (2)

Opposite: The worlds of reconnaissance and magnetic mines coincided with the Luftwaffe propaganda coverage of the destruction of the SS Protesilaus in January 1940. Protesilaus hit a TMB mine laid the previous month by U28 in the shipping channel south of Rotherslade Bay near Swansea. The ship was severely damaged, and the partial remains were towed to Swansea Bay and beached on the sands at West Cross, a popular site for beaching damaged vessels. The regular overflights of reconnaissance observed the drama of Protesilaus, and the story was eventually thought entertaining enough to be included in the Luftwaffe propaganda magazine 'Der Adler' in April 1941. The eventual article had two images of the vessel, one on the sands at West Cross and the second in the Palmer's Dry Dock inside King's Dock. The translated article is below, although sometimes the flowery language of propaganda can be challenging to translate efficiently!

'The British steamer cut in half

Nothing escapes German reconnaissance

Even before the last major attacks by the German Luftwaffe on Swansea, a large British freight steamer had met its fate in the Bristol Channel,

Severely damaged, the ship was just able to escape into the shallow water near the coast, where it completely fell apart under the influence of wind and waves. The British cannot afford to let as many tons of iron as a modern steamship lie idle. If the steamer can no longer be used as such, then at least the iron must be turned into scrap. Their attempts to salvage the steamer are only partially successful. While the rear half resisted all efforts, the front half of the ship was able to be towed away. She was sent to dry dock in Swansea, a port on the northern bank of the Bristol Channel. In the picture below, the front ship, marked by an arrow, can clearly be seen in the pumped dry dock.

The two images, a masterpiece of German long-distance reconnaissance, prove once again how closely all events on the British island are under observation. Photographs of the Air Force (2).'

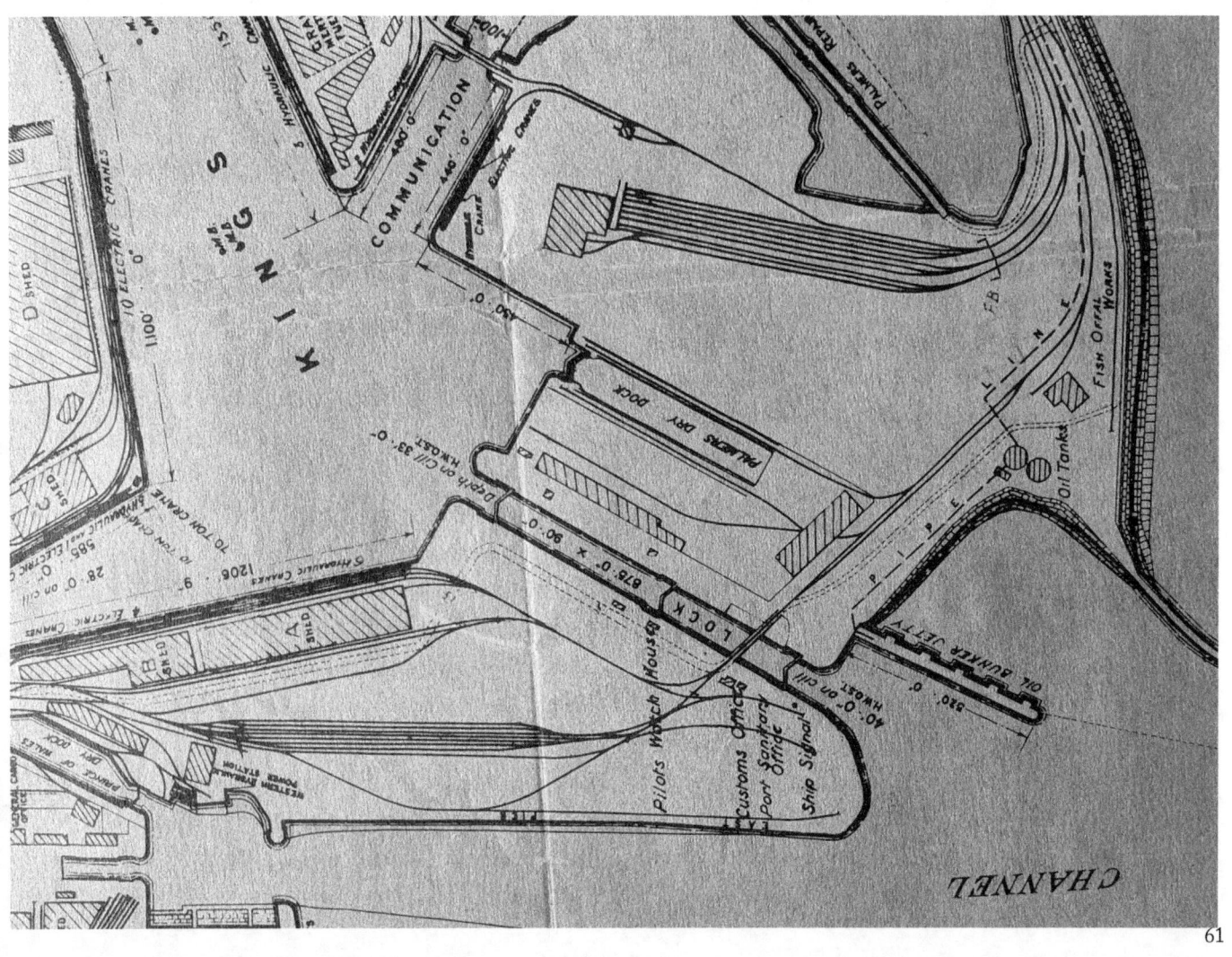

attempts to salvage the wreck and its eventual transfer from the beach at West Cross to Swansea Docks and made her into a feature article in Luftwaffe propaganda magazine Der Adler ('Der halbierte Britendampfer' 1941). U29 returned to the Bristol Channel with more mines off Swansea at the end of January ('War Diary of German Naval Staff (Operations Division)' 1940b: 125). The boat appears to have travelled the Welsh coast in February ('War Diary of German Naval Staff (Operations Division) Part A, Volume 6, 1-29 February 1940, 1948 | US. Naval War College Archives' 1948: 66). By 19 March 1940, U29 laid twelve mines and also sank three ships on the way out of the Channel ('War Diary of German Naval Staff (Operations Division)' 1940c: 87).

The TMB and TMC mines would have doubtless remained formidable weapons for a long time were it not for the intervention of the Luftwaffe. Senior German Air Force staff were great admirers of the magnetic mine and pressed for the need to have an air-dropped variant from the war's outset. Senior naval officers objected strongly to air-dropped mines, fearing they would be imprecise and risk a mine falling on land. Naval staff knew that the weapon's effect depended solely on the enemy's ignorance of how it worked. However, the Luftwaffe argued that the shortage of U-boats meant that mines could never be deployed in the numbers necessary for mass disruption unless air delivery was adopted. The Air Force argument carried the day, and air-dropped variants of the mines were constructed. The magnetic fuse was comparatively delicate, necessitating a parachute to limit the impact force upon the water. This was another unpopular step as it enabled the mine to drift on the wind, often for a considerable distance, compounding the fear that they would land on dry land. As a precaution, the parachute mines were given bomb fuses, which would explode the mine shortly after impact if, by that time, the fuse was not covered by at least 4m (13 feet) of water.

The German Navy pioneered the development of air-dropped mines in the 1930s, probably with an eye to the future development of its maritime air fleet. Dropping a technically delicate device such as the mine from the air wasn't easy. The aircraft had to fly level at a constant speed of about 330 kilometres per hour. This ensured the parachute-retarded mine hit the sea at the right angle to avoid destruction. Deployed correctly, the air mine was sufficient to sink a ship of about ten thousand tons. The ship had to pass within sixty metres of the mine for a detonation to occur. The immediate problem was the giant parachute needed to slow the bomb's descent. The slow rate of fall made it impossible to aim the mine accurately, so it could only be used in large river mouths or wide bays, unlike the surgical precision of a U-boat-placed mine (Marquard 1955: 377).

The Luftwaffe jealously watched the successful ground mine campaign develop and became eager to develop their own successes. Air Force units commenced laying parachute mines on 17 November 1939, regardless of the protests by the navy. Within days, the navy's worst fears had been realised. On 23 November 1939, the first magnetic mine was spotted on the mud flats near Shoeburyness. In an operation that forms one of the most famous chapters of bomb disposal history, Lieutenant Commander R.C. Lewis RN and Chief Petty Officer Baldwin defused the mine. After a day of careful work, the Admiralty was told that the first magnetic mine had been recovered. The British knew precisely the value of the information that had been obtained. On the evening of 23 November, Lieutenant Commander Lewis presented his findings to Winston Churchill and sixty senior naval officers. Within days, the scientific secrets of the mine were revealed, and countermeasures were being devised.

The technical experts at HMS Vernon knew that the ground mines were magnetically detonated, but at last, they had an actual example to work with. The crucial information was the polarity of the detonators and whether they worked in the horizontal or vertical magnetic fields set up by the metal hulls of ships. The Shoeburyness mine was actuated when subjected to a field of 50 milligauss, and it was a simple matter to reduce the magnetic field of any ship below 50 mg by winding a current-bearing coil around the hull of the ship to give her less North Pole down polarity. This countermeasure became known as 'degaussing'. A merchant ship could be effectively degaussed in three days, although this short delay often caused problems. A simpler and faster process known as 'wiping' was also devised, which would quickly alter the magnetic signature of a boat for a temporary period (up to six months). Wiping only took about twelve hours and could be done with a minimum of specialist equipment in any port. The German navy learned that the British had discovered the countermeasure by a rather clumsy Parliamentary statement describing the new installation of 'defense girdles against magnetic mines', which clearly referred to the degaussing coils being used. The news must have been rather depressing for them and once again illustrates the indifferent attitude of the British press to reporting sensitive issues ('War Diary of German Naval Staff (Operations Division)' 1940c: 88). The enduring threat of the mines off Swansea continued up to 16 March 1940 when German radio services intercepted Admiralty warnings to avoid Swansea (Fricke 1940: 105).

The changing circumstances of the war in April and May 1940 meant that the operational requirements for U-boats increased rapidly, and all available boats were taken off minelaying tasks and rearmed for torpedo and gun attacks. This was eventually confirmed by a direct order from Adolf Hitler on 2 April 1940 ('War Diary of German Naval Staff (Operations Division)' 1940d: 12). From now on, the Bristol Channel mine war would be conducted by the air force.

Once the technical nature of the mine had been laid bare, its desired effect was much reduced. The Navy's dire warnings that the Air Force would give the secret away had come true with a startling speed. The mine war intensified after that. Both sides invested considerable time and resources in producing more complex fuse systems and effective countermeasures. The U-boat command knew that Allied shipping had been fitted with degaussing equipment from April 1940. Towards the end of 1940, The TMB/C series mines were fitted with magnetic/acoustic fuses, which caused significant disruption until effective countermeasures were devised. However, the defusing of the Shoeburyness mine had already robbed the U-boat arm of one of its best assets: surprise.

A final rather unpleasant postscript to the story concerns the German Air Force. The incorporation of a bomb fuse into the air-dropped variant enabled the weapon to be used as a high-capacity parachute retarded blast bomb. This method of use proved irresistible to the Air Force, particularly as they faced a shortage of large conventional bombs. On the night of 16 September 1940, at least 25 magnetic mines were dropped on London. Seventeen of these weapons failed to explode due to the fuses being damaged on impact or hung up on their parachutes and failing to go into their arming cycle. Those that did explode invariably had a devastating effect, and many British towns were to bear the scars of the massive explosions that these weapons yielded. Both Swansea and Cardiff suffered dreadful damage on the occasions that parachute mines were used. This is the origin of the term 'land-mine' (Marquard 1955: 377–78).

Although the U-boat command moved its boats onto other tasks, the Luftwaffe continued to use mines against trade in the Bristol Channel. Throughout July 1940, regular mine drops were organised for Cardiff and Swansea. Even Llanelli was visited at the end of the month ('War Diary of German Naval Staff (Operations Division)' 1940e: 120,137,152,216,237,245). This resulted in considerable time and resources being expended by naval mine sweeping outside the ports for the whole of August ('War Diary of German Naval Staff (Operations Division)' 1940f: 24). As an attempt to maintain the pressure on the defences and to interrupt vital war production, missions were usually flown on nights when no other raids were taking place, thereby extending the amount of time an area remained under Red Alert. Further missions were flown in late October, abandoning the planned invasion of Britain and switching to a blockade policy resumed by He 111s of KGr 126 flying from Nantes in Brittany. This unit was reorganised as I/KG 28 in December 1940 and continued minelaying until July 1941. All areas considered suitable for U-boat minelaying were considered appropriate targets for aerial campaigns. With the realisation that the mines could cause massive damage on dry land, the minelaying Gruppen were often used to supplement air raids on the west coast ports. Further minelaying occurred between October and December 1941 with the transfer of Ju 88s of III/KG 30 from the Balkans to Melun in France.

Alban, J.R. 1994. The Three Nights' Blitz: Select Contemporary Reports Relating to Swansea's Air Raids of February 1941, Studies in Swansea's History, 3 (Swansea: City of Swansea)

Behrens, C.B.A. 1955. Merchant Shipping and the Demands of War (London: HMSO)

Boog, Horst. 1986. 'German Air Intelligence in World War II', Aerospace Historian, 33.2: 121–29

'Der halbierte Britendampfer'. 1941. Der Adler, p. 5

Fricke, Adm. 1940. 'War Diary of German Naval Staff

(Operations Division)' (US. Naval War College Archives) <https://www.usnwcarchives.org/repositories/2/archival_objects/34385> [accessed 9 January 2024]

Fricke, Kpt. 1939. 'War Diary of German Naval Staff (Operations Division)', (US. Naval War College), Archives <https://www.usnwcarchives.org/repositories/2/archival_objects/34365> [accessed 9 January 2024]

Generalstab des Heeres. 1940. 'Militärgeographische Angaben über England Textheft' (Abteilung für Kriegskarten und Vermessungswesen, IV,-Mil.Geo.)

———. 1941. 'Militärgeographische Einzelangaben Uber England Militärgeographische Objektkarten Mit Objektbildern 7 Süd-Wales' (Abteilung für Kriegskarten und Vermessungswesen, IV,-Mil.Geo.)

Generalstab des Heeres Abteilung für Kriegskarten und Vermessungswesen. 1940. Militärgeographische Angaben über England (Mappe A) (Berlin: Abteilung für Kriegskarten und Vermessungswesen)

German Air Historical Branch (8th Abteilung). 1939. The Course of the Air War against England (Berlin: German Air Historical Branch)

Hessler, Gunter. 1989. The U-boat War in the Atlantic 1939-1945, ed. by Andrew J. Withers (London: HMSO)

Marquard, Ernst R. 1955. The Planning and Development of Bombs for the German Air Force 1925-1945 (Maxwell Air Force Base, Alabama)

Nielsen, Andreas L. 1955. The Collection and Evaluation of Intelligence for the German Air Force High Command, p. 225

O'Neill, Robert J. 1968. The German Army and the Nazi Party (London: Cassell)

Payton-Smith, D.J. 1971. Oil: A Study of War-Time Policy and Administration (London: HMSO)

Savage, C.I. 1957. Inland Transport (London: HMSO)

Schmid, Joseph ('Beppo'). 1939. Proposal for the Conduct of Air Warfare against Britain (Berlin: German Air Force Operations Staff (Intelligence))

'War Diary of German Naval Staff (Operations Division)'. 1939a. (US. Naval War College Archives), Archives <https://www.usnwcarchives.org/repositories/2/archival_objects/34368> [accessed 28 February 2024]

'———'. 1939b. (US. Naval War College Archives) <https://www.usnwcarchives.org/repositories/2/archival_objects/34370> [accessed 12 April 2023]

'———'. 1939c. (US. Naval War College Archives) <https://www.usnwcarchives.org/repositories/2/archival_objects/34372> [accessed 28 February 2024]

'———'. 1940a. (US. Naval War College Archives) <https://www.usnwcarchives.org/repositories/2/archival_objects/34399> [accessed 29 February 2024]

'———'. 1940b. (US. Naval War College Archives) <https://www.usnwcarchives.org/repositories/2/archival_objects/34378> [accessed 28 February 2024]

'———'. 1940c. (US. Naval War College Archives) <https://www.usnwcarchives.org/repositories/2/archival_objects/34385> [accessed 28 February 2024]

'———'. 1940d. (US. Naval War College Archives) <https://www.usnwcarchives.org/repositories/2/archival_objects/34387> [accessed 28 February 2024]

'———'. 1940e. (US. Naval War College Archives) <https://www.usnwcarchives.org/repositories/2/archival_objects/34402> [accessed 29 February 2024]

'———'. 1940f. (.S. Naval War College Archives) <https://www.usnwcarchives.org/repositories/2/archival_objects/34404> [accessed 29 February 2024]

Opposite: The Great Western Railway (GWR) railway network from the valleys to the ports in 1930. The rail network was the final result of a century of expensive design, development and engineering. However it was only designed to move coal out of Glamorgan and proved extremely difficult to repurpose for other uses. At its height it was an engineering miracle of transportation.

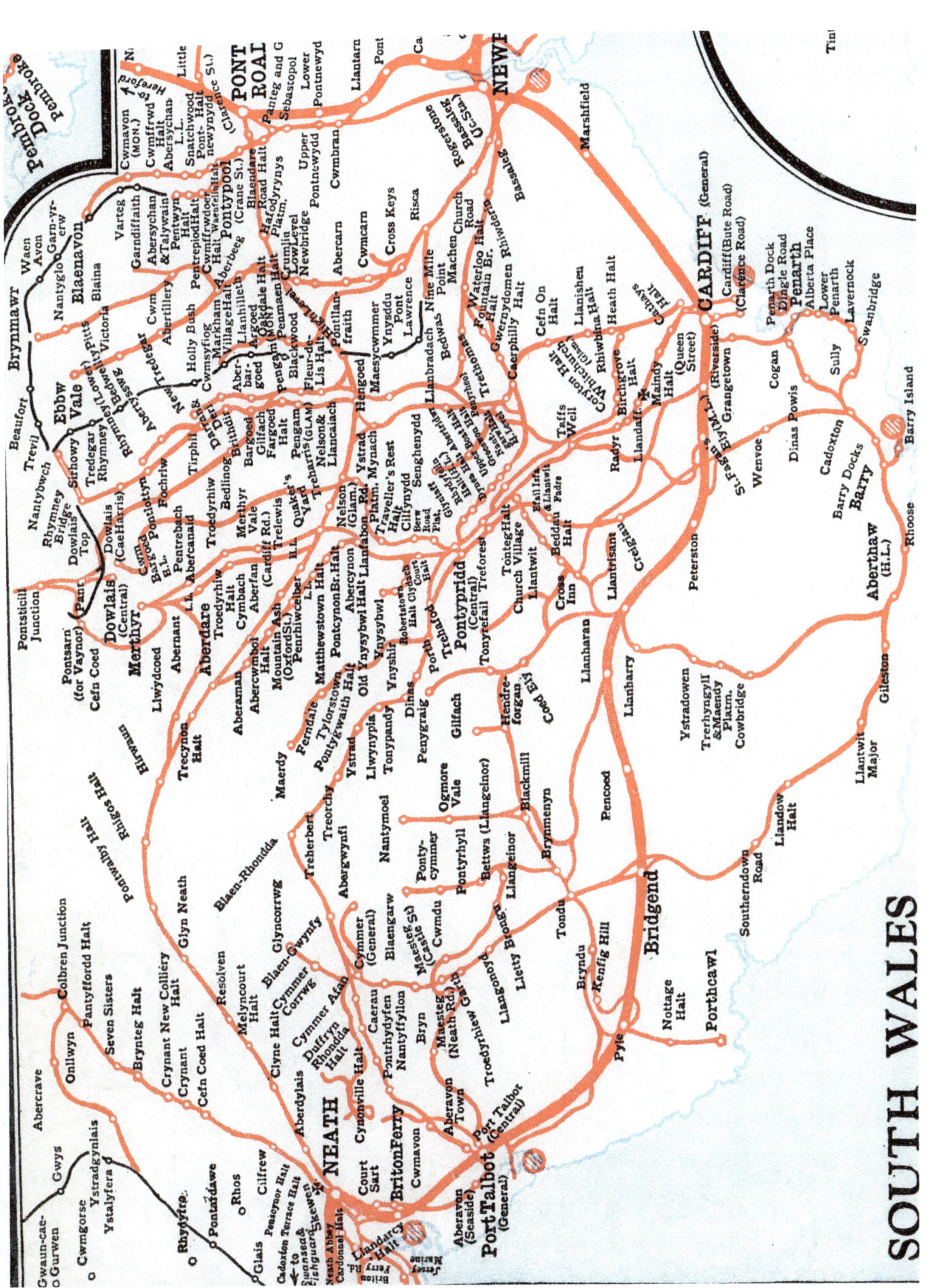

Großbritannien 1:250000

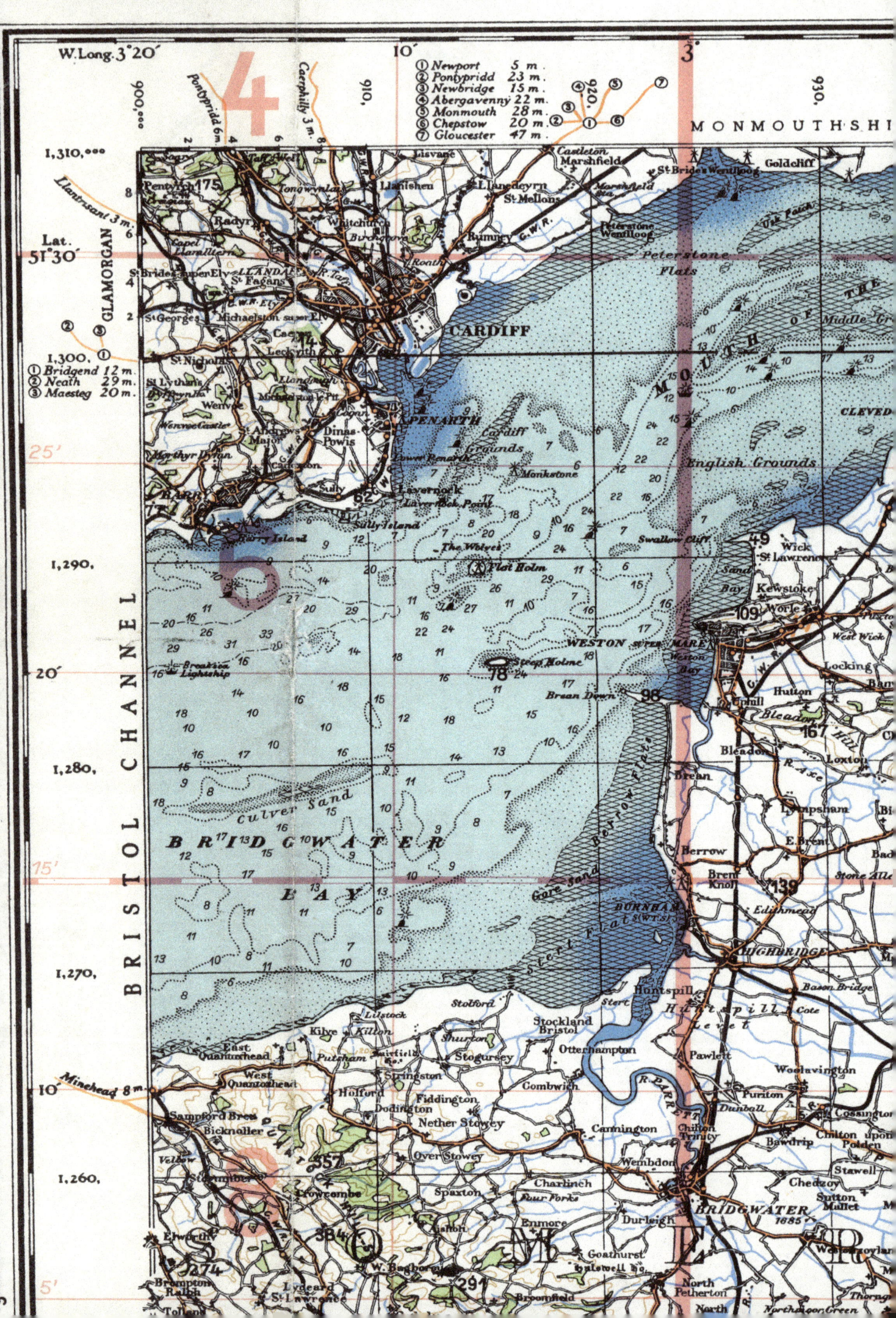

3. Reconnaissance over the Ports 1940-1941

A German air war against Britain needed accurate information. The intelligence maps and Study Blue research discussed earlier had adequate detail for most tasks, but modern bomb attacks needed better information. Both are needed to understand the target and assess the results after the bombing. After the fall of France in June 1940, German long-range reconnaissance units were quickly moved into French airfields to begin detailed surveys of British targets. The first missions in July and August 1940 supported a proposed invasion of Britain 'Operation Sea Lion'). Reconnaissance missions were flown over army, air and naval bases. By the autumn of 1940, the situation started to change. The Luftwaffe was being drawn into more strategic missions, such as understanding the west coast ports and how to disrupt imports into Britain (Galland 1953: 11). As we now know, this became a challenge that was never met, not least because, despite the intelligence preparations made that were discussed earlier, there was no clear-cut strategic plan for the conduct of the war against Britain (Galland 1953: 11–15; Koller 1956: 11–17). The task of surveying Britain, particularly the western side of the country, fell to *Fernaufklärungsgruppe* 123 (Aufkl. Gr.(F)123, an elite long-range air group that was flying aircraft with large survey cameras.

The smallest combat flying unit of the Luftwaffe was known as a *Staffel*, generally a unit of about nine aircraft. Aufkl.Gr.(F)123 was formed of three *Staffeln*. The first Staffel 1.(F)/123 was known as 'Knullenkopf' because of its unique aircraft badge, 2.(F)/123 was known as '*Der Adler mit dem Fernrohr*' (an eagle holding a telescope). The third *Staffel* 3.(F)/123 was known as 'The Iron Third' with a hammer and anvil as their emblem (Rabeder 2017: 20–23). These three units would become frequent and well-known visitors to the airspace over the Welsh ports in the coming months.

The main aircraft flown by the *Staffeln* was the Dornier

Opposite: An extract from the Luftwaffe *Fliegerausgabe* (Aviation Edition) for Wales and South-West England. This is a redrawn version of the British Ordnance Survey 'Quarter-inch' map (1: 253 440) dating from 1933. The original map was designed as a road map for motorists The map was found to be ideally suited to aviation and the Germans reprinted it at a European standard 1:250 000 scale and overprinted navigation detail in red. After the war the British decided vto follow the German example and the map was redrawn to conform to the European metric scale.

Right: German reconnaissance crews train on a model of a port. It was important to understand the principles of port operation and dock management. The Royal Navy was considered a primary target and crews were intensively trained in ship recognition to allow for precise identification of vessels. The commercial management of a port was also an important topic and it was useful to be able to interpret ships in differing states of activity such as repair, unloading, bunkering fuel, and preparing to use locks.

Do. 17. A bomber design from the early 1930s when speed took precedence over protection. The thin body of the bomber gave it its German nickname, Flying Pencil. Although regarded as fast in the 1930s, the plane was not fast enough to keep out of trouble with aggressive RAF fighter patrols, and its slower speed and inadequate defensive armament meant it was a dangerous plane to fly in over contested British airspace in 1940 (Koller 1956: 6). The reconnaissance bombers of *Aufkl. Gr.(F)123* carried very large and heavy survey cameras in their bomb bays, although they could on occasion also carry some 50kg bombs as well. In late 1940, the Do17s were gradually replaced by Junkers Ju 88 bombers (also adapted to carry cameras). The South Wales ports saw a combination of Do 17s and Ju 88s fly over them.

The *'Knullenkopf'* and 'Iron Third' *Staffeln* were moved into Buc airfield near Paris on June 1930 and readied for survey missions over the Bristol Channel by the following day.

The first reconnaissance flights we know of took place on 1 July 1940, with an overflight of Swansea. This began a sequence of flights covering Cardiff, Swansea, Llandarcy, and Llanelli between July and September 1940. There was clearly a rush to get good-quality photographs of Swansea, Cardiff and Newport to feed into the target analysis process at the Luftwaffe intelligence and air fleet headquarters. The original set of aerial photos of Wales had been taken secretly in 1938, and they were usually too poor to use for advanced technical targeting. New photos were essential to update the *Zielstammkarten*. The autumn of 1940 saw a series of hard months for the crews of *Aufkl.Gr.(F)123*. Flying over large areas of sea, the British weather and long missions over hostile territory all took their toll on men and machines. The RAF knew exactly what the *Aufkl. Gr.(F)123* were up to and attacked the reconnaissance

Below: A Dornier Do 17 P reconnaissance aircraft at Jersey in July 1940. The one is showing the insignia of the second *Staffel* of *Fernaufklärungsgruppe* 123 (The Eagle with the Telescope). This is likely to be one of the aircraft that regularly flew over South Wales in 1940.

Right: Officers from the same reconnaissance unit review film from a mission. They are working outside in the fine summer of 1940. They are reading the film in negative for speed. Any interesting images would then be printed for further analysis. British photo-interpreters criticised the Germans for viewing images in negative as they believed it wasn't an accurate method of working, although it fitted in with the Luftwaffe ethos of rapid working.

fliers every time they had the opportunity (Galland 1953: 25). Unlike the bomber aircraft, reconnaissance aircraft need good visibility and weather to take their photographs so any clear weather meant intense flying as more and more information was needed to feed into the bombing plans for the ports. Current records confirm that regular surveys of the ports carried on between July 1940 and March 1941.

References

Galland, Adolf. 1953. The Battle of Britain (London: AHB6 Air Ministry)

Koller, Karl. 1956. German Air Force Policy During the 2nd World War (London: AHB6 Air Ministry)

Rabeder, Harald. 2017. The Knullenkopfstaffel: Luftwaffe Long-Range Reconnaissance with Staffel 1.(F) /123 over France, Great Britain, the Mediterranean and over the Reich. (Wurzburg: Verlagshaus Wurzburg GmbH & Co. KG, Wurzburg)

Below: The first direct reconnaissance images of Wales were taken on 1 July 1940 from aircraft taking off from Jersey only hours after they had actually occupied the airport. The aircraft was a Do 17P as shown on the preceding page. These two images are from that initial mission. Below, the open fields of Mumbles are seen in the fine summer of 1940 with the open lands of the commons on the left side. The wreck of the SS Protesilaus can be seen on the sands at West Cross in the Bay (see page 60). Clyne Valley is still intensely wooded and the fields and gardens of western Swansea are still free from the urban density that we see today.

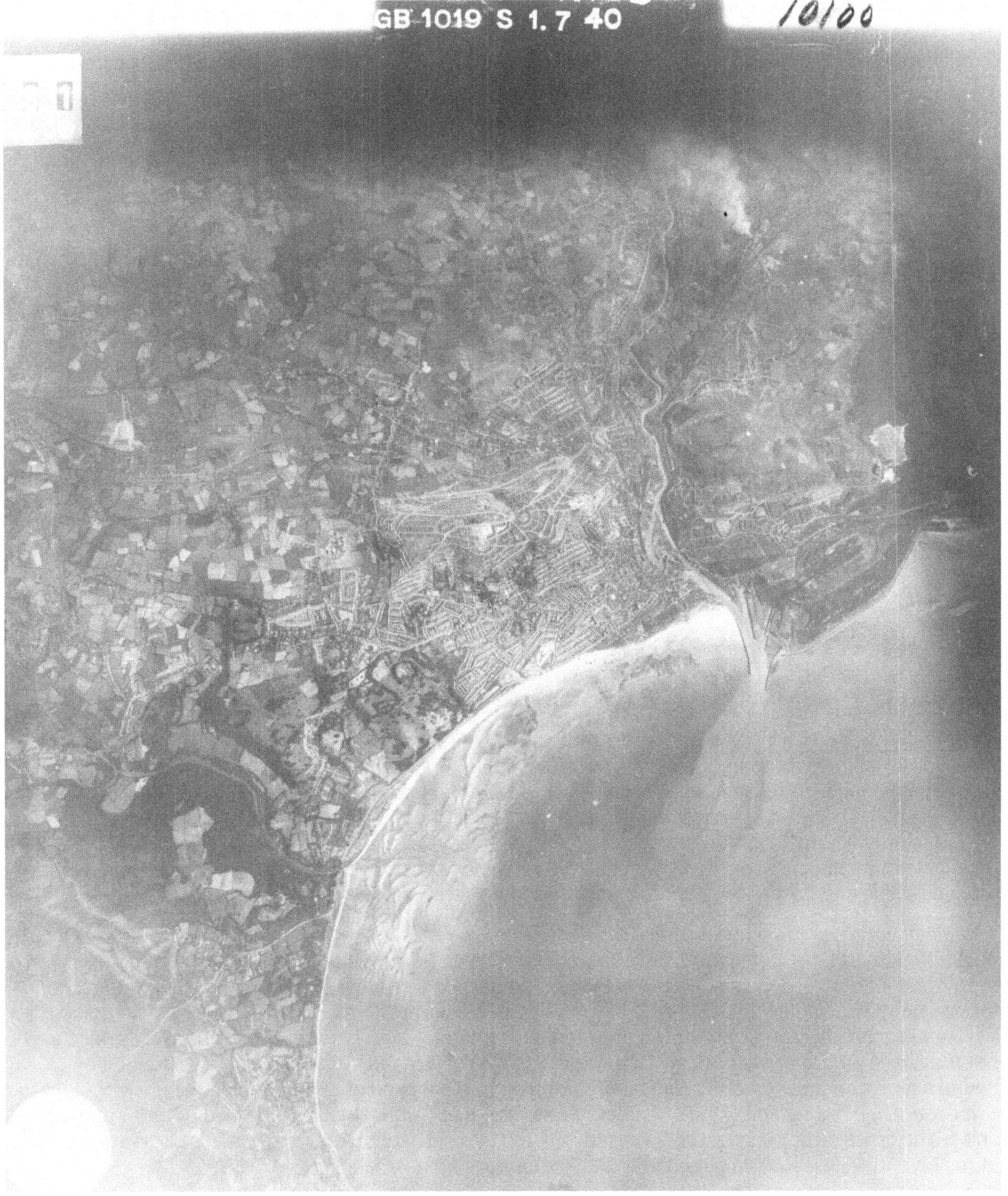

Above: Another shot from the 1 July 1940 mission. The aircraft is flying west and it is probably collecting overlapping images to allow for stereoscopic analysis of the ground. At this stage in the war, the air defences in Swansea were very weak and the aircraft could fly at altitudes above 5000m unhindered by interception or firing. The thick woods of Clyne at lower left give way to the open lands of Singleton Abbey and the park. The sinuous curves and roundabouts of the 1920s Townhill estate contrast strongly with the nineteenth-century gridiron street patterns of inner Swansea and the Lower Swansea Valley. The docks dominate the landscape to the right (West) of the picture and the dark areas of the extensive waste tips in the valley can be clearly seen.

Above: the newly delivered *Knullenkopf* Ju88s at Buc Airfield. The *Knullenkopf* emblem is on the engine casings.

Strangely and contrary to orders, the war diaries and unit administrative records for *Fernaufklärunsgruppe 123* were not destroyed during the war. We now have some opportunity to rebuild the events of a few important reconnaissance missions across Wales.

After a brief opportunity for some rest after the Fall of France the crews of long-range reconnaissance were quickly committed to new missions over Britain. *Staffel 1 (Knullenkopf)* were quickly installed at Buc Airfield near Paris. *Staffel 3* had already arrived at Jersey as described on the preceding pages. The French Air Force had hurriedly destroyed a lot of their aircraft and equipment in advance of the Germans arriving, but that didn't affect *Knullenkopf* as they were completely air mobile. *Knullenkopf* had received early versions of the new Junkers Ju88 reconnaissance bomber which was faster and more manoeuvrable should it come into contact with RAF fighters.

Knullenkopf's first mission over Britain included a flyover of Swansea to supplement the views gained on 1 July. At that time in July the Luftwaffe were keen to understand the organisation and capability of the Royal Air Force and missions were being prepared to explore large British airbases in preparation for bombing. The primary task of the 3 July mission was to examine airfields possibly defending Wolverhampton and Liverpool. The weather is cloudy and the English south coast was largely obscured, but the single aircraft leaves Buc at 11.40 and flies over Cherbourg avoiding radar interception by taking a long turn around Land's End before flying up to a checkpoint at Lundy Island and direct flight to Swansea. The crew noted that the Bristol Channel Route to Swansea and Cardiff were busy with many ships. The crossing of the coast at Swansea initiated a Civil Defence response as observers logged the intrusion and the height and direction of the intruder.

The aircraft proceeded to Wolverhampton and took images of the city. Although tracking the aircraft as it crossed a coastline or radar screen was relatively easy, it was much harder to track an aircraft that had penetrated the coast and had an unknown destination. Civil Defences had to wait until the aircraft encountered a listening post on its way inland.

From Wolverhampton, the aircraft flew north to Stoke-on-Trent and then on to Salesbury for a long turn to bring it over Liverpool from an unexpected northerly direction. All this time it was flying at varying heights to reduce its predictable speed and heading. After collecting images at Liverpool it continued directly South to Bristol. After photographing Bristol (either the docks or aircraft engine factories) it headed across country to pick up some views of the airbase at RAF Middle Wallop. From there it went to Southampton. Crossing Middle Wallop and travelling east of the Isle of Wight initiated a scramble response from the RAF and three Hurricanes from 238 Squadron chased the Ju88. The evasion

Above: The flight track of the 3 July 1940 mission, photographing Swansea on the outgoing leg before unwisely flying over RAF Middle Wallop on its return to France.

response from the Ju88 was to dive lower and use superior speed and manoeuvrability at lower altitudes to escape. The Hurricanes are wise to the tactic and follow the Ju88 down. The Hurricanes pursue the Ju88 across the Channel with the German sometimes flying a few metres above the sea. After a series of passes and attacks with all three attackers firing, the Hurricanes turn back at Le Havre. The damaged Ju88 returns to Buc Airfield at 15.35 with a severely injured crew and 285 bullet strikes.

The Luftwaffe staff had experienced for the first time the extreme aggression and professionalism of the RAF fighter crews. It is reported that in the following days, missions concentrate on monitoring shipping rather than risky coastline crossings.

4. Newport

Newport's port is old, and its original town centre dock was a busy port from medieval times. The take-off point for Newport's prosperity was the creation of the Monmouthshire and Brecon Canal, allowing coal to come down straight into the port. The fact that Monmouthshire did not have much of a large-scale iron industry meant that coal was exported straight out of Newport instead of being channelled off into other industries as happened at Swansea and Cardiff. The canal and its associated network of tramways meant that Newport was a vigorous coal exporter, rivalling nearby Cardiff for annual tonnage until the 1850s. Some of the best Welsh steam coal collieries were within ten miles of the port, which provided a lucrative trade up to 1945.

Newport took off with the building of the Alexandra Docks (North and South). The North Dock was opened in 1875, and the South Dock was expanded between 1893 and 1914. Newport's South Quay was massive for its time, with over a kilometre of lineal quayage on the south side, making it attractive to large ships and complex cargoes (Bird 1963: 226–27).

To complement the scope and ambition of the docks, in 1914, Newport opened a truly massive entrance lock, reportedly inspired by the Panama Canal locks' dimensions, built with an eye to future-proofing (Dawson 1932: 85–87). Newport's coal trade was of immense value to the GWR. By the 1930s, there was railway siding space for over 12,000 coal wagons, which enabled efficient sorting and processing of coal quality before rapid loading onto ships via extensive suites of coal

Left: The *Stadtplan* for Newport showing the strategic assets edged in red. This map was part of the original *Einzelangaben* pack from 1940. Feature 61 is the Neptune Works which was considered a strategic engineering works.

Below: The impressive coal loading wharves on the northern side of South Dock in the early 1930s. Most of this coal went to France and the wharf was considered a strategic asset al least until France fell in June 1940.

hoists, many of which had been upgraded to the newer types of 20-ton coal wagon (the traditional Welsh coal truck was 10-tons).

The high level of metalworking and engineering skills in the local population made Newport attractive for ship repair businesses. Newport had five dry docks, two of them (the Tredegar and Eastern No. 2) being particularly large. These larger dry docks were big enough to handle Royal Navy Light Cruisers, particularly effective vessels with large calibre guns. The Luftwaffe was particularly interested in these docks.

The long straight quay on the South side of South Dock (a linear quay) was particularly attractive to ships specialising in large quantities of general cargo. Two things were needed to make the most of this: cranes and storage. Firstly, lots of electric and hydraulic cranes for speedy loading and unloading. By 1934, at least twelve of Newport's new hydraulic cranes were classed as 'heavy-lift' cranes that could move thirty tonnes or more loads. These cranes would move tanks and equipment in wartime, particularly the heavier, larger American tanks of 1943-44. Equally, the German Army would have preferred to unload their armoured vehicles with this kind of crane. Secondly, large transit sheds (to allow goods to be measured and sorted after unloading or before shipment) were vital. Newport had a particularly large transit shed (No. 9 Transit Shed), which greatly interested German Air Force analysts because they believed it held large quantities of aircraft components.

Newport's docks and the large sea lock were clearly strategic. South Dock's long, open quays were ideal for bulk handling goods and imports and rapidly unloading convoy ships. Before the fall of France, Newport exported large quantities of coal for the French industry. The town had been examined in great detail in early 1940, and the coal, iron, and steel industries and ship repair were considered very important. The significance of the town is highlighted by the German Army's decision to prepare a 1:10 000 scale map of the urban area (Generalstab des Heeres 1941b) in case there was ever a need for occupation or military action.

Newport was seen as a busy industrial town with

Below: An oblique view of the docks from the *Militärgeographische Angaben Bildheft* Military (Geographical Information Picture book) from about 1938. The Luftwaffe were particularly interested in the large factory building (No. 9 Transit Shed) in the centre of the image. Originally the building was a World War One box factory. The GWR bought the building and converted it into a large transit shed. The Luftwaffe analysts believed it was full of aircraft components.

108. Hafen von Newport (BB 27).
Zahlreiche Kanäle und Wasserstraßen am Unterlauf des Usk in Monmouthshire. Blick auf die Alexandra-Docks an der Mündung des Usk (links oben — rechts unten) von Südwesten.

GB 7, BB 27, Nr. 2: Alexandra-Süd-Dock in Newport.
Blick auf den Mündungstrichter des River Usk. Im Vordergrund links große Schleuse zum Alexander-Dock und Kohlenkräne.

Above: An oblique view of Newport from the *Militärgeographische Einzelangaben Objektbilder (*Object images book). This image has been copied from the book on the opposite page, although the detail has been lost in the reproduction process.

Below: A GWR sketch map of the investments made in Newport in the early 1930s. Newport had massive coal export facilities and was increasingly developing its multi-functional capabilities as the war began.

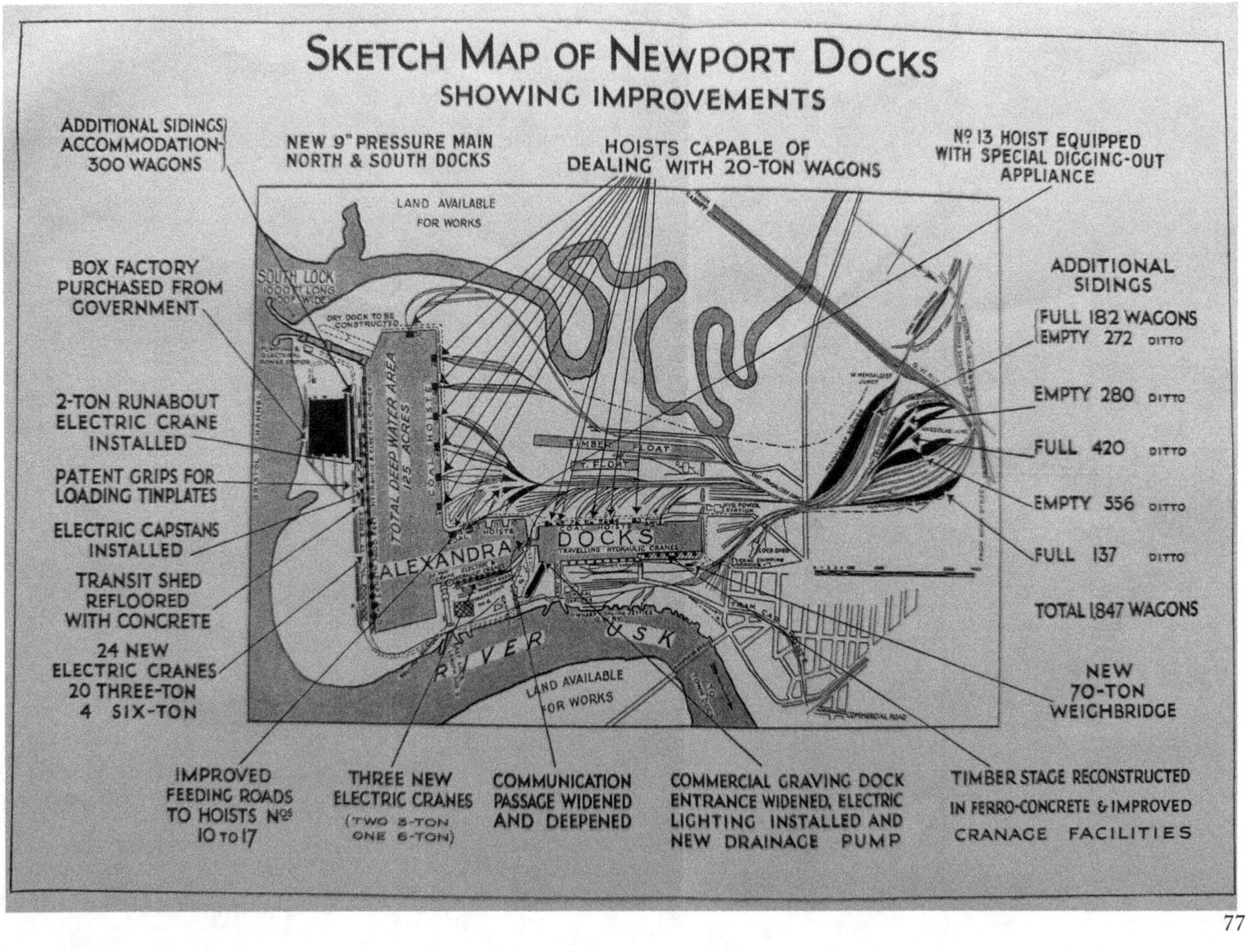

Geheim!

Zielstammkarte (L)

Land: Großbritannien (S)
England (Monmouthshire)

Ort: Newport (Bristol)
(Nähere Lage)
N.O. von Cardiff.

Geogr. Werte: (Lage d. S.-Schleuse)
51° 33′ 05″ N.
2° 59′ 15″ W.

Ziel-Nr. G.B. 45 57

Kartenbl.-Nr. Engl. 27/1:100 000

E.B.Nr. Engl. 102/1:63 360

---

1. Bezeichnung des Zieles: South und North Dock mit Seeschleuse.

Vgl. mit Ziel-Nr. G.B. 83 53: 2 Trockendocks mit Werkstätten am North Dock.

2. Bedeutung: Wichtiger Exporthafen (für Kohle und Erzeugnisse der eisenverarbeitenden Industrie. Einfuhr v. Erz, Holz und Rosinen).

---

3. Beschreibung des Zieles:

a) Verkehrsanschlüsse: Wasser- und Bahnanschluß.

b) Ausdehnung insgesamt: O.N.O.–W.S.W.: 1 250 m.   Bebaute Fläche:
N.N.W.–S.S.O.: 1 580 m.   Höhe ü. M.: 0 m

c) Art der Anlagen und Einrichtungen,
Bauweise, Bauausführung, Luftempfindlichkeit, Brandgefahr:

Ein geschützter Binnenhafen bestehend aus 2 Becken in L-Form:

a) **Das Südbecken:** In der S.-Ecke die durch 2 Einfahrtsmolen geschützte neue Schleuse mit drei Schleusentoren. Gesamtschleusenmaße 180 × 30 m und 120 × 30 m.
An der O.-Seite der äußersten Schleuse Kessel- und Pumpenhaus (Schornstein).
Westlich der Einfahrt ein neues Trockendock in Arbeit. Am S.-Kai 4 lange Lagerhäuser für Transitgut. Etwas weiter zurück hinter den beiden westlichen Häusern ein riesiger überdeckter Schuppen von 45 350 qm Grundfläche mit Laderampen für Bahntransport.
Am O.-Kai alte Einfahrt mit 3 Schleusen (150 × 22 m). Am N.- und W.-Kai 11 hohe Kohlenschütten, 8 davon für Eisenbahnwaggons mit 20 t Ladung. Im N.-Schlauch des S.-Beckens Durchfahrt mit Drehbrücke zum

b) **Nordbecken.** Am W.-Kai 9 Kohlenschütten, 5 davon für 20 t Wagen. Dahinter Holzlagerplätze und Holzteiche.
Am N.-Ende dieses Kais hydraulische Kraftstation für die am O.-Kai beider Hafenbecken stehenden 26 Kräne für Stückgut. In der S.O.-Ecke 2 Trockendocks (G.B. 83 53).
150 m ostw. des Beckens ein ca. 60 m hoher Kabelmast, dessen Kabel zu einem gleichen Hochmast auf dem jenseitigen Ufer des River Usk führt.

Einsturz- und Brandgefahr.

d) Erzeugnisse:

e) Erzeugungsmenge im Monat:
Maximal und normal,
bei wieviel Schichten und Arbeitern?

f) Belegschaft:
Männer, Frauen, Volkszugehörigkeit,
politische Einstellung, Unterbringung.

Opposite: The *Zielstammkarte* (Target Master Map document) for the main docks at Newport. This was created as part of the *Studie Blau* research in 1939. This cover sheet provides the textual information on the target as an explanation for the annotated photograph overleaf. A full explanation of this type of record is in the Annexes.

Secret!	**Location:** Newport (Bristol)	**Target=No G.B. 45 67**
Target master card (L)	(Nearby location) N.E. of Cardiff	Card sheet=No.Engl. 27/1:100 000
Country: Great Britain (S)	Geogr. location	GB No. Engl. 102/1:63 360

1. Name of the Target: South and North Dock with Sea Lock

Compare with target=no G.B. 83 53: 2 Drydocks with workshops at North Dock

2. Significance: Important export port (for coal and products from the iron processing industry. Import of ore, wood and food)

3. Description of the Target

a) Professional connections: Water and rail connections.

b) Total dimensions: E.N.E.-W.S.W.: 1 250m Built-up area:
N.N.W.-S.S.E.: 1 580m height(above sea level): 0 m

c) Type of systems and equipment, design, construction, vulnerability to air, risk of fire

A sheltered inland port consisting of 2 L-shaped basins.

a) The southern basin: In the southern corner, the new lock with three lock gates, protected by 2 entrance moles. Total lock dimensions 180x30m and 120x30m. boiler and pump house (chimney) on the east side of the outer lock. west of the entrance a new dry dock in progress. At the S Quay 4 long warehouse for goods in transit. A little further back behind the two western houses is a huge covered shed of 45,350 square meters with loading ramps for rail transport. At the E Quay old entrance with 3 locks (150x22m). On the N. and W.-Quay 11 high coal dumps, 8 of them for railway wagons with 20 t load. In the N. fork of the S. basin passage with swing bridge.

b) North Basin. At West Quay 9 coal loaders, 5 of them for 20 t wagons. Behind them are wood storage areas and wood ponds. At the north end of this quay there is a hydraulic power station for the 26 general cargo cranes on the east quay of both harbour basins. In the SE. Corner 2 dry docks (GB 83 53). 150 m E.W. of the basin is a cable mast about 60 m high, the cable of which leads to a similar high mast on the other bank of the River Usk.

Collapse and fire hazard.

d) Products:

e) Production quantity per month:
Maximum and normal
how many shifts and work?

f) Workforce:
Men, women, ethnicity, political views, accommodation

Above: The Master Target Map related to the information on the preceding page, with a translation opposite. This image is dated October 1941 which shows that politically, an abandonment of air war against Britain was not contemplated. No. 9 Transit Shed has its own Target Number GB 20 21. The prefix '20' indicates the Luftwaffe are convinced the shed is related to aircraft components.

GB 45 57 b c
For official use only

Newport
Port facilities

Generalstaff 5 Division October 1941

Map 1 : 100 000
GB/E27

Picture No. 1063b/40-58 (L.fl. 3)
Record from 30.11.40

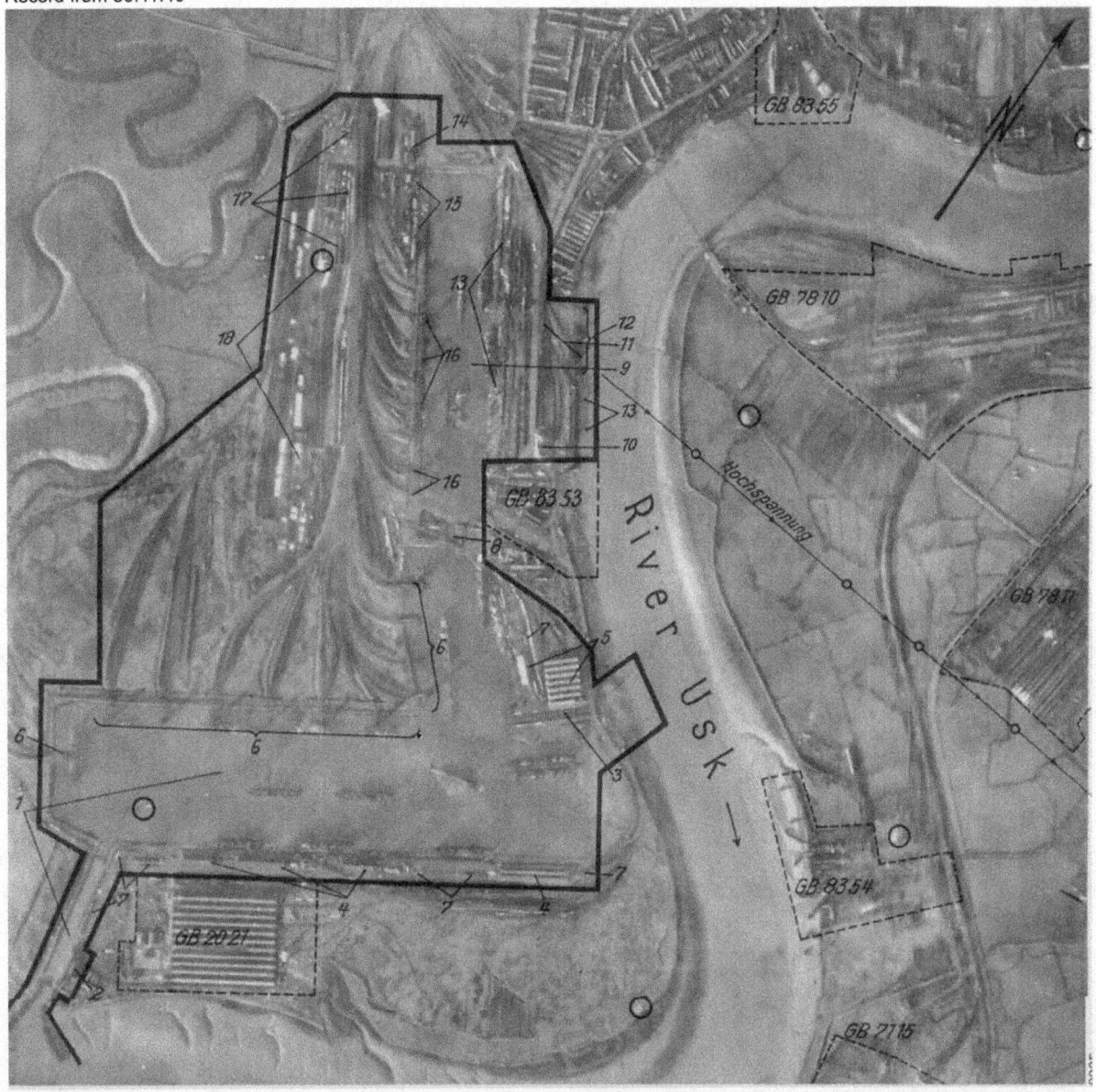

South Basin
1. South dock, in the SW corner closed to the sea by a new lock with two lock gates 30m wide.
2. Boiler and pumping station, solid gable roof, high chimney.
3. at the East side old entrance lock (out of service, entrance already silted up). abAut 22m wide.
4. On the South side 4 long warehouses for transit goods, solid, flat and gable roof.
5. Further warehouse and 1 larger warehouse for transit goods are located on the East side with a solid flat and gable roof.
6. On the N and W. sides 11 High coal sheds for railway wagons. 8 of them are for 20 t wagons.
7. Several small warehouses and company buildings on the wastewater facilities are arranged according to massive different types of roofs.
8. Passage with rotating bridge to the north basin

North Basin
9. North dock with 19m wide entrance from the south basin.
10. Customs and administrative buildings, massively different roof types.
11. 650m high cable mast.
12 3 additional coal sheds for railway wagons on the west bank of the River Usk.
13. On the East side and on the banks of the River Ulk several cranes and unloading systems.
14. Hydraulic power station for the cranes in both harbour basins, massively different roof types, high chimney.
15. Warehouse and mill building partly multi-storey, massive, different types of roof, ash, 2 elevator systems.
16. 9 coal chutes for railway wagons, 5 of them for 20 t wagons.
17. Warehouses and sheds (wood storage), solid, different roof types.
18. Timber camps and timber ponds with several small storage buildings.
  o= Barrage balloons

Superelevation near the object: two 60m cable masts, high-voltage masts and chimneys

GB 20 21 replenishment store Newport
GB 71 15 Aluminum works on the River Usk
GB 78 10 Ironworks "Lysachts Orb-Iron works"
GB 78 11 Steelworks "British Mannesman Tube Works"
GB 83 53 2 dry docks with workshops at North Dock
GB 83 54 Mountstuart Dry Dock on the River Usk.
GB 83 55 Tredegar shipyard and dry dock.

Above and opposite: Although the weather in November 1940 was generally poor for flying, the reconnaissance units were intent on flying as much as possible over areas that were either of concern or that they needed more information about. These two images of a cloudy Newport obscured with mist and smoke are from late November. A few barrage balloons had been moved into the area and the white plumes of steam engines can be seen across the town.

railway repair, ship repair, oil storage and iron and steel fabrication facilities. There was also a significant capacity for aluminium fabrication, so the Germans believed Newport could become a centre for airframe manufacture. In 1940, Newport held about twenty per cent of British aluminium manufacturing capacity. Newport also had a significant power station, a vital link in the South Wales electricity network.

Newport's bombing targets

Newport's port area had ten important bombing targets, although there were more in the outer parts of the urban area, as hospitals and army barracks were also identified. Newport was also recognised as the central telephone cable hub for Risca, Pontypool and Abergavenny (Generalstab des Heeres Abteilung für Kriegskarten und Vermessungswesen 1940a).

Newport has a large entry in the *Militärgeographische Angaben Textheft*, the Military Geographical Information (Generalstab des Heeres 1940b: 173). The entry illustrates the level of detail the military geographers preferred. There is a population figure, probably based on the 1931 Census and recording nearly ninety thousand residents. The importance comes next, with Newport regarded as a main transhipment port within the Bristol Channel. The implication being that Newport was transferring goods from larger vessels into smaller coasters and rail wagons for further distribution. This explains why the marshalling yards in the west of town were also highlighted. The *Textheft* entry also includes what will be a recurring theme in the Welsh

ports, the prominence of mining timber and the storage ponds used to manage the immense quantities imported annually. The massive extent of land devoted to pitwood storage across the GWR ports convinced the Germans that it was a strategic commodity. The German navy planned to conduct its own strategic campaign against the timber trade (Hessler 1989: 12–13). The imports and exports are recorded as we expect and have seen from the GWR publicity discussed earlier. The wharfside cranes were important to the army. Cranes with a lifting capacity of thirty tonnes or more. The reason for the interest was simple. In 1940, the weight of the German army's main battle tank was just about 22 tonnes and the army preferred unloading them dockside from ships (Ellis and Doyle 1976: 74–78). Although there is reference to a coldstore, Newport comes across as very much an industrial port with coal, iron, steel and ship repair. The later interest in the large Transit Shed No.9 came from the Luftwaffe interpreting the site as a centre of aircraft spare parts (Target GB 2021 *Nachschublager*). Evidently the military geographers were short of good quality photos of Newport with only one poor quality photo in the *Militärgeographische Bildheft* derived from a pre-war aerial view of the docks (Generalstab des Heeres

1940a: 109). The intelligence on Newport is completed with a small street plan of central Newport (Generalstab des Heeres 1940c: 73).

In the *Mil.-Geo. Einzelangaben* pack, there is a 1:10 000 map of Newport (a *Stadtplan*) based on original British Ordnance Survey maps but carefully reprojected from the British 1:10 560 scale to the continental 1:10 000 scale. An expensive and quite technical task (Generalstab des Heeres 1941b).

The accompanying photo book contains two poor-quality views of the docks looking west. In typical German fashion, all the photos in the photo-book are perforated so they can be quickly torn out and passed around attacking army units (Generalstab des Heeres 1941a: 15, 30).

References

Bird, James. 1963. The Major Seaports of the United Kingdom (London: Hutchinson)

Dawson, James W. 1932. Commerce and Customs: A History of the Ports of Newport and Caerleon (Newport: R.H Johns)

Ellis, Chris, and Hilary Doyle. 1976. Panzerkampfwagen: German Combat Tanks 1933-1945 (Kings Langley: Bellona)

Generalstab des Heeres. 1940a. 'Militärgeographische Angaben über England Bildheft' (Abteilung für Kriegskarten und Vermessungswesen, IV,-Mil.Geo.)

———. 1940b. 'Militärgeographische Angaben über England Textheft' (Abteilung für Kriegskarten und Vermessungswesen, IV,-Mil.Geo.)

———. 1940c. 'Stadtdurchfahrtpläne England (ohne London)' (Abteilung für Kriegskarten und Vermessungswesen, IV,-Mil.Geo.)

———. 1941a. 'Militärgeographische Einzelangen über England Objektbilder zu den militärgeographischen Objektkarten 1:250 000 und 1:10 000 der Mappe 7 Südwales' (Abteilung für Kriegskarten und Vermessungswesen, IV,-Mil.Geo.)

———. 1941b. 'Stadtplan von Newport Mit Mil.-Geo.-Eintragungen GB7, BB27' (Berlin: Abteilung für Kriegskarten und Vermessungswesen, IV,-Mil.Geo.)

Generalstab des Heeres Abteilung für Kriegskarten und Vermessungswesen. 1940a. 'Großbrittannien Und Irland Funkstellen, Fernsprech Und Telegraphennetz', Militärgeographische Objektkarte von England (Berlin: Generalstab des Heeres Abteilung für Kriegskarten und Vermessungswesen (IV. Mil-Geo))

———. 1940b. Militärgeographische Angaben Über England Textheft (Berlin: Abteilung für Kriegskarten und Vermessungswesen)

Hessler, Gunter. 1989. The U-boat War in the Atlantic 1939-1945, ed. by Andrew J. Withers (London: HMSO)

Above: Newport Target GB 71 15 was identified as an Aluminium manufacturing plant with the prefix code of 71 denoting non-ferrous-metal industries. The Luftwaffe were very concerned in fining any manufacturing industries that contributed to building Spitfire aircraft and other aircraft. Aluminium plants across Britain were identified as potential targets.

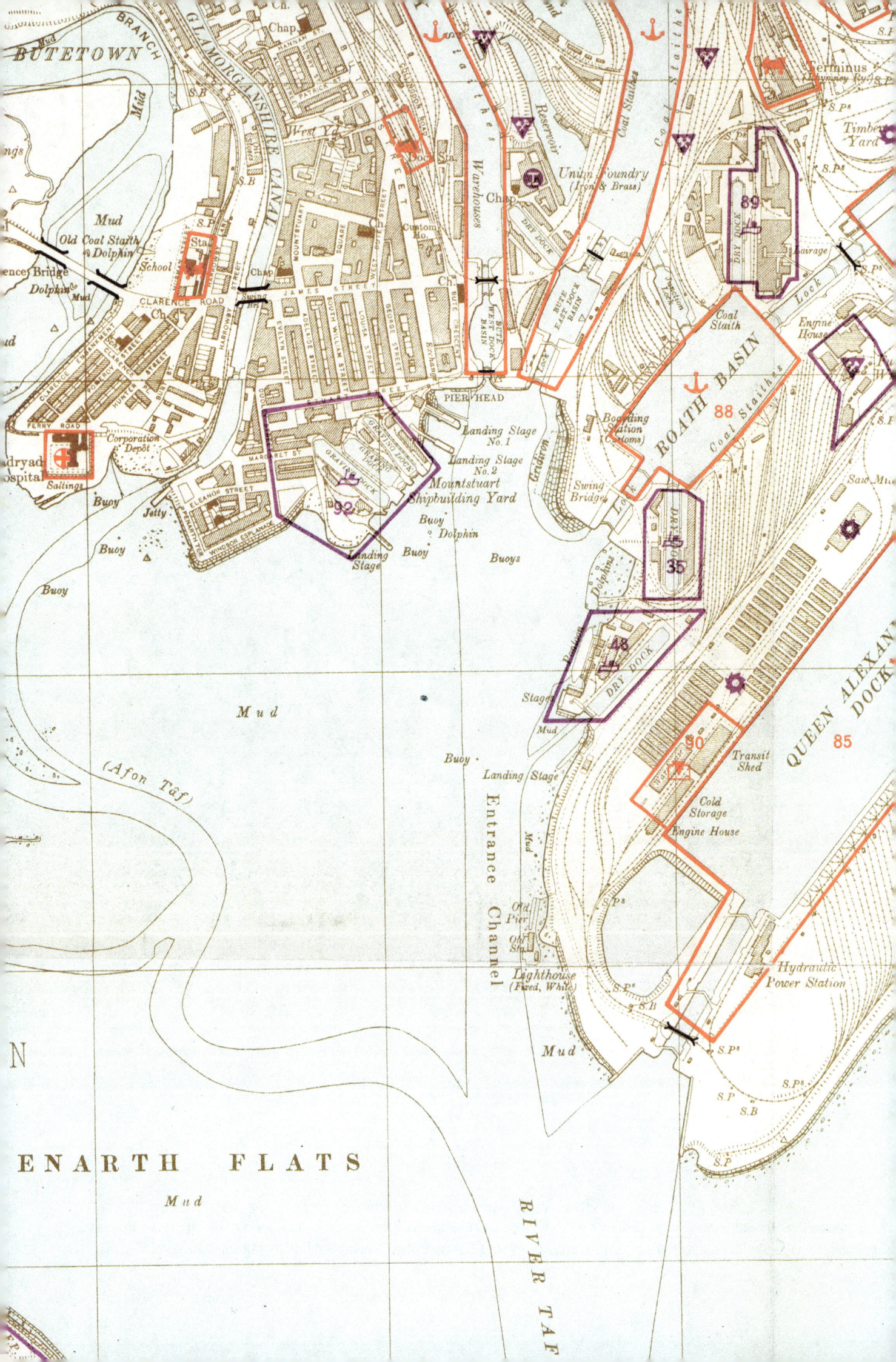

5. Cardiff

Cardiff's port history began with a small quay on a bend of the River Taff. Now long disappeared, its location survives in the name of Quay Street. Cardiff's serious industrial expansion began with the creation of the Glamorganshire Canal in 1794, which allowed larger loads of coal to be brought down the Taff's river system from as far north as Merthyr. A 1798 extension to the canal allowed access to the bay, and coal shipping increased rapidly to Bristol, Ireland and France. In common with Swansea, Cardiff altered the course of its river in the 1850s to improve port facilities by freeing up more wharf space and land for railway yards. However, the big change in Cardiff was the opening of the Bute West Dock in 1839. The Bute West gave Cardiff a dock with luxurious lengths of loading wharves for coal exports. The land between the canal and the dock became Bute Town, one of Cardiff's most famous districts (Chappell 1939).

Adjacent to Bute West, the flat plain of East Moors was well-suited to dock developments, and Bute West was followed by Bute East Dock in 1858, Roath Dock in 1887, and ultimately, the massive Queen Alexandra Dock, one of the largest walled docks in the world, in 1907. Between 1858 and 1910, the flat lands surrounding the docks and basins became ideal locations for a multitude of port industries, shipbuilding and repair, with over fifteen dry docks, including two very large docks suitable for Royal Navy heavy cruisers. The southeastern wharves of Queen Alexandra Dock became a complex hub of modern bulk coal loading machines capable of filling the largest coal ships in a matter of hours. The opposite side of the dock became a large general cargo wharf for industrial and domestic goods for the growing population.

By the 1930s, Cardiff was the primary port on the GWR network. Its railway connections were considerable and heavily integrated into the port facilities. Efficient rail links via the Severn Tunnel and into the Midlands ensured Cardiff had a growing dominance in general and industrial imports and exports. Cardiff's coal business had been considerably enhanced by clever diversifying into food imports and storage. Live cattle were imported for auction, slaughter, and butchering, with Roath Basin having nearby chill rooms and cold stores ensuring good support for meat distribution. Live cattle came from South Africa and Canada for distribution into Wales and the Midlands. Roath Dock became a centre for grain imports with large storage silos and advanced equipment for rapid processing at the Spillers Mills. The GWR had also invested in a floating grain elevator, which allowed the largest grain ships to be rapidly emptied.

Cardiff had a massive capacity for frozen and cold storage. Queen Alexandra Dock alone had over 8000 cubic metres of cold storage and four massive transit sheds, which gave it immense capacity to unload food and general imports. GWR had invested in modern crane technology with over eighty cranes, including many 'heavy-lift' cranes, ensuring a quick turn-around for modern merchant ships. In total, Cardiff had twenty-six transit sheds, allowing ships to unload quickly, and cargoes could be immediately under weatherproof cover for sorting and dispatch. The cold stores originally intended for meat were also attracting the sea-fishing industry and by 1932, Cardiff was bringing ashore about 10,000 tons of fish annually (Appleby 1933: 135).

A look at Cardiff's import data for the 1930s indicates that Wales' domestic iron and steel industry was nowhere near providing enough steel for the British market. Annually, a huge tonnage of iron ore was imported alongside massive quantities of American semi-finished

Left: Cardiff Bay and the dock entrances shown on the *Stadtplan* (map) in 1940. The docks are edged red and ship repair facilities are edged violet. This area was to be the main strategic interest of the Luftwaffe in 1941.

steel components (billets and bars) for the industrial Midlands manufacturing industry. Another key import was pitwood. The wood for Welsh coal mines didn't come from the forests of Wales, it came from Russia, Norway, Sweden and Canada, with over half a million tons of wood brought in during 1932, which was in fact, a massive decline from the peak years of the late 1920s when a million tonnes of wood came in every year (Appleby 1933: 165–66). In fact, senior staff in the German navy regarded the Welsh pitwood trade as a strategic material and even prepared several plans to specifically attack the Russia/Wales timber trade (Hessler 1989: 12–13).

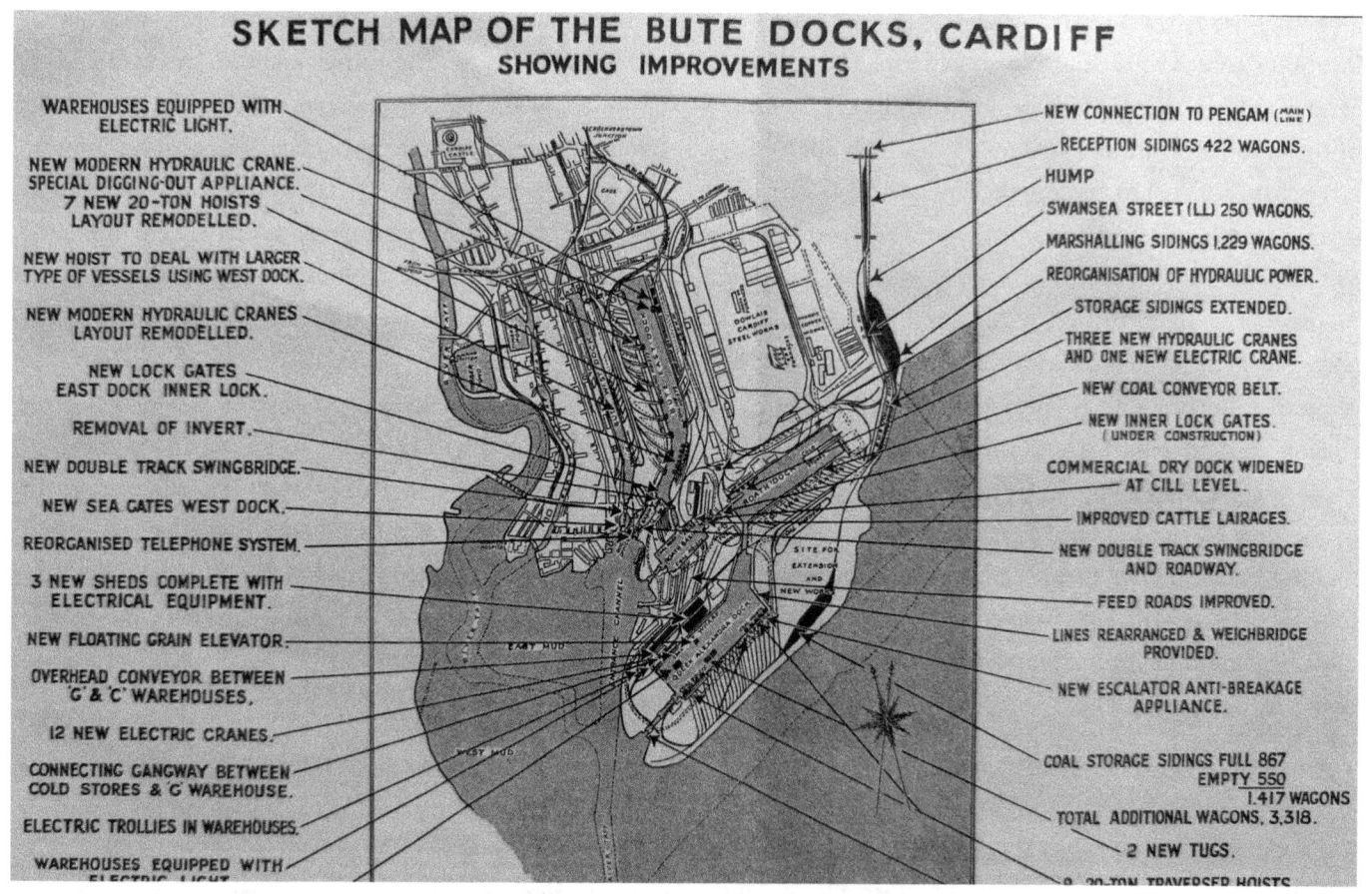

Above: A sketch map of the GWR improvements to Cardiff in the 1930s. GWR invested heavily in the future of Cardiff as a general port. Roath and Queen Alexandra Docks were big enough for long linear quays with generous spaces for transit sheds. Live cattle imports from Canada were a a regular feature and both cattle markets and butcheries were built on the north side of Queen Alexandra. Increased provision for electric lighting and machinery and improved road networks began the process of moving goods movement away from rail and on to the roads.

Opposite: The incredible industrial landscape of the Dowlais works was a masterpiece of combination of bulk transit and manufacturing of heavy steel products. Dowlais made rails, railway wagons, and all manner of steel components for cranes and other vehicles. Iron ore could be imported via the north wharf of Roath Dock directly to the Dowlais furnaces and pig iron moved easily to the finishing processes in the centre of the photograph. Finishing could include making steel girders for buildings, and carcasses for coal wagons. Waste gas provided fuel for malt houses at the top left of the picture. Imported timber from the Bute East Dock import wharf could be taken into the timber yards and wagon works to manufacture hundreds of twenty-ton coal wagons for the Glamorgan coal mines.

In the 1930s, the rail networks and open spaces of the eastern side of Roath Dock (bottom of the picture) proved attractive to massive investment in grain import infrastructure led by Spillers Limited. This February 1941 picture shows busy grain ships unloading American and Canadian grain at the grain elevators.

Below and opposite: The *Zielstammkarte* for Cardiff's Queen Alexandra Dock (Target GB 45 59). Cardiff's large rectangular docks (Roath and Queen Alexandra) were heavily developed for the general trade which made them important locations and complex targets. The sheer size of the port made it difficult to attack from the air. The cold stores, frozen food, grain silos and mills, and the extensive ship repair made Cardiff very significant. The main attack points of Queen Alexandra Dock were the grain mills and particularly the cold stores. The cold stores and their associated supporting power stations and rail networks were considered a *Schwerpunkt* (main emphasis) of any bombing. Transport of frozen meat from the ports to British markets relied almost exclusively on refrigerated meat wagons. The Luftwaffe knew this ,although destroying them was immensely difficult. The rail systems around the cold stores were an easier target. At times in 1941, the shortage of refrigerated wagons meant that the GWR meat vans (MICA A and B) were considered more important than armoured vehicles, such was their scarcity. The Luftwaffe analysts believed that attacks on the cold stores and associated rail networks with large calibre bombs (250 and 500 kilogrammes) would be effective. Although their susceptibility to incendiary attack is highly doubtful. The mention below of vulnerability to fire (*Brandgefahr*) indicates that this assessment is pre-war or early 1939. Experience would prove that incendiaries were rarely effective against such industrial targets. The other notable feature on this image is identification of the ship repair facilities such as F (Mountstuart Yards) and E (The Channel Yards). These were to become of vital significance once the convoy system had been adopted for the Atlantic merchant trade.

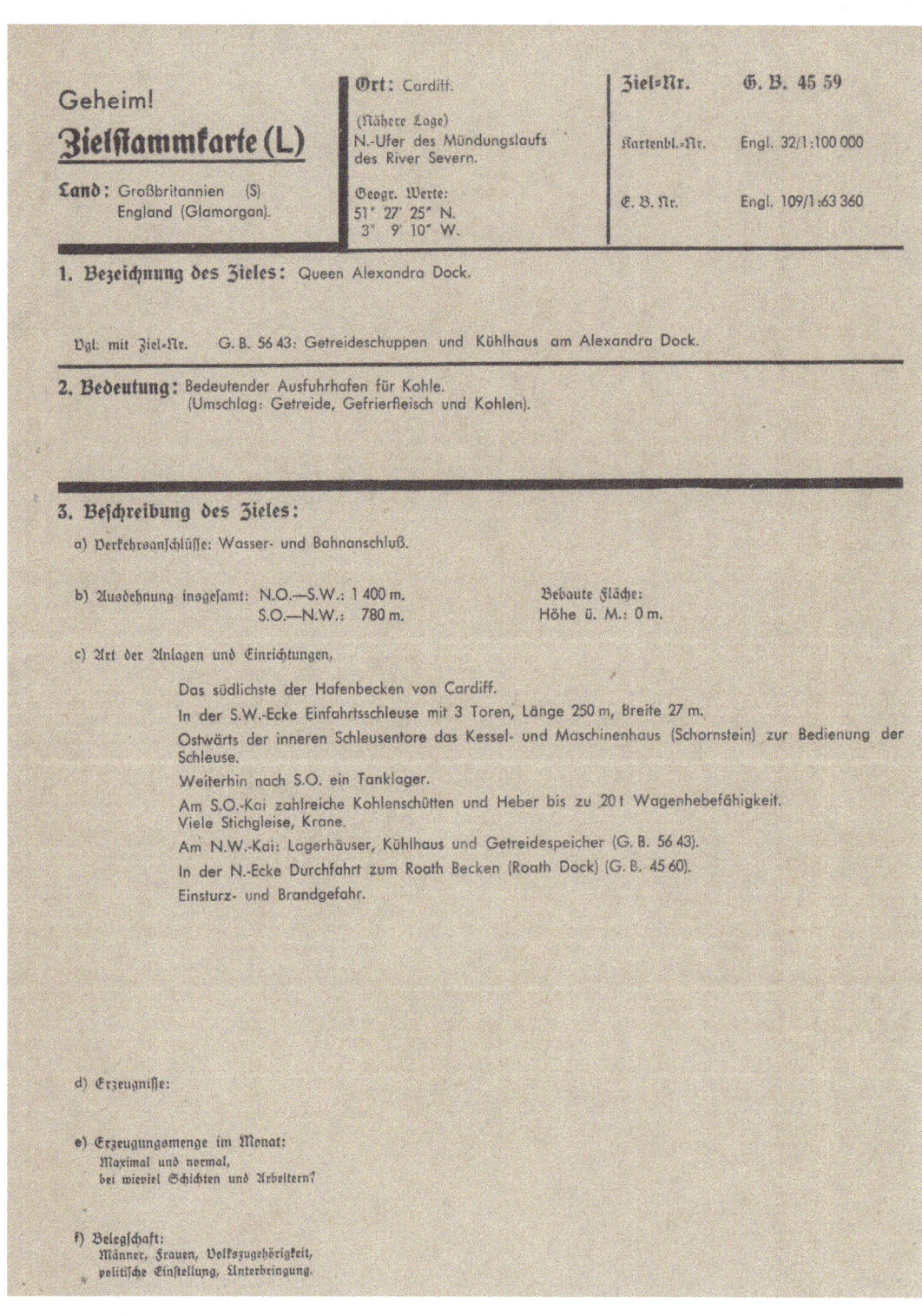

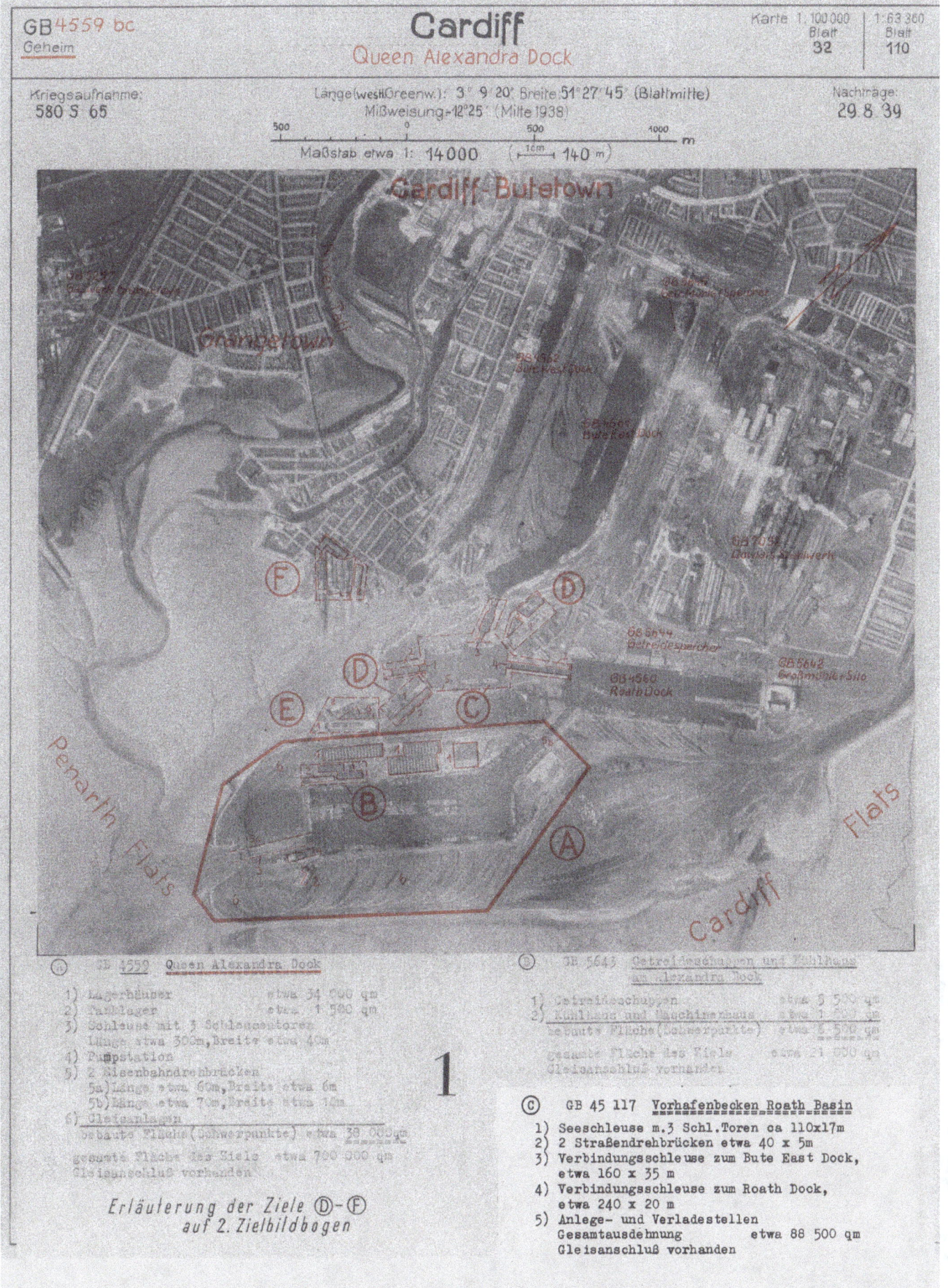

Overleaf: Centred on a very busy Mountstuart Yard on 28 February 1941. The yards are full of merchant ships being repaired or modified to combat against magnetic mines. Over on the other side of the Entrance Channel opposite Mountstuart Yard, the Channel Dry Dock holds a very large oil tanker.

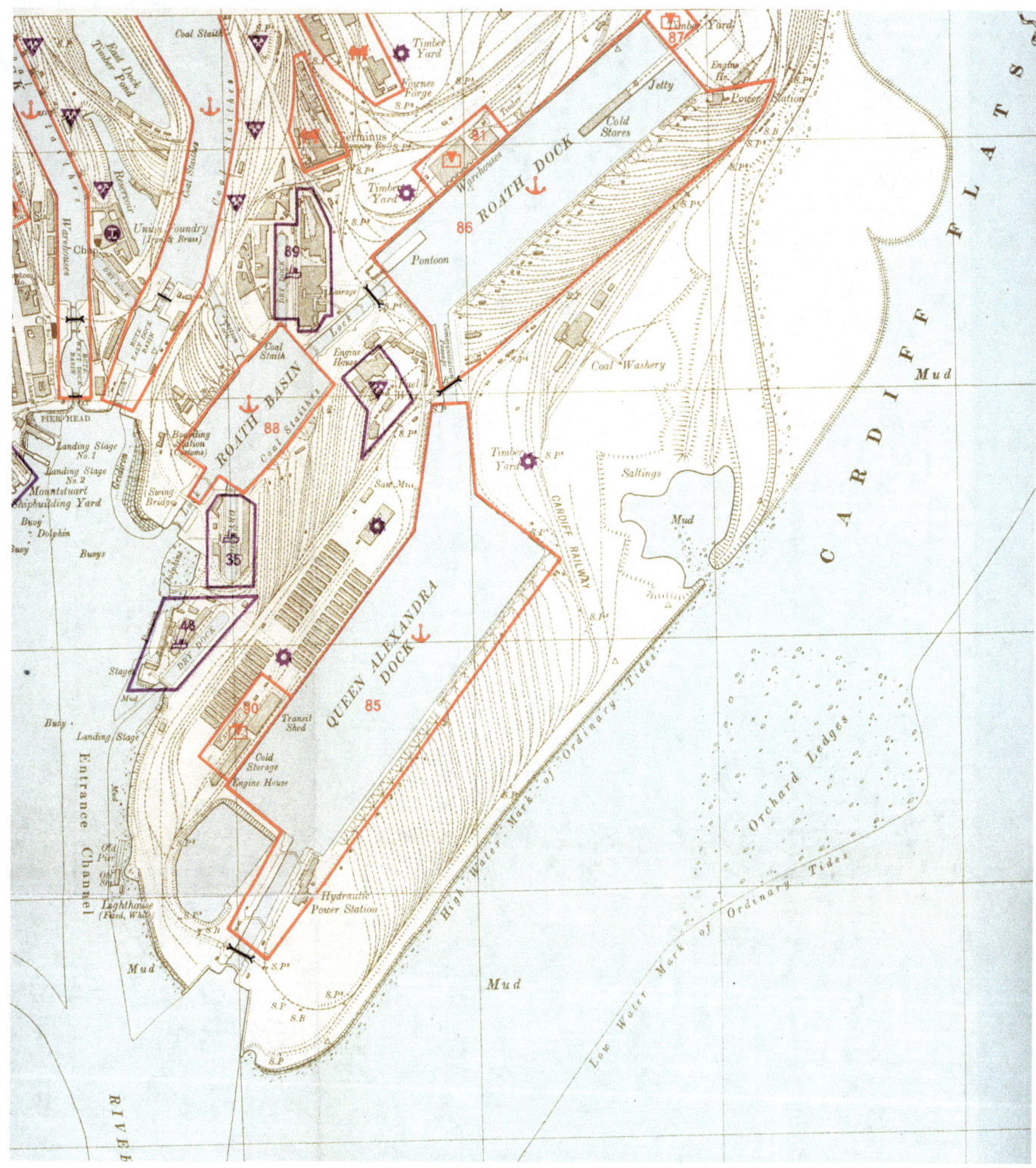

Above: The Queen Alexandra and Roath Docks as shown on the *Stadtplan* for Cardiff. The map shows the long sinuous loops of the coal loading lines as they track up to the coal drops. This map is based on the pre-war Ordnance Survey map, so the later developments of the grain and cold stores are not shown. This is why the Luftwaffe had to survey the ports in the summer and autumn of 1940, to ensure they knew about recent buildings.

Opposite: Open-source intelligence gathering at work. The top photograph is a GWR publicity shot of the docks from the early 1930s. The lower photograph is the same shot copied, re-interpreted and included in the 1940 *Militärgeographische Eizelangaben Objektbilder* (Military geographical details object images) handbook.

Translation: 'On the right in front is the Queen Alexandra Dock with tank stations and pumping station (chimney on the right in front). Right long side: coaling plants; Left long side: Coldstore and warehouses. Rear transverse site: timber storage area and briquette factory (chimney). To the rear right: Roath Dock, to the left of it (middle) the small Roath Basin with passage to the rear (middle) to the long Bute East dock, next to it the narrow Bute West dock.'

AERIAL VIEW OF THE BUTE DOCKS, CARDIFF

GB 7, BB 32, Nr. 85: Queen Alexandra Dock im Hafen von Cardiff (Glamorganshire).
Rechts vorn das Queen Alexandra Dock mit Tankanlagen und Pumpwerk (Schornstein, rechts vorn). Rechte Längsseite: Bekohlungsanlagen; linke Längsseite: Kühlhaus und Lagerhäuser. Hintere Querseite: Holzlagerplatz und Brikettfabrik (Schornstein). Nach hinten rechts: Roath Dock, links davon (Mitte) das kleine Roath Basin mit Durchfahrt nach hinten (Mitte) zum langen Bute East-Dock, daneben links das schmale Bute West-Dock.

36

Above: Dowlais and Roath Dock on 23 November 1940. The Dowlais steelworks was one of the most spectacular integrated steel plants in the world. Building at the site began in 1881: By the end of the nineteenth century the works was producing massive quantities of pig iron and mild steel. Modernisation of the plant in the 1930s resulted in a massive boost in capacity enabling the plant to produce over a million tons of iron and steel annually. The plant depended on massive imports of iron ore. One of the most notable sources of good-quality ore was from Sweden and Norway via the port of Narvik. The disastrous Norwegian campaign of 1940 was a British attempt to take control of the iron ore industry and ensure supplies for Dowlais whilst denying them to Germany. The end of availability to acquire iron ore meant that Dowlais imported increasing quantities of American semi-finished steel products The works is shown in a German image from the 1940 *Militärgeographische Eizelangaben Objektbilder* (Military geographical details object images) handbook

The lower part of the photo shows Roath Dock with grain ships unloading at the Spillers Mills. The ferro-concrete mill reflects more light than its surroundings. The mill is shown opposite in an image from the *Objektbilder*. Attacking such a complex industrial target required a large supply of large or very large calibre bombs. Although the Luftwaffe knew how to attack and destroy the plant, they never had sufficient resources to mount the sustained air attacks that would be needed.

At bottom left goods and supplies are being stacked in the open because the shortage of goods wagons and locomotives was preventing the port to be cleared of supplies coming in from convoy ships. At some points in 1940, Cardiff ceased to function as an effective port because it was overloaded with stores and supplies that could not be moved.

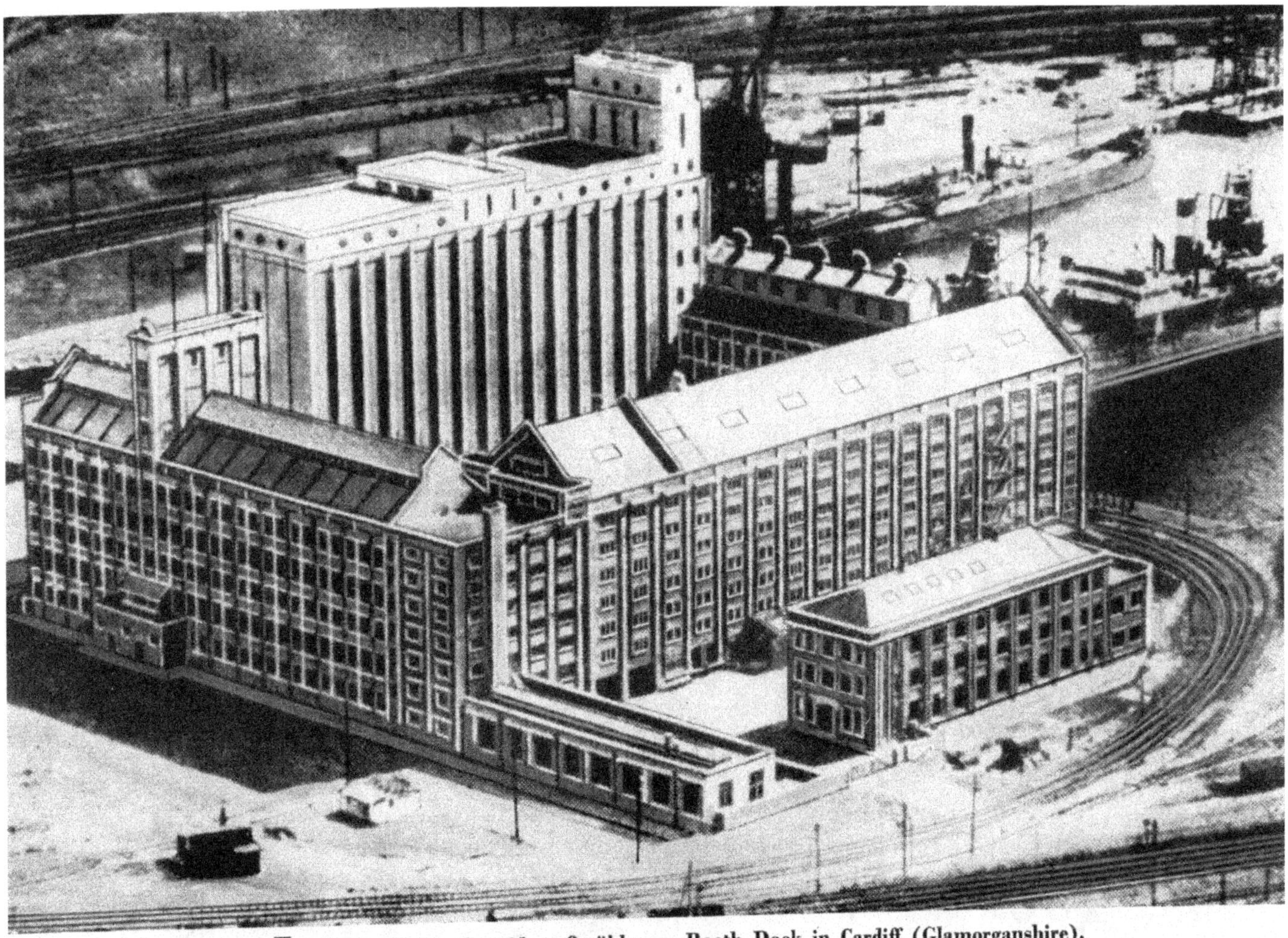

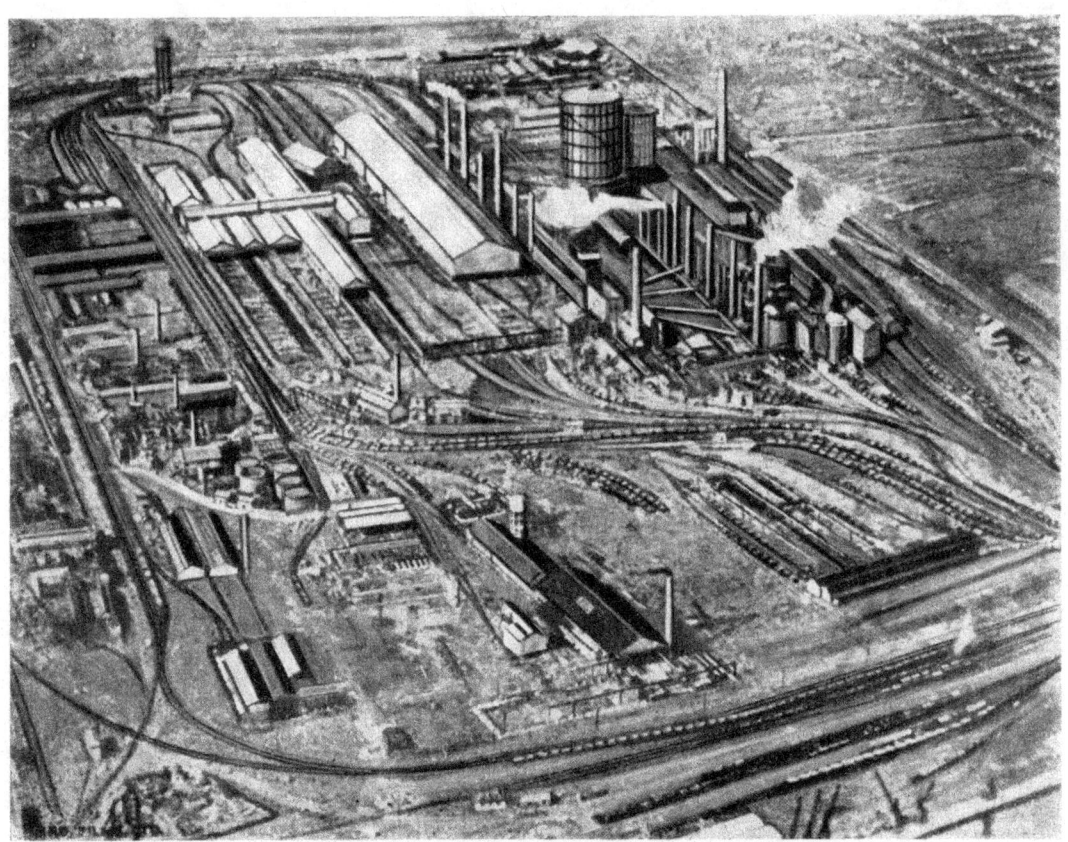

GB 7, BB 32, Nr. 87: Getreidegroßmühle am Roath Dock in Cardiff (Glamorganshire).
Spiller's Großmühle und Getreidespeicher; Speichervermögen 25 000 t; Tagesleistung etwa 480 t Weizen.
Förderanlagen auf der Mole 120 t Stundenleistung.

GB 7, BB 32, Nr. 102: Dowlais Stahlwerke in Cardiff.
Luftbild der Eisen- und Stahlwerke Guest Keen Baldwins Iron & Steel Co. Ltd. (Dowlais), ostwärts vom Bute Dock gelegen.
47 ha Ausdehnung; Stahl- und Walzwerk, eigene Kokerei, 6 SM-Öfen; Erzeugung: 7000 t Koks, 9000 t Roheisen, 10 000 t Rohstahl;
Herstellung von Maschinenteilen, Panzerplatten, Flugmotorenteilen. 1939: 6000 Arbeiter.

Above: A wide-angle view of the port area. This photograph was taken shortly after 3 p.m., hours after the city suffered its heaviest air raid when over a hundred bombers dropped one hundred and fifteen tons of explosives and thousands of incendiaries. It was important for the Luftwaffe to send reconnaissance flights into an area as soon after heavy air raids as possible in an order to understand the extent of damage and success of the bombing attacks. This became even more important after the switch to night bombing. These later missions became more dangerous as anti-aircraft defences and local RAF bases were on high-alert to prevent effective survey of the bomb damage. The Target No. GB 70 32 indicates that this mission was primarily to investigate damage to the Dowlais works which may have been the *Schwerpunkt* (Central aiming point) of the air attack. The indifferent accuracy of the raid meant that many of the high explosive bombs landed on the surrounding streets rather than the Dowlais works. The Luftwaffe used many large calibre bombs of five hundred kilogrammes in this raid, again confirming that they were intending to destroy the industrial buildings, but many of these bombs landed on houses.

The Spillers grain mills in Roath dock look busy and there are two vessels unloading chilled or frozen meat at the Queen Alexandra cold stores seen as the white rectangle on the right side of the dock. Despite the heavy attack, the working and functions of the port were not affected and people carried on.

Above: Another image from the 3 January 1941 flyover after the heavy attack. This photograph is centred on Leckwith Moors to the west of the Cardiff urban area. It is likely that Leckwith became the site for a series of bonfires that were lit to attract bombers. This process had already been successful in English towns. Eventually, Leckwith had a 'SF' or 'Starfish' site (which was a 'Special Fire'). when it had trenches filled with oil and petrol. Once a raid had started the trenches were set alight in the hope that bomber crews would drop their bombs on the fires. Although this may sound a rough and ready action, the principles were based on a sound understanding of the German bombers' electronic navigation aids. The burnt areas on this photo show where the bonfires were lit. The bomb craters in the fields show that many bombs were dropped here instead of the urban areas east of Leckwith. Bomb decoys eventually became extensive networks protecting Cardiff and Swansea.

Although the Luftwaffe had this photograph as part of the attack evaluation in early January 1941, it took them a while to understand what was actually happening.

6. Penarth

Two kilometres southwest of Bute West lies the Penarth Dock. A tidal harbour at the mouth of the River Ely was converted into a dock in the 1850s (Appleby 1933: 63). The dock was built to cater to some companies that were unhappy with the shipping and commercial arrangements at Bute West. Penarth was integrated into the Taff Vale Rail Company's network in the 1860s, giving it access to the Rhondda, Aberdare and Merthyr valleys and became a coal dock specialising in rapid transhipment of coal between the railways and the ships. Penarth was a considerable exporter of coal and coke in the 1920s and exported over two million tons of coal in 1930 alone (Appleby 1933: 171). The GWR invested in new lock gates and crane improvements in a bid to rejuvenate trade, but by 1936 the dock was largely closed to commercial shipping (Bird 1963: 221).

Below: The GWR plan of Penarth in 1933. Despite having excellent coal dispatch facilities, the poor economics of the coal export trade were too strong for Penarth and the decline of its commercial viability was rapid after the economic crash of the early 1930s.

Left: Coal wagons queueing in front of the coal drops at Penarth during its peak trade years in the late 1920s.

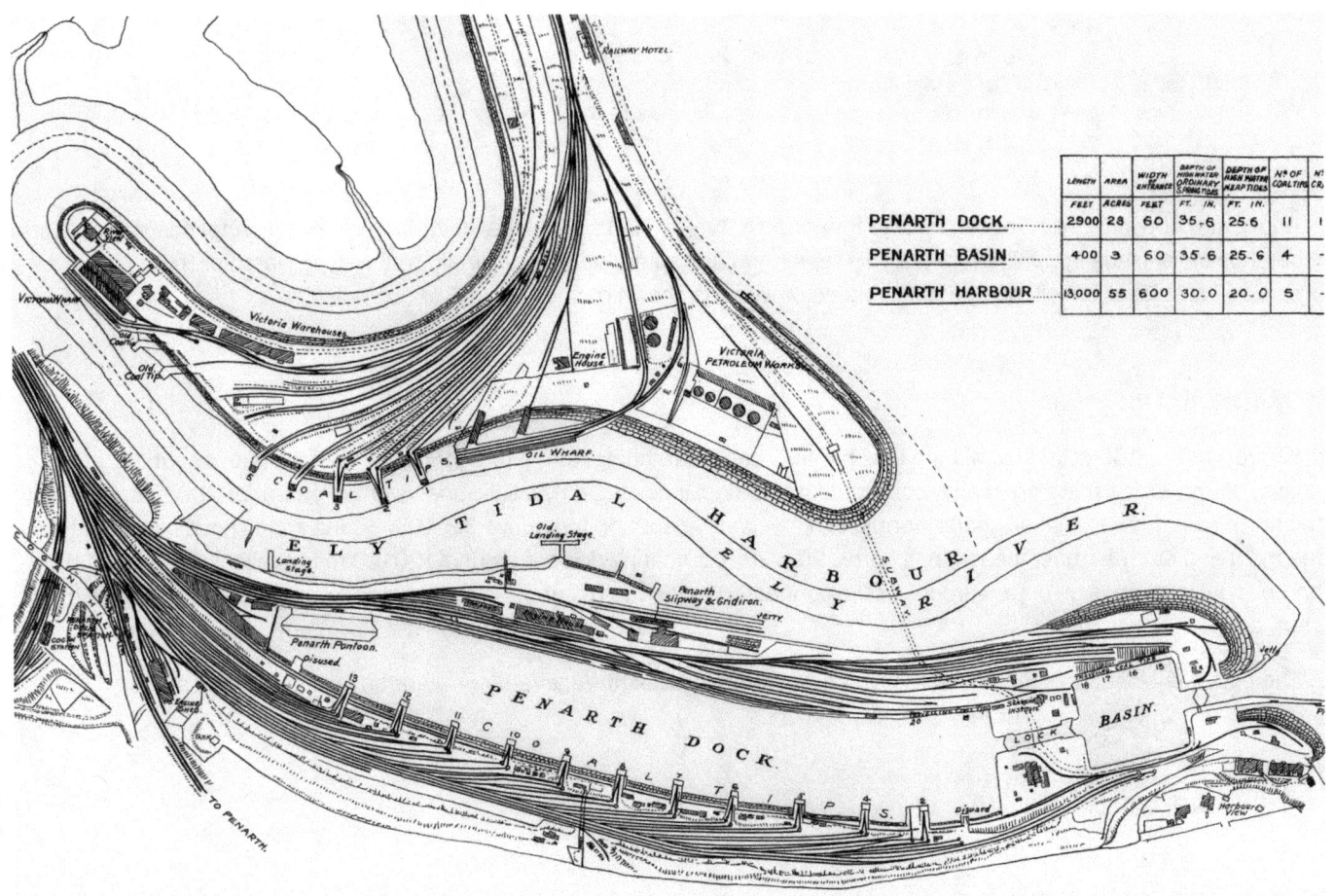

Geh. Kommandosache Ausfertigung **Geheim** **Zielstammkarte**	Ort: Penarth (Glamorgan)	Ziel-Nr. G.B. 45 183
		Kartenbl.Nr. Engl.32/1:100.000
Land: Grossbritannien England.	Geogr. Werte: 51° 27' 00" N 3° 10' 30" W	E.B.Nr. Engl.109/1:63.360

1. Bezeichnung des Zieles: Hafenanlagen

Vgl. mit Ziel-Nr. G.B. 21 55, G.B. 45 59, G.B. 83 58, G.B. 52 57.

2. Bedeutung: Kohlen-Ausfuhr-Hafen.

3. Beschreibung des Zieles:

a) Verkehrsanschlüsse: Vollbahnanschluss

b) Ausdehnung insgesamt: 204 ha Wasserfläche   Bebaute Fläche: einige 100 qm

c) Bauweise, Bauausführung, Luftempfindlichkeit, Brandgefahr:

Etwa 100 m breites und 1 km langes von O nach W sich erstreckendes, im W spitz zulaufendes Hafenbecken mit etwa 1,2 km Quailänge. Auf der S-Seite hauptsächlich Kohleverladungsanlagen, dabei 4 hydraulische mit 200 t Stundenleistung. Auf der Nordseite ein kleiner Warenspeicher. Wassertiefe an den Quais 6,5 - 10 m bei Springhochwasser. Schleuse zwischen Haupt- und Vorhafen mit ca. 90 x 20 m Ausmass. 1 Schwimmdock von etwa 120 x 20 m ist vorhanden. Dem Hafenbecken vorgelagert ist ein Vorhafenbecken, mit dem Haupthafen durch Schleuse verbunden, gegen See mit Stemmtor abgeschlossen.
Der Hafen wurde im Juli 1936 für den allgemeinen Verkehr geschlossen. Für aufliegende Schiffe wurde ermässigte Liegegebühr bewilligt.

Above and opposite: The *Zielstammkarte* for Penarth. Target GB 45 183. The *Militärgeographische Angaben* gave Penarth a quite positive listing in 1938 as having ship repair and accommodation for a small-Cruiser-type warship. There was also provision for at least ten oil-storage tanks. Some of which is shown on the *Objekt Bild* opposite.

Translation of the above:

'Approximately 100 m wide and 1 km long harbour basin stretching from E to W, tapering in the W with about 1.2 km of quays. On the S side there are mainly coal loading facilities, including 4 hydraulic ones with an output of 200 t per hour. On the north side there is a small goods storage facility . Water depth on the quays 6.5-10m during spring floods. Lock between the main and outer harbour measuring approx. 90 x 20m. 1 floating dock of around 120 -20 m is available. In front of the harbour basin there is an outer harbour basin, connected to the main harbour by a lock and closed off from the sea with a stem gate.

The port was closed to general traffic in July 1936. Reduced demurrage fees were granted for ships lying afloat.'

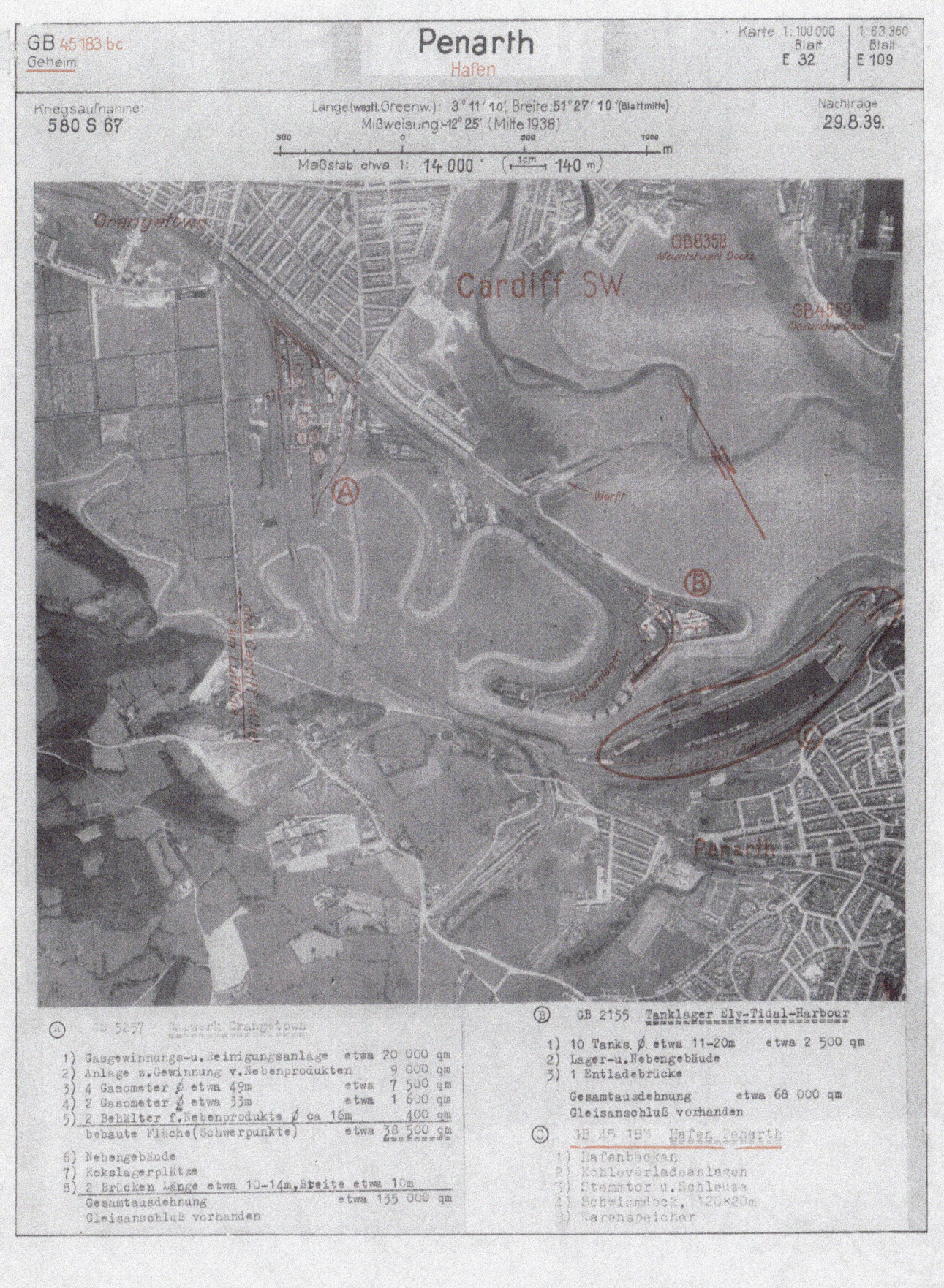

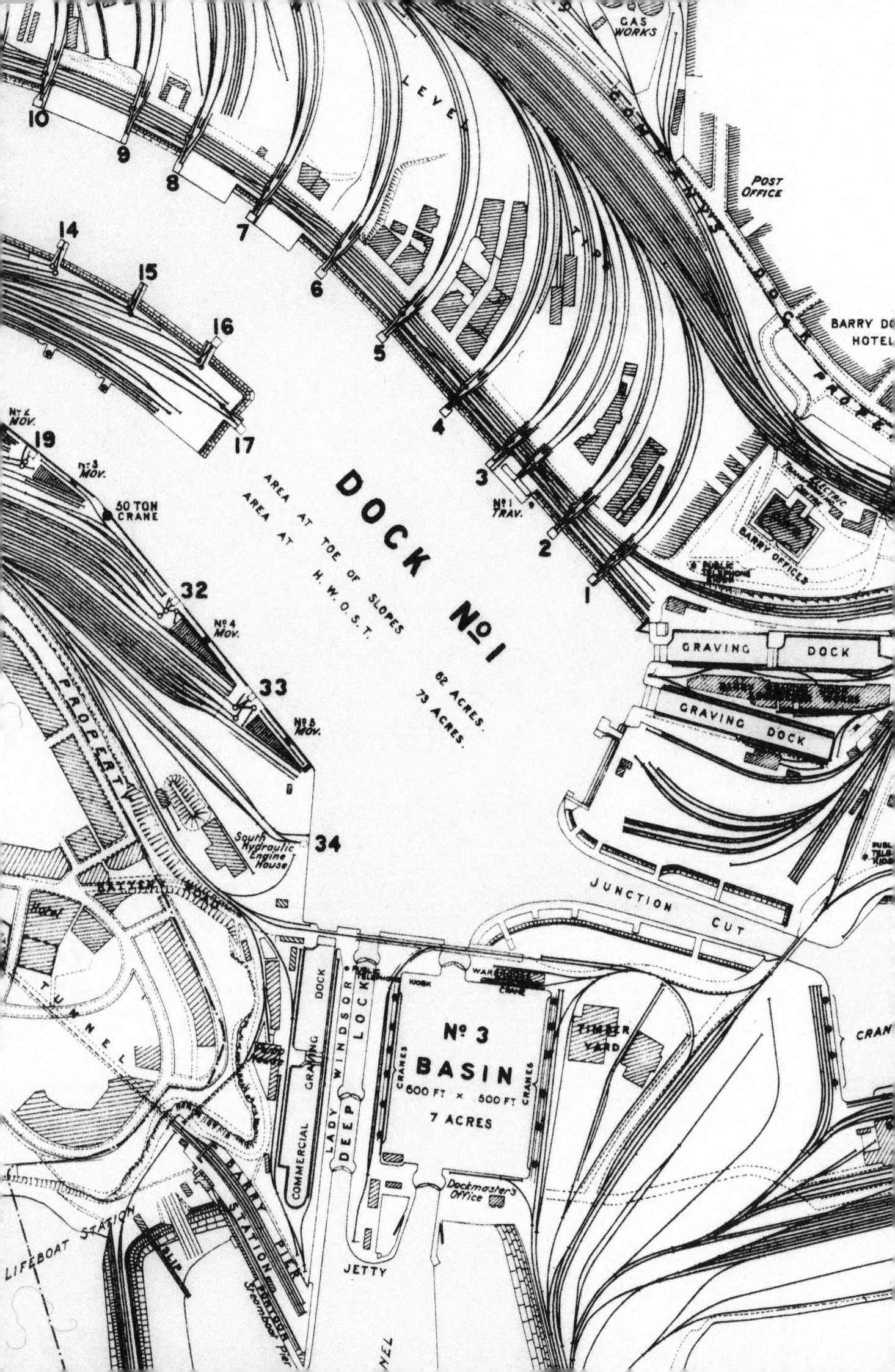

7. Barry

The political and commercial dissatisfaction with the Cardiff Bute Docks also initiated the development of Barry Docks. A perfect spot for docks was seen adjacent to Barry Island. Several coal firms saw merit in developing an independent dock free of Cardiff's charges and constraints. The slightly longer rail distance from the Rhondda was believed to be offset by the virtues of a modern independent dock system. Dock No. 1 opened in 1889, followed by Dock No. 2 in 1898. the half-tide Basin into Dock No. 1 was considered Dock No. 3, although considerably smaller than the two main docks.

Eventually both docks were equipped with coal drops to allow for lifting the coal from coal trucks and into the holds of the colliers. The GWR also modernised Barry with new hoists capable of handling the twenty-ton coal wagons.

Barry's advantage was that the lock entrances were very close to deep water, allowing quick access into the Bristol Channel. From the start, Barry was constructed with coal export as the priority. The integration between rail links, marshalling yards, coal hoists and ship accommodation was probably the best in the Bristol Channel. Good wharf layouts meant quicker turnaround times for coal loading. A combination of older coal hoists and new equipment for handling twenty-ton coal wagons meant that Barry had the flexibility to deal with a wide range of collieries, including those who had not yet invested in the handling equipment for the larger coal trucks and

Below: A sketch map of the GWR improvements made to Barry in the early 1930s. Barry became a storage centre because of the flat open space south of Dock No. 2. Eventually, the Supply Reserve Depot was erected here although the main transport element was road not rail. Left: An extract from the GWR plan of Barry from the early 1930s, showing the coal drops and shipyards of Dock No.1.

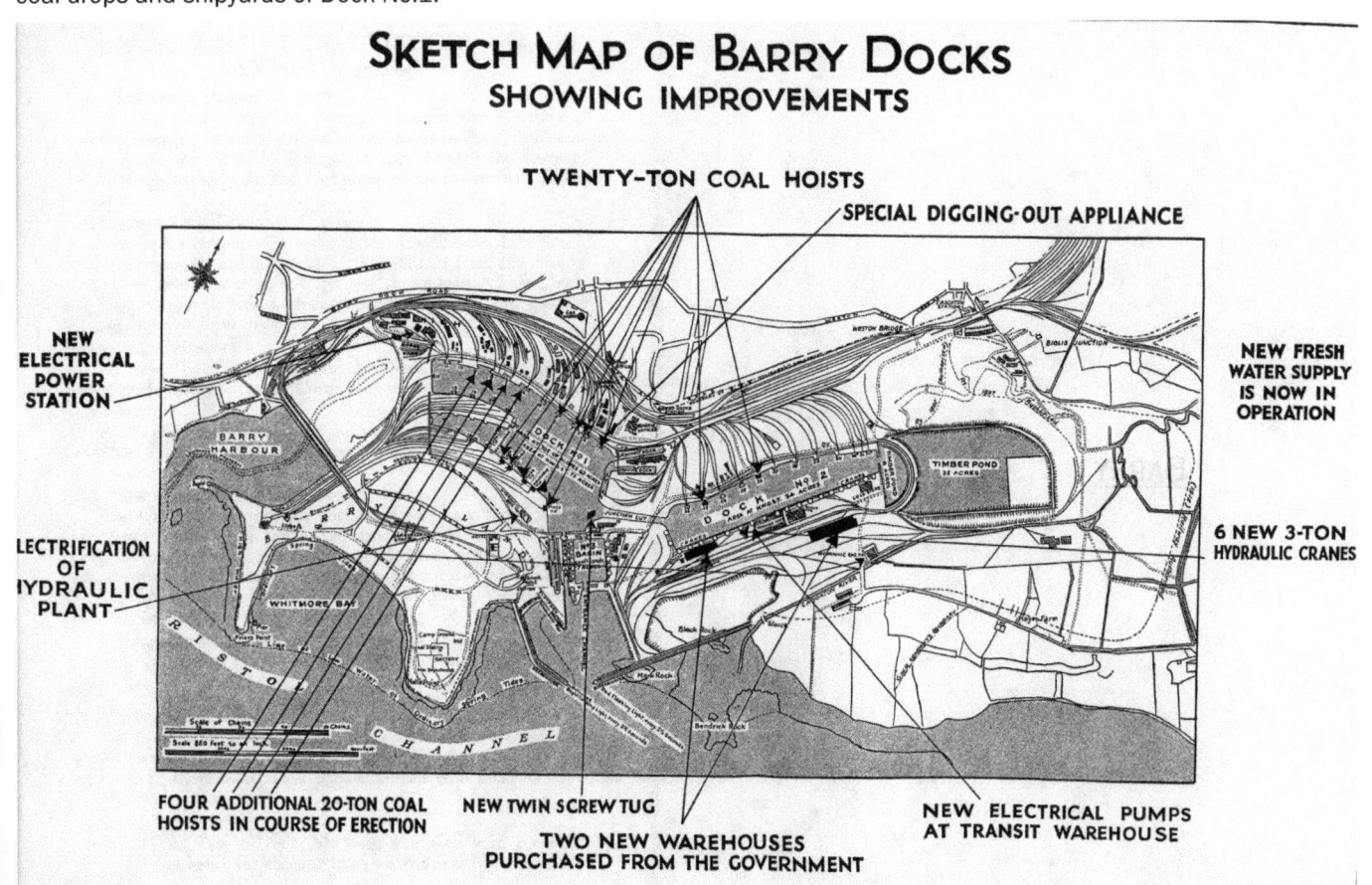

still used thousands of ten-ton coal trucks. Barry held the coal industry record for coal handling, with a peak of eleven million tons a year in the 1920s. By the 1930s, this had dropped slightly, but Barry still exported seven million tons annually in the 1930s. The GWR constantly enhanced Barry's coal handling capability, adding twelve twenty-ton coal hoists in the early 1930s (Appleby 1933: 105)

Barry's success was too big to be kept within the confines of the coal industry, and it developed a wider function as a general merchandise port. Further investment after World War One saw better cranes, wider electricity cabling for powering machinery, large transit sheds (some with elaborate internal floors and racking) and cold stores. With an eye to the future, Barry improved road vehicle handling with new roads and roundabouts. Eventually, Barry would become a preferred port for government stores with the Supply Reserve Depot (SRD) foundation at Dock No.2. The SRD became a strategic storage depot for key wartime supplies. After 1943, the United States army had great affection for the supply and storage facilities of Barry.

The food industry also liked Barry. Rank built a large grain store and flour mill at Dock No. 2 adjacent to the cool and cold storage. other industries followed, including ship repair, wagon repair and oil storage. Grain and flour were significant imports by the 1930s.Barry was also important in importing pitwood from Russia, Norway, and Canada for the Glamorgan coal industry. Dock No. 2 had a sixteen-hectare timber pond for pit prop storage. Several Luftwaffe images show the pond stocked with mining timber.

Below: An extract from the Barry *Zielstammkarte*. The Three docks are listed and the Luftwaffe recognise the quality of the modern coal-loading equipment. Again, optimistically they have suggested the docks may be suitable for incendiary attack (*Brandgefahr*)

1. Bezeichnung des Zieles: Barry Hafenbecken Nr. 1, 2 und 3.

Vgl. mit Ziel=Nr. G. B. 56 48: Getreidegroßmühle mit Silo und Kühlhaus im Hafenbecken Nr. 2.
G. B. 83 59: 3 Trockendocks am Hafenbecken Nr. 1.

2. Bedeutung: Sehr wichtiger Umschlaghafen besonders für Cardiffkohle (11 000 000 t Kohle jährlich).

3. Beschreibung des Zieles:

a) Verkehrsanschlüsse: Wasser- und Bahnanschluß.

b) Ausdehnung insgesamt: O.—W. 2,3 km.   Bebaute Fläche:
   N.—S.: 0,7 km.   Höhe ü. M.: ± 0 m.

c) Art der Anlagen und Einrichtungen,
   Bauweise, Bauausführung, Luftempfindlichkeit, Brandgefahr:

   Hafenbecken Nr. 1, das größte westliche Becken.
   Am N.-Kai 12 Kopfgleise mit hohen Kohlenschütten und Hebern. An der Mittelkaizunge Kohlen-schütten und Kräne zum Verladen anderer Güter.
   Am S.-Kai wiederum hohe Kohlenschütten.
   3 Trockendocks (G. B. 83 59) im S. O.-Teil des Beckens.
   120 m nördlich der N. W.-Ecke und 120 m westlich der S.-Kante des Beckens je eine elektrische Kraftstation mit Kesselhaus und Schornstein.

   Hafenbecken Nr. 2, das östliche, schmalere Becken.
   Am N.-Kai 10 hohe Kohlenheber und Schütten an Kopfgleisen. Am N.O.-Kai kleiner Holz-hafen mit Durchfahrt und Drehbrücke.
   Am S.-Kai eine große Anzahl von Kränen, in der Mitte hohe Mühlengebäude (G. B. 56 48).
   360 m südlich der S. O.-Ecke des Beckens Kessel- u. Maschinenhaus (Schornstein) für den Hafen-betrieb.
   Von den 40 modernen Kohlenverladeanlagen in beiden Becken heben 11 je 20 t.
   Für alle Ein- und Ausfuhrwaren sind auf den Kais beider Becken und im Hafengelände neuzeit-liche Lagerhäuser und zahlreiche Kräne bis zu 50 t Tragkraft, ferner im Hafen ein Schwimmkran von 125 t Leistung vorhanden.

   Hafenbecken 3 zwischen S. O.-Kai des Hafenbeckens 1 und dem Außenhafen.
   Ein kleineres Becken zur Entlastung der Schleuse für den Hafenverkehr.
   An beiden Seiten je eine Schleuse von 24 m Breite. Neben dem W.-Kai des Beckens eine Ein-fahrtschleuse, die durch 3 Paar Schleusentore je nach Bedarf geteilt werden kann.
   Einsturz- und Brandgefahr.

Above: The *Objektphoto* for Barry Docks (Target GB 45 62). The docks are listed and described with their dimensions. Feature 13 is a coldstore (*Kuhlhaus*). This was a priority target and is marked with (*Schwerpunkte)* to emphasise its significance.

Geheim
GB 4564 c

Ba
Hafenbec

A Hafenbec
B 3 Trocke
C Getreide

Maßstab 1:9130

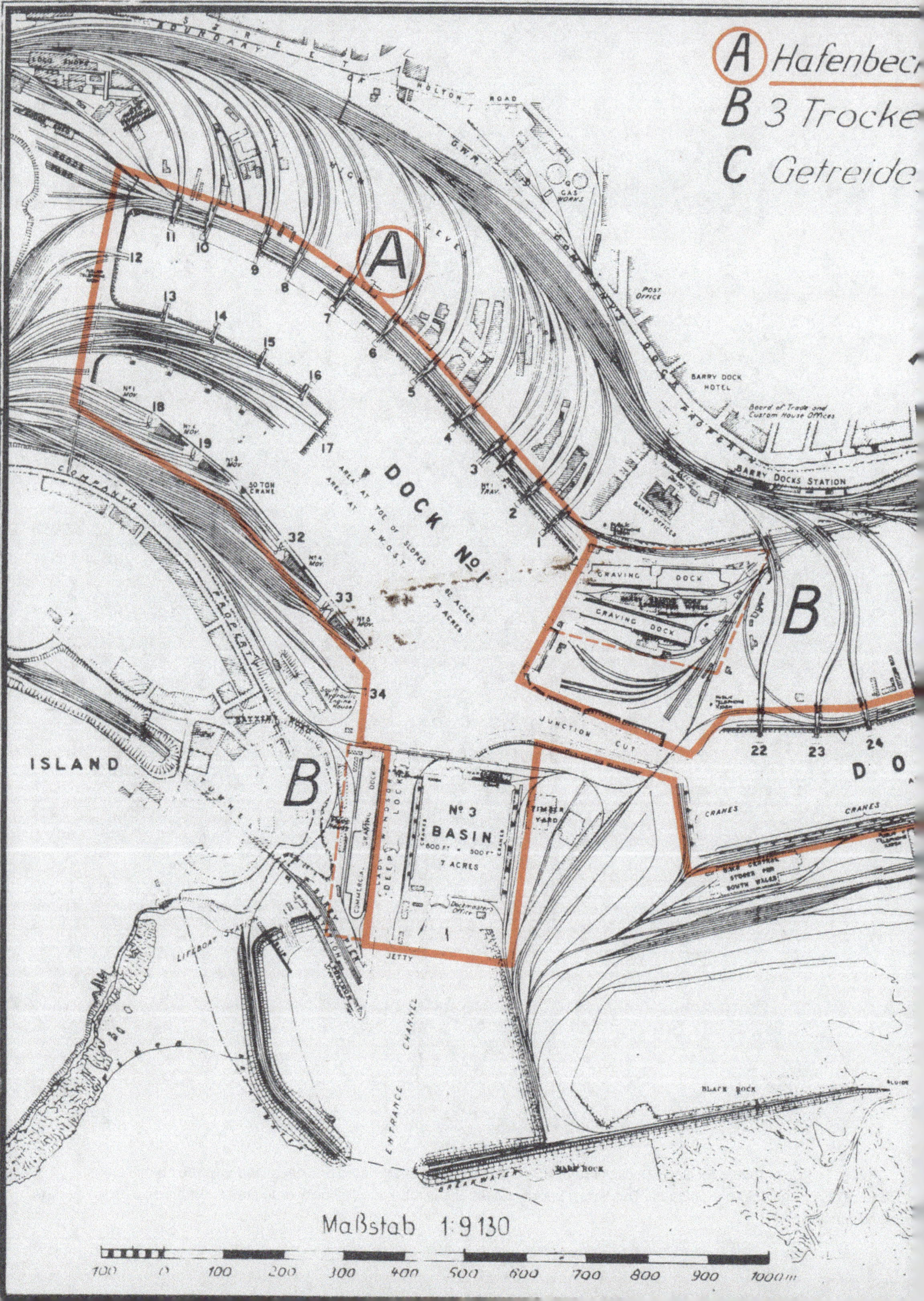

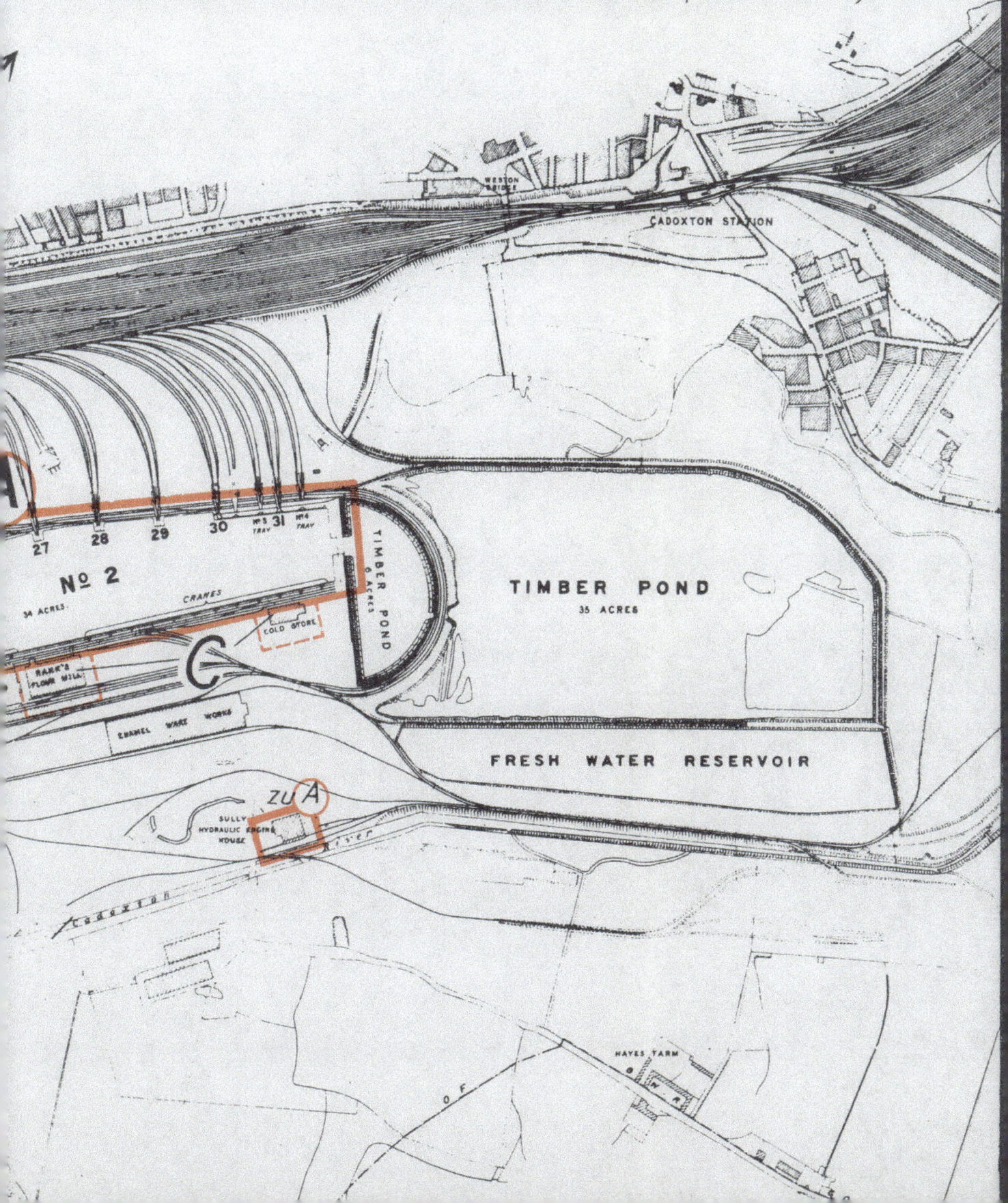

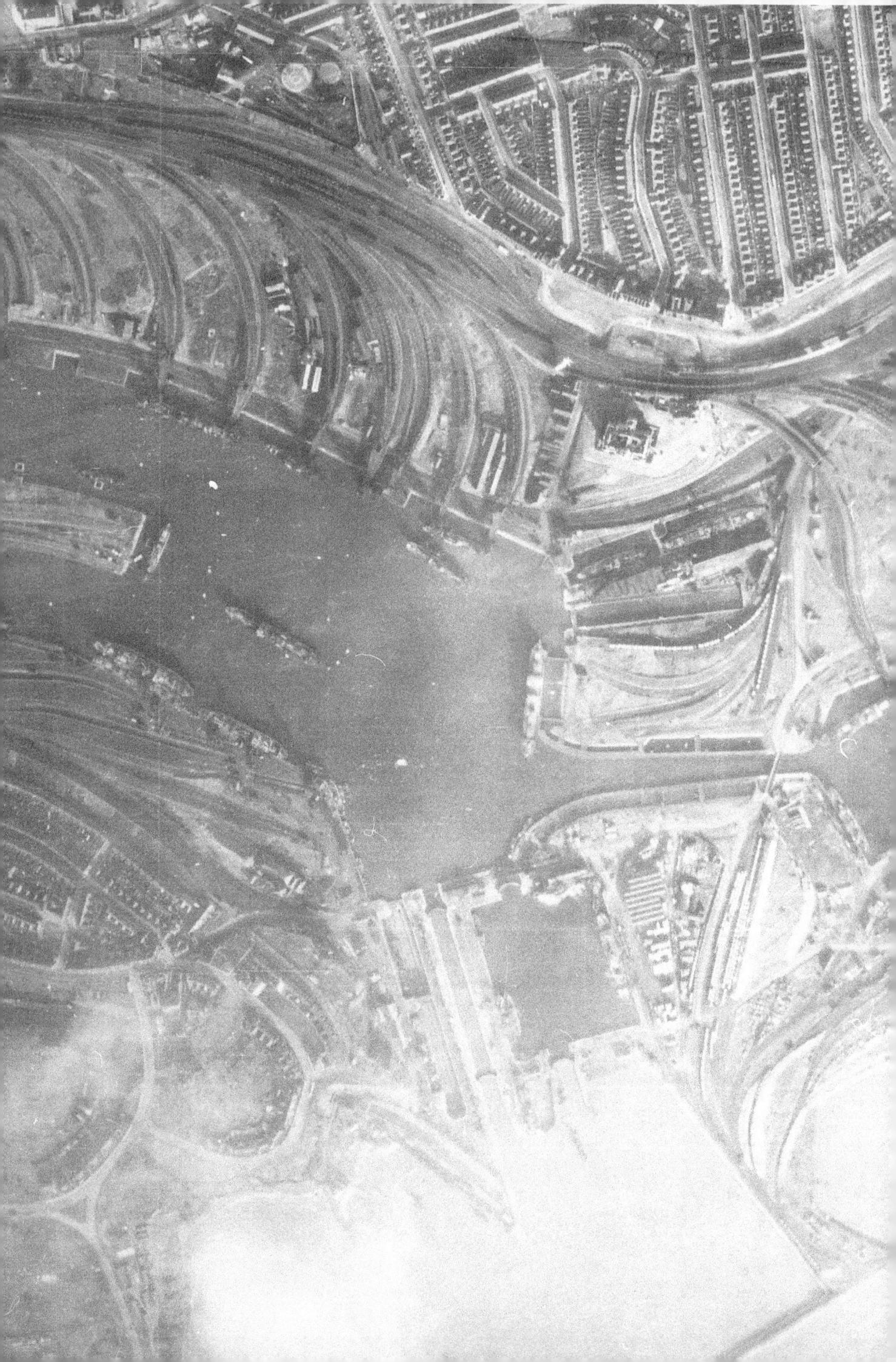

Previous pages: A Luftwaffe *Bildskizzen* (Sketch plan) of Barry from November 1939. This likely to have been derived from the Study Blue research. Sketches from Ordnance Survey maps were often used where photographs were not available. It is interesting to see that both the grain silo and the cold stores were noticed.

The following page is an image from 28 February 1941. The docks are very busy Dock No. 1 on the left has a number of oil tankers, general cargo ships and may even be loading up coal on the northern side of the dock. February 1941 was the height of the coal movement crisis where a shortage of coal wagons and problems with the Severn Tunnel meant that coal could not be transported to the South-East of England. This forced the Ministry of Supply to risk coaster traffic moving out of the Bristol Channel and around Lands End. The grain wharf in Dock No. 2 is quiet although a ship can be seen unloading frozen food into the cold stores. Further right, the timber pond is stocked with pit props and other timber.

The newly erected light-coloured warehouse buildings of the Supply Reserve Depot (SRD) can be seen lower right. These warehouses were steerage for essential equipment arriving from North America. Such stores included fire hoses, trailer pumps, vans and lorries, and engine parts. The SRD was intended to rely on road transport rather than rail connections and the road network with roundabouts can be seen. Roads were considered more flexible and resilient to air attack. This period of the war saw a gradual transition of a great deal of strategic supplies to road delivery.

Above: A view of Dock No. 1 and the oil terminal north of Barry Island in November 1940. The Luftwaffe analyst has marked the oil storage target and the protecting Barrage Balloon. It may seem strange to think that the presence of a single balloon could have much impact for protection, but even one balloon could discourage bomber crews from low-level precision attacks and force them into higher altitudes. The number of oil tankers here indicates the importance of oil imports into Barry.

Opposite: A closer look at the Supply Reserve Depot from November 1940. The Luftwaffe took some time to understand the growing importance of road transport because German industry tended to concentrate on railway networks for industrial use and distribution. At the top right, goods stored in the open show the growing storage problem faced by Barry. At the extreme top right, mining timber is stored in the timber ponds. The cold store wharf at the top of the image is busy unloading frozen meat.

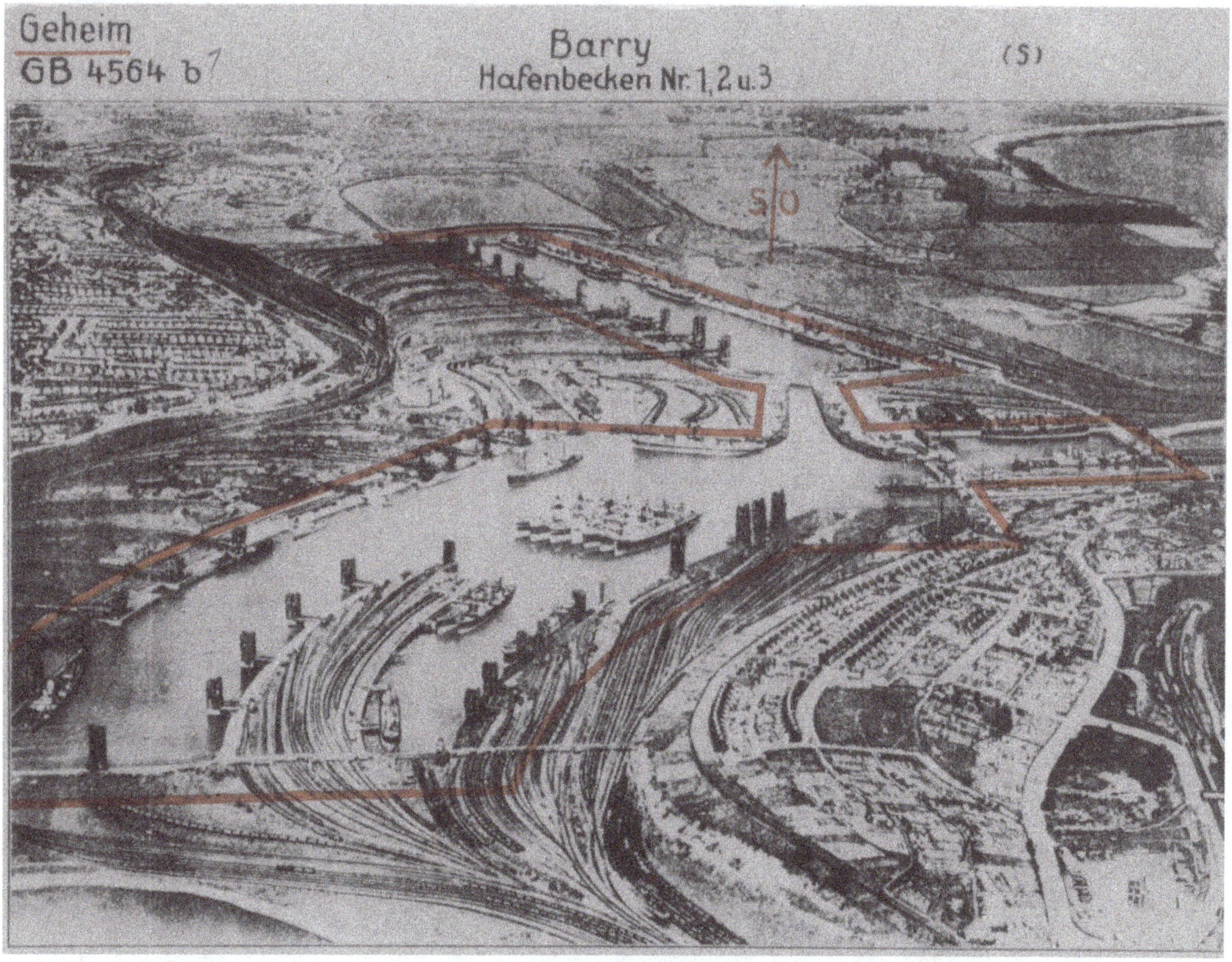

AERIAL VIEW OF BARRY DOCKS (LOOKING EASTWARD)

Top: An aerial view of Barry with Dock No.1 in the foreground. This is from the Luftwaffe *Zielstammkarte* dossier. The target area is edged red. Below is the original GWR publicity photograph from the early 1930s. This indicates the original image was obtained by the Luftwaffe as part of the Study Blue research in 1938-39.

Opposite: Barry Island in November 1940.

8. Port Talbot

Port Talbot (Aberafan) has a long history as a port, although much of the town's historic identity is swallowed up by the dominant steelworks (Jones 1988: 7, 34). Coal was moved down the Afan Valley to a site originally known as Llewellyn's Quay, probably from the 1600s or earlier. By the 1750s, a tram line had replaced the pack horse route, and by 1811, iron was also being moved through the valley. Copper ore was imported for the copper works at Cwmafan by the 1830s, and a wharf near Llewellyn's Quay was built to handle ore (the original Copper Works Wharf).

The prevailing wave direction and longshore drift of this part of Swansea Bay meant that the mouth of the Afan was blocked by sand dunes, creating a lagoon where the Afan's outlet to the sea was forced eastwards. This lagoon eventually became the focus of dock developments in the 1830s. With clever engineering, a new lock system converted the lagoon into a floating harbour. This float allowed for further expansion of wharves and dockside activities and encouraged further industrial growth. The growing demand for more accommodation of bigger ships accompanied plans for steelworks expansion. By 1898, a larger dock system had been created to serve the Port Talbot Steelworks and the nearby Margam Iron Works.

In the 1930s, the GWR developed Port Talbot's general cargo quays with transit sheds, sidings and new hydraulic cranes (Appleby 1933: 59). Even so, Port Talbot remained a centre of coal export with a substantial sideline in finished iron and steel products such as railway goods, and tin-plate. Port Talbot also played an important part in importing pitwood for the Afan Valley coal mines and acting as the port for the Rio Tinto Company copper smelting works.

Left: Port Talbot on the *Stadtplan* in 1940. Below: A sketch plan of the Port Talbot dock improvements of the early 1930s.

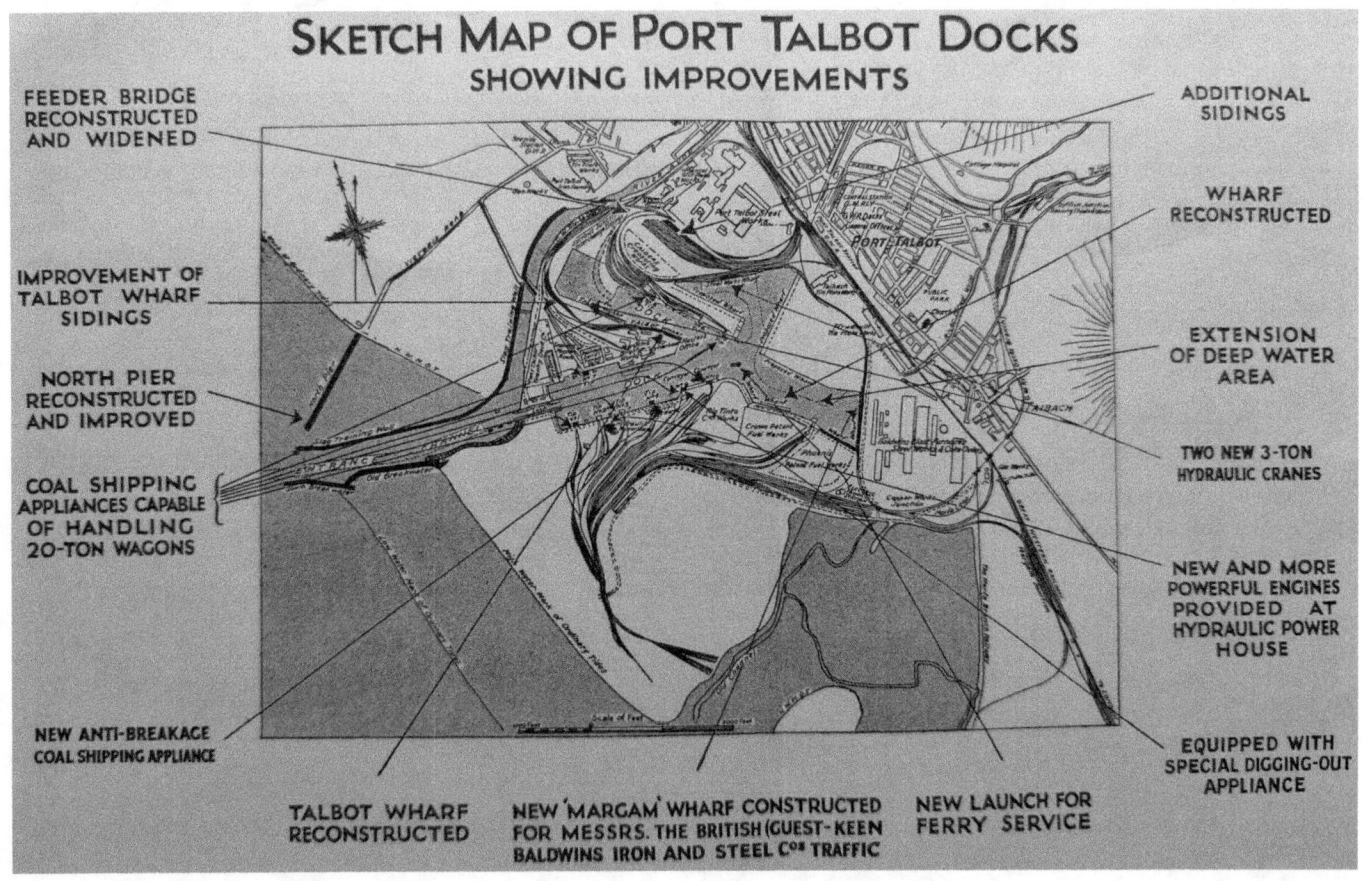

> **Geheim!**
> **Zielstammkarte (L)**
>
> **Land:** Großbritannien (S)
> England (Glamorgan)
>
> **Ort:** Port Talbot
> *(Nähere Lage)*
> N.-Ufer des Bristol-Kanals,
> 11 km ostsüdostwärts v. Swansea.
>
> **Geogr. Werte:**
> 51° 34' 55" N.
> 3° 47' 45" W.
>
> **Ziel-Nr.** G. B. 45 65
> **Kartenbl.-Nr.** Engl 26/1:100 000
> **E. B. Nr.** Engl 101/1:63 360
>
> **1. Bezeichnung des Zieles:** Port Talbot Hafenbecken mit Seeschleuse und Trockendock.
>
> Vgl. mit Ziel-Nr. G. B. 70 63: Stahlwerk Guest Keen Baldwin, Port Talbot.
> G. B. 70 67: Hochofen- und Stahlwerk, Port Talbot.
>
> **2. Bedeutung:** Ausfuhr: Kohle, Eisen- und Stahlwaren.
> Einfuhr: Eisenerz, Eisen, Stahl, Holz.
>
> **3. Beschreibung des Zieles:**
>
> a) Verkehrsanschlüsse: Zahlreiche Gleisanschlüsse.
>
> b) Ausdehnung insgesamt: 27 ha.   Bebaute Fläche:
>   Wassertiefe: 8 m.
>
> c) Art der Anlagen und Einrichtungen.
>
> Unregelmäßig geformtes Hafenbecken.
> Zugang zur Swansea Bay im W. durch Einfahrtsschleuse (130×30 m). Das ostw. anschließende, neuere Hafenbecken hat am S.-Ufer moderne Kohlen-Verladebrücken mit Hebe- und Kippvorrichtungen bis zu 20 t Waggons. Zahlreiche Gleisanschlüsse und Abstellgleise vorhanden. Die hydraulische Kraftstation liegt unmittelbar am S.-Kai, 250 m südostwärts der Einfahrtsschleuse. An der N.W.-Ecke dieses Hafenbeckens, 200 m nördlich der Einfahrtsschleuse, 1 Trockendock (130×20 m) und einzelne kleinere Werftgebäude.
> An N.-Ufer gleichfalls moderne Verladeeinrichtungen mit Gleisanschlüssen, sowie Hafenbetriebsgebäude und Lagerschuppen.
> Die Stahlwerke (G. B. 70 63) im N. und G. B. 70 67 im O. der Hafenanlagen haben eigene leistungsfähige Verladeeinrichtungen.
> Einsturzgefahr.

Above and opposite: The *Zeilstammkarte* for Port Talbot. The sketch plan (*Bildskizzen*) rather than a photo indicates this research was part of the Study Blue research in 1938 -39.

Translation:

'Irregularly shaped harbour basin

Access to Swansea Bay in the W. through an entrance lock (130x30m.) The new harbour basin to the east has modern coal loading bridges with lifting and tilting devices for up to 20 t wagons on the S bank.

Numerous track connections and sidings available. The hydraulic power station is located directly on the S quay, 250 m southeast of the entrance lock. On the N.W. Corner of this harbour back, 200 m north of the entrance lock, 1 dry dock (130x20m) and individual smaller shipyard buildings.

On the N bank there are also modern loading facilities with railway sidings, as well as port operations buildings and storage sheds.

The steelworks (G.B. 70 63) and in the N. and G.B. 70 67 in the E. of the port facilities have their own efficient loading facilities.

Danger of collapse'

Obviously, the emphasis is in the Port Talbot and Margam Steelworks and the buildings are assessed for attack by large bombs (but not incendiaries) as shown by the word *Einsturzgefahr.* at the end of the description.

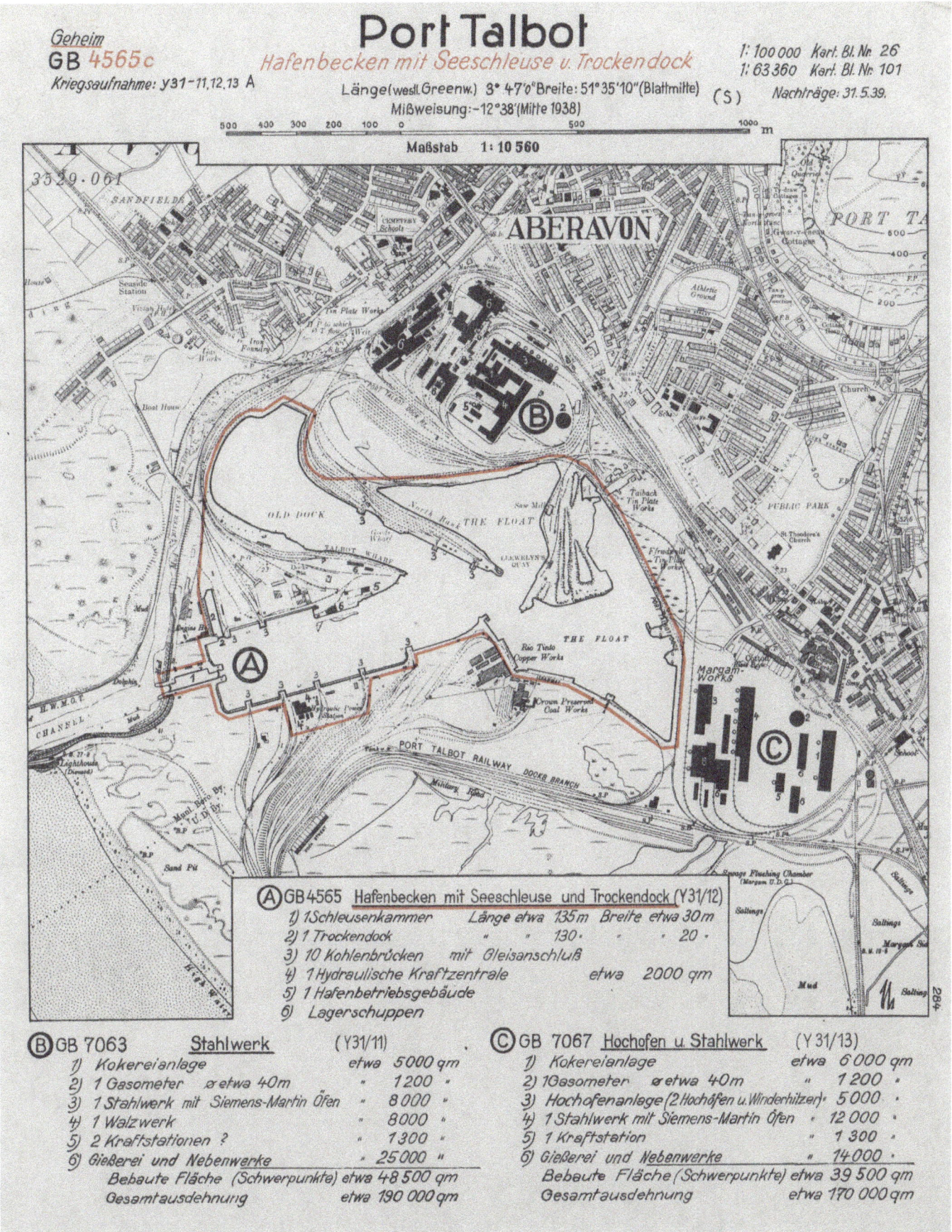

The main targets in Port Talbot were the built up areas of the steelworks *(Bebaute Fläche)*. Which were both identified as main aiming points *(Schwerpunkte)* by the Luftwaffe analyst. This is because the buildings at these steelworks were much more compact than the open expanses of newer steelworks, so the likelihood of effective destruction by large bombs was much improved.

Overleaf: The incredible industrial landscape of Port Talbot on 3 September 1940. The building of the docks and steelworks irreversibly transformed the environment of the Afan river mouth and the dune belts of Swansea Bay.

9. Llandarcy (Swansea)

Llandarcy is not a GWR port, but it deserves its own listing because of its national strategic significance. The genesis of the Llandarcy refinery has its origins in the complex politics and finances of the early oil industry before World War One. The formidable businessman William Knox D'arcy skilfully navigated the tortuous politics of Persia and the Ottoman Empire in the early 1900s to obtain exploration licences for parts of both countries. By 1912, with the involvement of the British government, the Anglo-Persian Oil Company was formed to exploit the newly discovered Persian oil fields. Oil had already become a commodity of great sensitivity to the Royal Navy, as warships were already heavy users of this new strategic resource. The early history of the oil industry is complex, and for Britain, much is obscured by the murky politics of British Middle Eastern policy and the deterioration of the Empire (Payton-Smith 1971: 7–25).

In the aftermath of World War One, oil production and supply had been established as a strategic commodity. Technicians, economists and imperial politicians debated where to place oil refining. Whether at the source of oil in Persia, or at new British refineries on major estuaries. It was never an easy debate. Refining crude oil usually involves a series of condensation and distillation processes that mean a substantial loss in outputs, so a tonne of crude oil results in about 850 kg of refined product (motor spirit, lubricants, DERV). Economic sense suggests the refineries should be close to the source of the oil, for example, in Abadan in Persia (later Iran). It was less clear on the advantages of importing crude oil and refining this domestically. Royal Navy and trade experts believed it best to refine oil at source and ship refined products. By the 1920s, there was little appetite for establishing new refineries on the British mainland.

The Anglo-Persian Oil Company saw things differently and took a business decision to build two British refineries, one at Grangemouth on the Forth estuary and Llandarcy on the Bristol Channel (Payton-Smith 1971: 190–92). Swansea was an ideal location for the tanker terminal, allowing for large imports of crude oil from Abadan and the export of refined products to the global economy (Appleby 1933: 29).

Llandarcy was a remarkable development in the early 1920s. Although created in a Welsh economy thoroughly versed in the brutal consequences of coal-based industry, Llandarcy was something else…radical and forward-looking and probably feeling cleaner than old coal. Anglo-Persian took pains to communicate that oil was not in Wales to compete with King Coal, but the writing was already on the wall for maritime coal -fired propulsion and modern fuels for aviation.

Built in an era when planning and community impact were non-existent and allowed uncontrolled sprawl over the green countryside, the extent of the refinery must have been revolutionary. Over two hundred and sixty hectares (about 650 acres) of land were taken for tank farms and industrial processes. Pipelines and storage transformed the coastline between Swansea's Queen's Dock and the main site. Tank farms had a capacity for over seventy-five million gallons of oil and refined products. By the 1930s, Llandarcy/Swansea was the fuel supply hub for Suez, Port Said, Antwerp, Hamburg, Danzig, Oslo, and Copenhagen (Appleby 1933: 31)

Left: An interpreted image of the Llandarcy oil storage from February 1941. The targets at Llandarcy were a combination of oil refining (GB 65 51) and oil storage (GB 21 56 and 21 58). The damaged tanks are outlined in white, with anti-aircraft defences marked as 1, 2, and 4 and barrage balloons also marked. The damage in this image was mainly from a heavy bomb raid in August 1940. Llandarcy is the location of one of the most significant moments in bomb disposal history when a bomb disposal officer defused an unexploded bomb which had an additional device intended to kill bomb disposal staff. The discovery of the extra device saved the lives of many bomb disposal staff.

```
a) Verkehrsanschlüsse: Vollbahnanschluß; eigene Werkgleise.

b) Ausdehnung insgesamt: NNO-SSW etwa 2,2 km   - etwa 1 565 000 qm.
                         OSO-WNW  "   0,8 "

   Bebaute Fläche: Etwa 123.900 qm.

c) Bauweise, Bauausführung, Luftempfindlichkeit, Brandgefahr:

   Aufgelockerte Bauweise, entsprechend der Brand- und Explosionsgefährlichkeit
   des Materials. Massive Fachwerkbauten z. größten Teil mit Sattel- und Flach-
   dächern. Im N-Teil (Erdölverarbeitung) liegen

   1) Destillations- und Raffinationsanlagen, etwa 40 Gebäude mit hohen Schorn-
      steinen, Rohrleitungen u. etwa 90 Vorfüll- u. Auffangtanks (∅ etwa 5-10 ;
      liegende Kesselbatterien (etwa 150 Kessel),

   2) Kraft- und Heizwerk, 4 massive Gebäude mit 2 hohen Schornsteinen,

   3) Schmieröl-Gewinnungsanlage, 1 Halle u. 6 massive Gebäude,

   4) Zwischenproduktverarbeitungsanlage u. Lagerung, 3 Hallen, 4 massive Ge-
      bäude u. mehrere kleine Schuppen, etwa 25 liegende Kessel.

   5) Verladebahnhof, 2 Güterschuppen. Zwischen den Ziff. 2-5 liegen
      etwa 82 Tanks mit ∅ etwa 3-13 m,

   6) mehrere Lagerhallen (Abfüllhalle usw.), am NO-Rand liegt

   7) Verwaltungsgebäude u. Laboratorium, 4 massive Gebäude u. mehrere
      Nebengebäude.

   Im gesamten S-Teil (Tanklager) sowie im N-Teil verstreut und in
   einer Teilanlage (etwa 500 m SO) stehen

   8) etwa 166 Treibstoff- u. Rohöltanks, für Fertig- bezw. Rohprodukte
      (∅ etwa 6-36 m).

   Erhöhte Brand- u. Explosionsgefahr, Einsturzgefahr.
```

Above and opposite: The Zielstammkarte for Llandarcy Oil Refinery. The original assessment of Llandarcy was before the war as part of Study Blue, but revision of the intelligence information continued throughout 1941. Although it was a large storage refinery, the Luftwaffe believed it was a rather old and outdated installation and they may have been right as improvements to the refineries only took place after the war had ended.

Translation:

Medium-sized, somewhat outdated facility

a) Transport connections: mainline railway connection, own factory tracks

b) Overall extent NNE-SSW about 2.2 km, ESE about 0.8 km

approximately 1,565,000 sq.m

Built area 123 900 sqm

Dispered construction, corresponding to the fire and explosion hazard of the material, massive half-timbered buildings, e.g. Most of it has a saddle and flat roofs. Located in the N part (petroleum processing).

1) Distillation and refining plants, around 40 buildings with high chimneys, pipelines and around 90 pre-filling and collecting tanks (around 5-10 horizontal boiler batteries (around 150 boilers),

2) Power and heating plant, 4 massive buildings with 2 high chimneys

3) Lubricating oil extraction plant, 1 hall and 6 massive buildings

4) Intermediate product processing and storage 3 halls, 4 massive buildings and several small sheds, around 25

GB 65 51 b c	**Swansea**	Genst. 5. Abt.	März 1941
(3. Ang.)	Öl-Destillation und Raffinerie mit Tankanlage		
Nur für den Dienstgebrauch	„National Oil Raffinery Llandarcy Platform"	Karte 1 : 100 000	
Bild Nr. 916b/40-666 (Lfl. 3)	Länge (westl. Greenw.): 3° 51' 30" Breite 51° 38' 43"	GB/E 26	
	Mißweisung:– 12° 18' (Mitte 1940) Zielhöhe über NN 60 m		
Aufnahme vom 1. 10. 40	Maßstab etwa 1: 11 300		

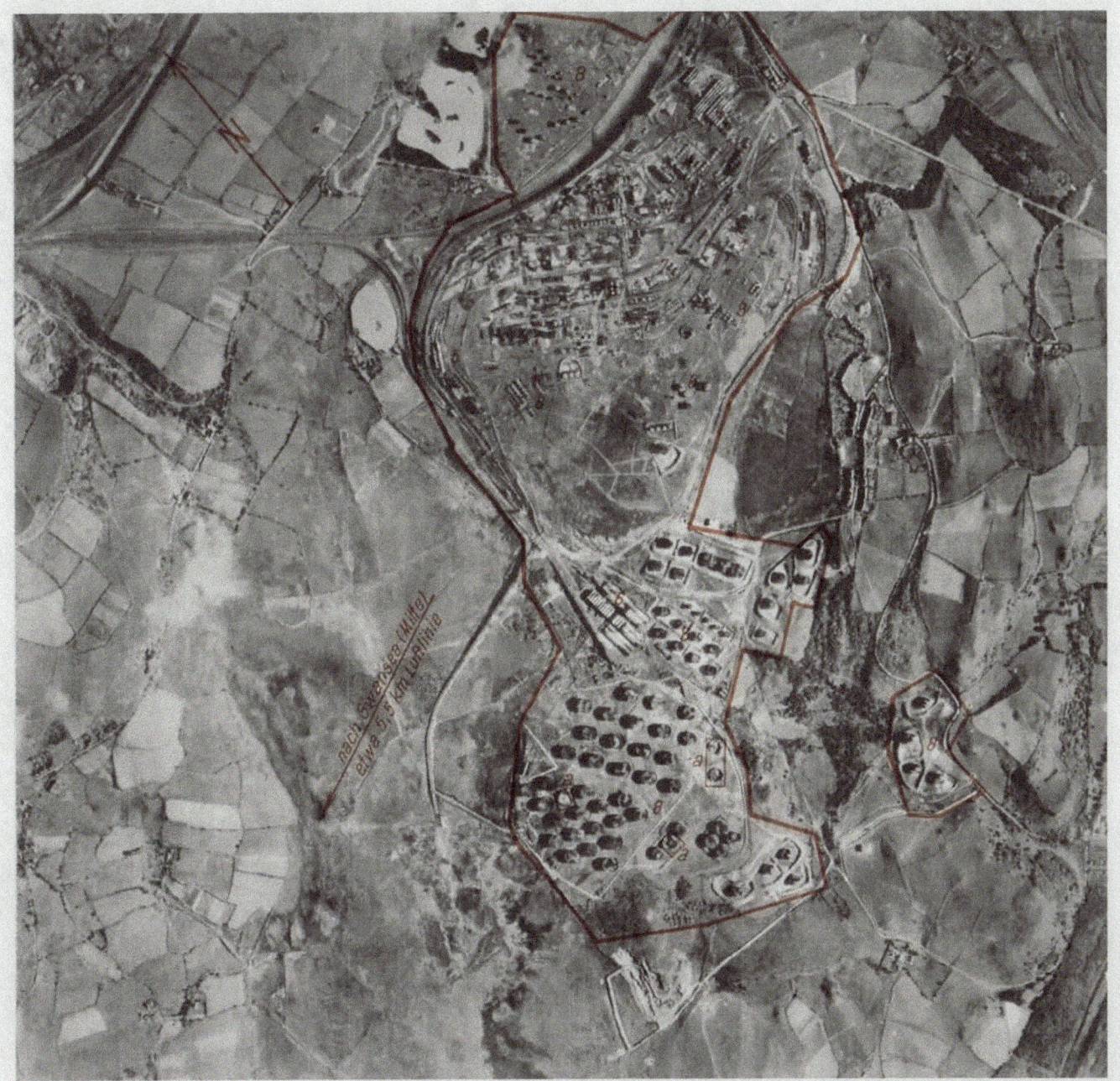

horizontal boilers

5) Loading station, 2 goods sheds, between numbers 2-5 there are around 82 tanks with around 3-13m

6) several warehouses (filling hall, etc.), located on the NE edge

7) Administrative building and laboratory, 4 4 massive buildings and several outbuildings.

Scattered in the S-part (tank farm) and in the N-part and in a partial range (about 500 m SE).

8) around 166 fuel and crude tanks, for finished or raw products (around 6-36m)

Risk of fire and explosion. Danger of collapse.

45 120

1391 Z45 Briton Ferry

10. Briton Ferry

Despite its small size, the small dock at Briton Ferry was in the centre of a lot of industry. In 1932, the dock provided wharves and storage for at least eleven companies, including four tinplate works and Briton Ferry Iron and Steelworks. There was also a small Shell-Mex and BP motor spirit depot. The German Air Force was also aware of the activity around the dock.

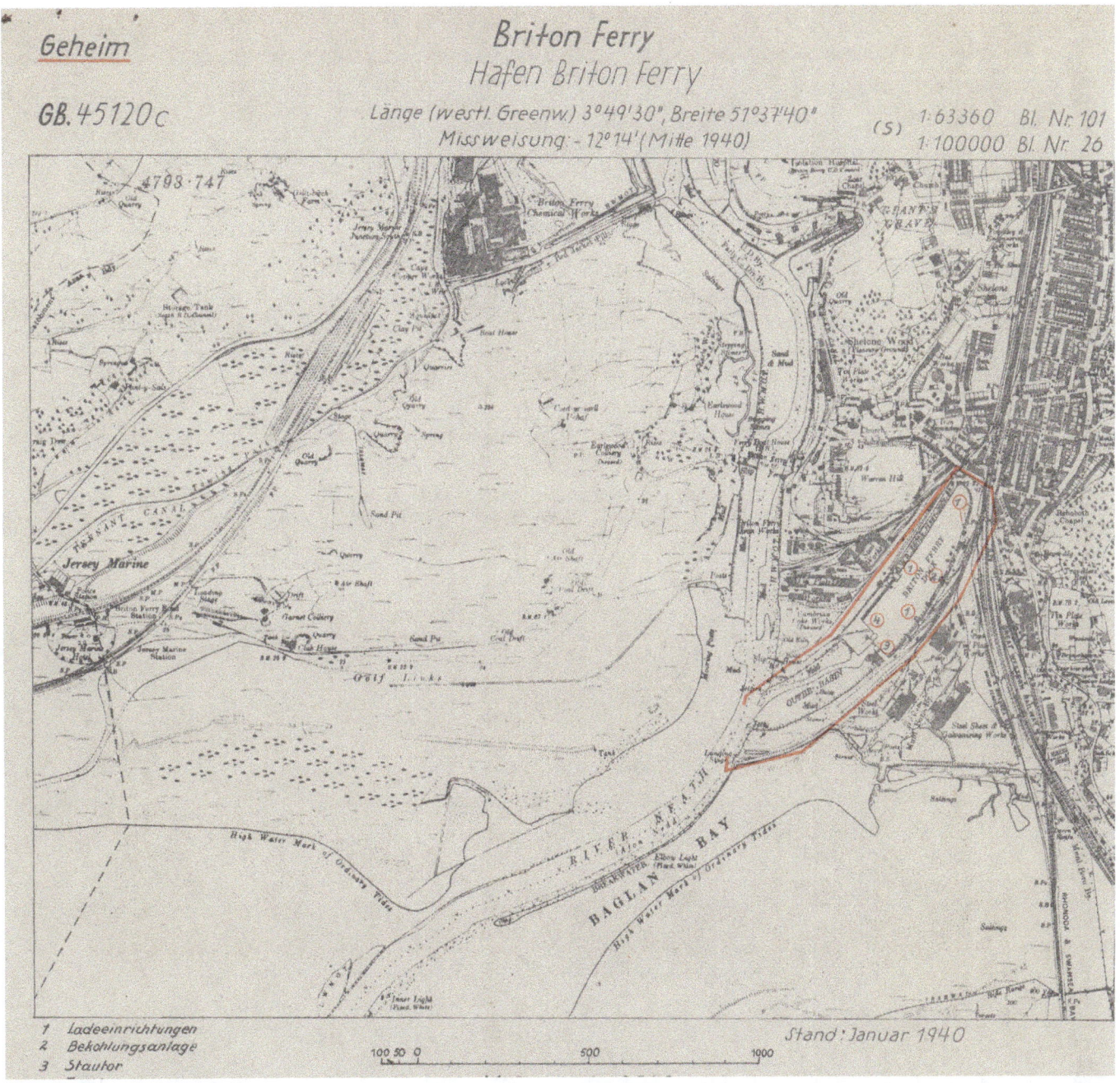

Left: The Briton Ferry dock and the mouth of the Neath River in February 1941. (Target GB 45 120).

Above: A *Bildskizzen* (Photo sketch) of the target from 1940. There were a number of small industries around the dock and the Luftwaffe wondered whether it could be used for small-scale export of oil and lubricants.

Geheim!

Zielstammkarte (L)

Land: Großbritannien (S)
England (Glamorgan)

Ort: Briton Ferry
(Nähere Lage)
50 km W.S.W. Cardiff.

Geogr. Werte:
51° 37′ 40″ N.
3° 49′ 30″ W.

Ziel-Nr. G. B. 45 120

Kartenbl.-Nr. Engl. 26/1:100 000

E. B. Nr. Engl. 101/1:63 360

---

1. Bezeichnung des Zieles: Briton Ferry Hafen.

Vgl. mit Ziel-Nr.

2. Bedeutung: Keine militärische Bedeutung.
Industriehafen für die umliegenden Werke der Kohlen-, Eisen- und Stahlindustrie.
Zufahrtstiefe bei Hochwasser 5,5 bis 7,6 m.
EINFUHR: Eisenerz, Stahl, Eisen.
AUSFUHR: Kohle, Eisen- und Stahlerzeugnisse, Weißblech.

---

3. Beschreibung des Zieles:

a) **Verkehrsanschlüsse:** Durch River Neath zum Bristol-Kanal.
   Eisenbahn- und Straßenanschluß.

b) **Ausdehnung insgesamt:** N.O.–S.W.: 1000 m
   N.W.–S.O.: 200 m

   Bebaute Fläche:
   Höhe ü. M.: ± m

c) **Art der Anlagen und Einrichtungen,**
   Bauweise, Bauausführung, Luftempfindlichkeit, Brandgefahr:

   Langgestreckte Hafenanlage.

   Im N.O.-Teil das innere Hafenbecken, 500×120 m; anschließend nach S.W. das äußere Hafenbecken, 400×120 m, dazwischen ein Stautor.

   3,5 km lange Zufahrt von S.W. zwischen Leitdämmen durch das Wattengebiet der Mündung des River Neath.

   Gleisanlagen und Ladeeinrichtungen auf beiden Seiten des Innenbeckens. Auf dem S.O.-Kai eine Bekohlungsanlage. In der S.W. Ecke des Innenbeckens ein Tanklager.

   Einsturz- und Brandgefahr.

   FLUGHINDERNISSE: Im N. u. O. hügeliges Gelände bis zu 400 m Höhe.

d) **Erzeugnisse:**

e) **Erzeugungsmenge im Monat:**
   Maximal und normal,
   bei wieviel Schichten und Arbeitern?

f) **Belegschaft:**
   Männer, Frauen, Volkszugehörigkeit,
   politische Einstellung, Unterbringung.

| GB 45 120 b c | Briton Ferry | Karte 1 : 100 000 |
| N. f. D. | Hafenanlage | Engl. Bl. 26 b |

Bild Nr. F 31b/41./017 v. 15.I.41 Geogr. Lage: 3°49'30" W, 51°37'40" N, Höhe ü. d. M. — m Stand: III. 41.

Maßstab etwa 1:18000 (1 cm = 180 m) Lft. Kdo. 3

Ⓐ GB 45 120 Hafenanlagen
   1) Ladeeinrichtungen
   2) Bekohlungsanlage
   3) Stautor
   4) Tankanlage

Ⓑ GB 45 124 Hafenanlage
   5) Anlegestellen
   6) Kohlenverladeeinrichtungen

Ⓒ GB 10 226 Swansea, Flugplatz (bc vorhanden)

Ⓓ   Flakstellungen
   7) Unterkunftsbaracken

Left and above: The *Zielstammkarte (L)* for Briton Ferry (Target GB 45 120). Briton Ferry was considered of potential interest because of its proximity to Llandarcy and various other targets on the Jersey Marine side of Swansea Bay. It was a long way down the priorities for an attack.

11. Swansea

In common with Newport and Cardiff, Swansea's port has a long history (Jones 1920: 77–85). An initial 'push' to the transformation of the port came with the creation of the Swansea Canal in 1798, creating a hinterland of trade particularly coal and iron along the Tawe Valley (Pollins 1954). Although Swansea has a substantial early industrial history, the port's significant expansion began with the creation of the Town Float (later the North Dock) in 1852 (Jones 1922: 184–91). Despite delays and setbacks largely related to local politics and finances, a series of dock developments followed, each progressively larger than the last and reflecting changes in industrial needs, shipping technology and railway integration. The first true dock was South Dock (1859), giving long and level wharves for the coal export and timber industries. Moving developments to the eastern side of the river mouth allowed for massive expansion of industry and railway integration. Prince of Wales Dock (1881) became a coal export dock, and the larger King's Dock became a hub for coal export and general cargoes. The large expanse of Queen's Dock was dedicated to the oil industry.

Despite Swansea's perceived dedication to the coal and metalliferous industries, there was a significant diversification into general cargoes. The North Dock and its half-tide basin were dominated by the Weavers Flour Mills, a feature to become particularly important in the coming conflict. By the 1930s, the old North Dock was defunct and being filled in, although the half-tide basin (known as Weavers Basin) was to last until the 1980s.

Although being somewhat small and reliant on frequent dredging of its lock entrance, South Dock became host to a diverse collection of industries. In 1901, a fleet of deep-sea trawlers was established, creating an impetus for a lively fish market and eventually cold storage. By the 1930s, South Dock markets and cold stores handled over thirteen thousand tonnes of fish annually. The warehouses and stores around the dock were always busy with small general cargoes.

The transfer of big commercial interest to the east side of the river began with the altered perceptions of Port Tennant as a potential site for larger docks once the river bridges replaced ferries in the 1860s. By 1881, the Prince of Wales Dock was open, marshalling yards and space for coal-handling equipment. Seven coal hoists were supplemented by over thirty cranes, which allowed for both coal export and general cargo imports. Subsequent enlargement of the dock in the following years increased linear quay space. The increasing size of merchant ships led to increased demand for more space, and the adjoining King's Dock was opened in 1909.

King's Dock was a step change in dock provision. Able to cope with the largest ships of the day and at over 28 hectares of water, it was a massive space reclaimed out of the curve of Swansea Bay. All the coal hoists could handle 20-ton coal wagons and over sixty heavy cranes, making the dock an attractive place for imports and coal export. In fact, Swansea had over a hundred cranes servicing the Prince of Wales and Kings Docks, even more than Cardiff. By the early 1930s, GWR

Left: Swansea on the *Militärgeographische Enzelangaben Stadtplan*. (Military Geographical details Town map). This is based on a British Ordnance Survey map from the early 1930s. Areas of strategic interest are edged red or violet. The areas of interest can be as distinct as the market or expansive such as the docks. Swansea's commitment to rail as the means of industrial transport is clearly seen, most being edged red. The Town Hall (No. 41 in red) is the old town hall rather than the new Guildhall, which dates the map to being from the early 1930s or earlier. Feature 17 in violet on the side of the North Dock is the Weaver's Grain Mills. The building usually associated with the grain mills was the Weaver's silo which was on the northern side of the Half-Tide Basin. The grain mill marked 17 was the *Schwerpunkt* (main aiming point) of the Three Nights' Blitz in February 1941. A range of industries are also identified in the Lower Swansea Valley.

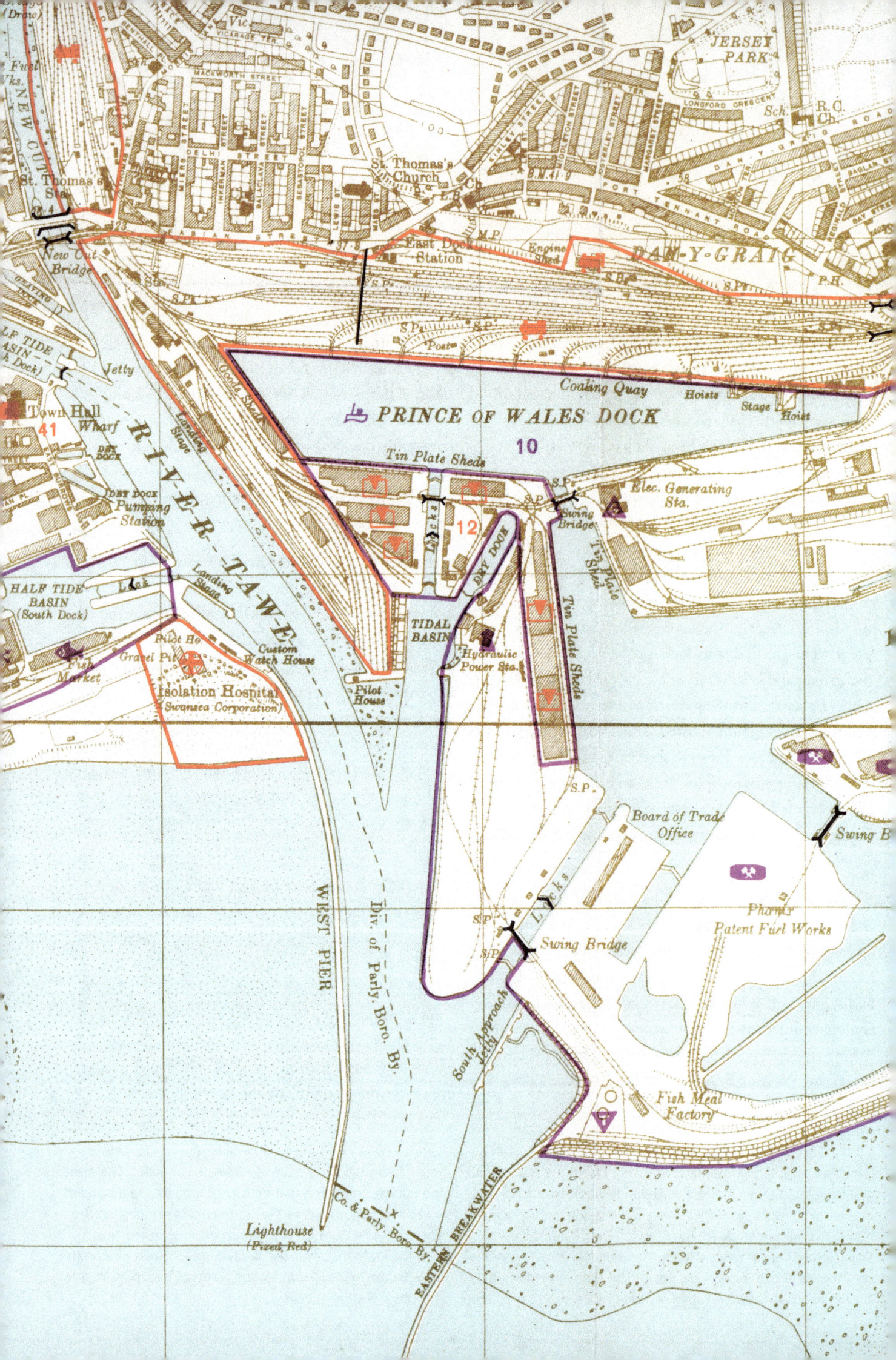

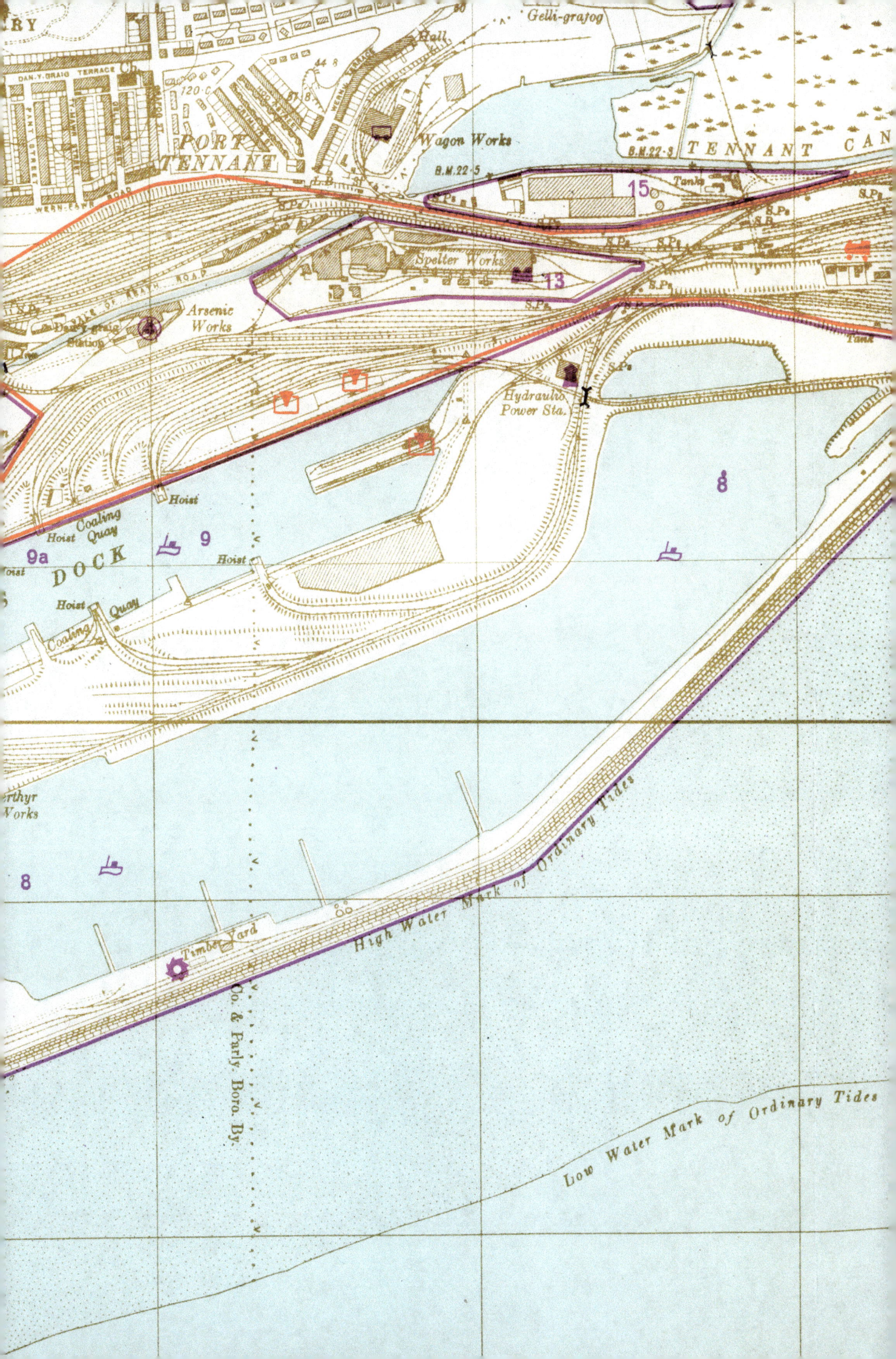

had added over forty-four thousand square metres of transit warehouses (Appleby 1933: 27–29). The increase in general cargoes drove the need for more transit and sorting space, and King's Dock even had railways running through 'D' Shed to facilitate all-weather despatch or reception of goods (Appleby 1933: 97).

Although coal and coke continued to dominate Swansea's export trade, there was also diversification into finished iron and steel products for railways, tinplates, grain, and flour. As with Cardiff, imports were dominated by finished and part-finished iron and steel (pig iron and steel billets and bars), pitwood for local mining, grain and flour (for processing and re-export), and a lively but declining copper ore business. But the biggest tonnages, both in and out, were for oil and petroleum products through the Queen's Dock.

Previous pages: Another extract from the Swansea *Stadtplan* showing the full extent of Swansea's Royal docks. The transit sheds between Prince of Wales and King's Dock were considered very important. The following page is a reconnaissance image taken 3 September 1940. The Weaver's grain silo is prominent at altitude because the concrete reflects more light than its surroundings. Ironically, this makes pillboxes and military and industrial architecture easier to identify from altitude. A barrage balloon flies over the South Dock basin. King's Dock is busy and general cargo is being unloaded into the large 'D' Shed just right of centre.

Above an image from the same 3 September 1940 flight showing Clyne Valley and West Cross. There is a significant amount of wooded landscape in Clyne and around Singleton Park.

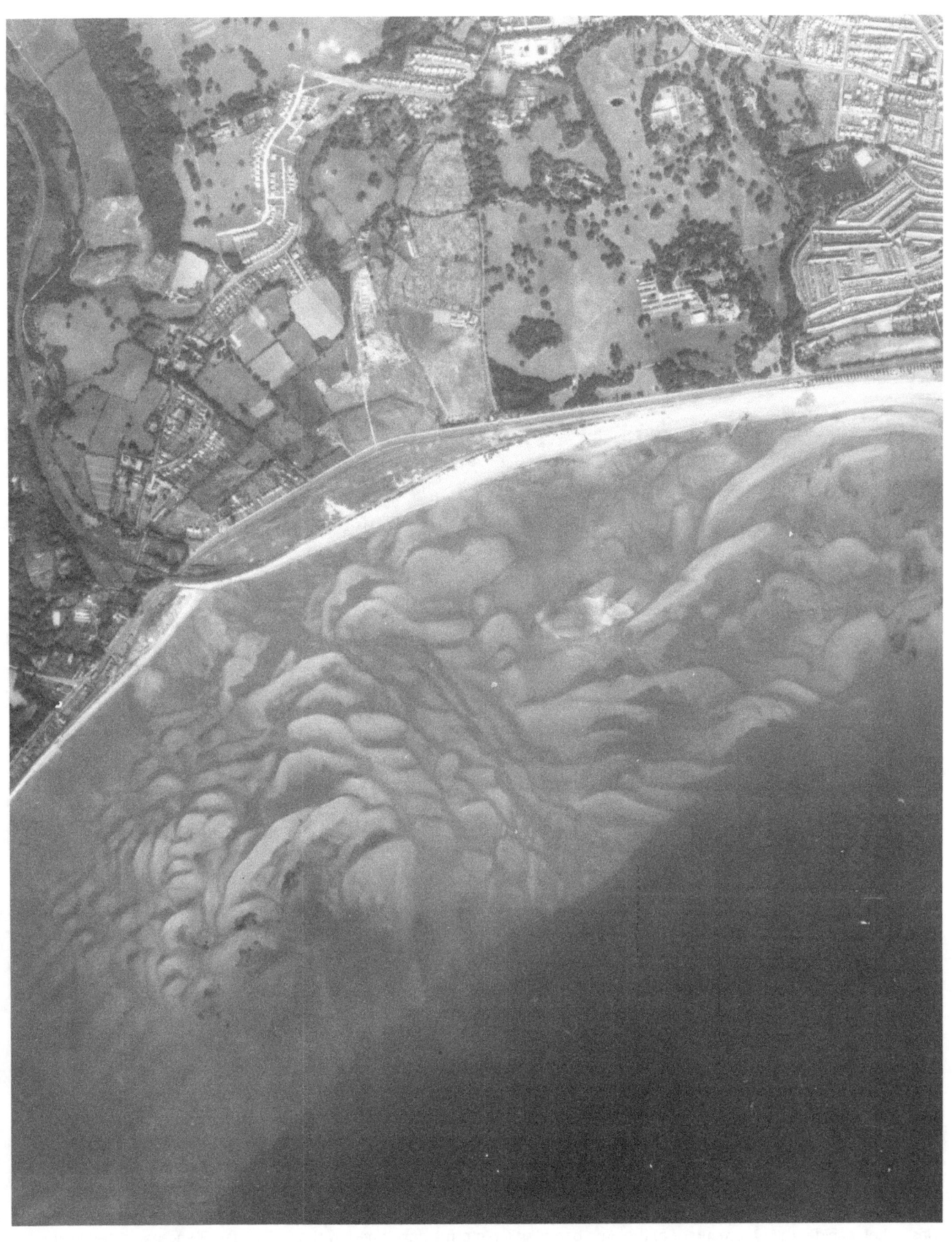

Above: An enlargement of the 3 September image opposite. The tide is out and the sandbanks of the bay are shown to good effect. The wooded landscape of Singleton Park is seen, along with allotments covering fields on the western side of the Singleton Estate.

Above and opposite: Probably the most famous of the reconnaissance photographs, originally published in my 1993 book. . This is a survivor from a series of flights made between a heavy bombing raid on 17 January 1941 and the three nights attack between 19 and 21 February 1941. Swansea and Cardiff were at the focus of the western port attacks during the opening months of 1941. It is fortunate that the Nazis had already decided to turn their attention to the invasion of the Soviet Union and equally, the Luftwaffe was short of aircraft and pilots after an incredibly hard winter of air warfare, otherwise the raids would have been heavier. Although the *Schwerpunkt* (main target) of the February raids was the grain mills marked 56 50 in the image above, the inclusion of a large quantity of incendiaries on the night of 21 February confirms that the strategy of area attack was beginning to take over from the Luftwaffe precision bombing strategy. The dropping of magnetic mines on the urban areas confirms the change from precision bombing to area 'terror' bombing. Swansea was, albeit accidentally, a precursor of the area bombing fire storms developed by the RAF in 1943 and perfected by the American air forces in 1945. If in 1941, the Luftwaffe had the resources that the RAF were given by 1943, Swansea would have been completely destroyed with weeks of incendiary air attacks, not just three nights.

The Luftwaffe analyst has marked Swansea's bombing targets on the images, but has also marked areas of damage in white outline. People often question why Kilvey Hill has such a large number of craters. The reason is that bombs fell in similar density across all of central Swansea, but the craters are easier to identify on the hill. Urban damage was often cleared up or made safe as quickly as possible, but the craters on Kilvey remain to this day.

Above: an enlargement of the central part of the opposite image. The Luftwaffe analysts often misunderstood the function of the North Dock-Half-Tide Basin has been confused (No. 83 65) believing it all to be a ship repair dock. The South Dock was a centre for fish, frozen food and general stores (No. 4567), and was seen as a significant food-related target. In the centre of the image the white line around the block of Castle Buildings highlights incendiary damage from the 17 January raid.

Above and opposite: Another image from the 15 February 1941 mission. This image shows more of the docks, east side and the Lower Swansea Valley. The Weaver's grain mill is shown on the left (No 56 50). The large Queen's Dock is at the bottom. This image shows the Lower Swansea Valley and the huge extent of industrialisation and associated waste tips that blighted the whole area. At the top of the picture are the tips of the Cambrian Spelter works, Landore Siemens Steel works, and the Llansamlet Copper and Arsenic works. There were by 1941 over 130 hectares of toxic waste tips in the area. That does not include the devastation of the tipping on Kilvey Hill to the east and Hafod to the west. Another notable feature of this photograph is the lack of any tree cover on Kilvey Hill and the land north of the hill. This is a consequence of two centuries of atmospheric pollution from the industries of the valley.

Bomb craters have been identified by the Luftwaffe analyst quite a long way north of the aiming point of the grain mills at 5650. Bomb damage to buildings is usually displayed as white boxes, although the damage to the White Rock Copper Works is industrial dereliction rather than accurate bomb aiming.

Tir John North power station (50 56) is on the east side of Kilvey Hill, and the Anglo-Persian oil tanks (21 56) are at the eastern end of Queen's Dock.

Opposite: At extreme left of this image is the huge mountain of copper waste of Pentre Hafod and on the opposite side of the river are the White Rock and Middle Bank tips. These are only a fraction of the tips left behind by the Vivian family industries when they abandoned the sites in the 1930s.

Above: The pre-war *Bildskizzen* for Weaver's Mills. Swansea's grain stores had been identified by Steinmann's team as part of the Study Blue research. Translation opposite.

A. GB 5650 Grain Mill (Weavers Flour Mills Ltd.)

   1) Mill building with power station around 7300 square meters
   2) Silo about 700 square meters

B. GB 8365 Dry Dock b North Basin

   3) 1 dry dock
   4) Work shed about 1800 sqm

C. GB 8364 Commercial Dry Dock No. 1 & 2

   5) Dry dock
   6) Dry dock
   7) 1 pumping station about 950 square metres
   8) 5 work sheds about 850 square metres
   built-up area (Schwpkt) approximately 1800 square metres

D. GB 4567 South Dock with Basin

   9) 1 lock
   10) 1 lock.
   11) 1 power station approximately 700 square metres
   12) 1 fish storage building about 2300 square metres
   13) 2 ice factories approximately 4000 square metres
   14) 2 storage buildings approximately 4000 square metres
   15) Unloading stations

Built up area (Schwpkt) about 11,000 square metres

(The 'Schwpkt' or 'Schwerpunkt tag indicates bomb aiming points.)

Secret!	Location:	Target=No G. B. 45 67
Target master card (L)	(Nearby location) N shore of the Bristol Channel	Card sheet=No. Engl. 26/1:100 000
Country: Great Britain (S) England (Glamorgan)	Geogr. location 51° 37' 15" N. 3° 55' 48" W.	GB No.Engl. 101/1:63 360

1. Name of the Target: South Dock with Basin

Compare with target=no

2. Significance: Important inland port for fish imports and coal exports

3. Description of the Target

a) Professional connections: Water and railways

b) Total dimensions: E.N.E - W.S.W.: 920 m.   Built up area: 11 000 sqm
　　　　　　　　　　　S.S.E.- N.N.W.: 220 m.   Height above Sea level: 0 m

c) Type of systems and facilities,

　　From the River Tawe through a 2-gate lock (114m x 18.3m) into the basin, the S-quay of which is entirely taken up by a fish market hall.

　　To the W. there is a 90.5 m long and 18.00 m wide open bridge passage, on the N. quay of which there is a power station, and on the S. quay there are large warehouses with solid roofs.

　　Then to the west is the South Dock. On the N. -quay there are 2 high coal sheds. On the S.-quay there is a storage shed for handling goods.

　　There are plenty of rail connections and numerous hydraulic and electric cranes on all quays in the destination.

　　Collapse and fire hazard

Above and opposite: The *Zielstammkarte* for Swansea South Dock (GB 45 67) in translation. The dock area was considered suitable for high explosive and incendiary attacks, hence the 'Collapse and fire hazard' comment at the bottom of the notes. Opposite is the *Objektphoto* for the South Dock. This image also records the other targets in the Swansea area (although there were several others outside the port area and in the Lower Swansea Valley). Swansea's docks were the most significant on the northern shore of the Bristol Channel because of the combination of food and oil targets. Coal loading facilities were considered important as long as France was a military power as Swansea exported large quantities of coal to France. That significance ended after France was defeated by the Germans. After that food and fuel become the priorities. The image also records the target numbers and descriptions of the nine other significant targets in the Queen's Dock area. GB 50 56 Tir John Power Station, GB 71 21 Magnesium works, and a series of large ship repair facilities.

| GB 45 67 b c | Swansea | Karte 1 : 100 000 |
| N. f. D. | Hafenanlage | Engl. Bl. 26 d. |

Bild Nr. F.31a/41./010 v. v. 15.II.41. Geogr. Lage: 3°55'48" W, 51°37'15" N, Höhe ü. d. M. — m Stand: III. 41.

Maßstab etwa 1:13 500 (1 cm = 135 m) Lfl. Kdo. 3

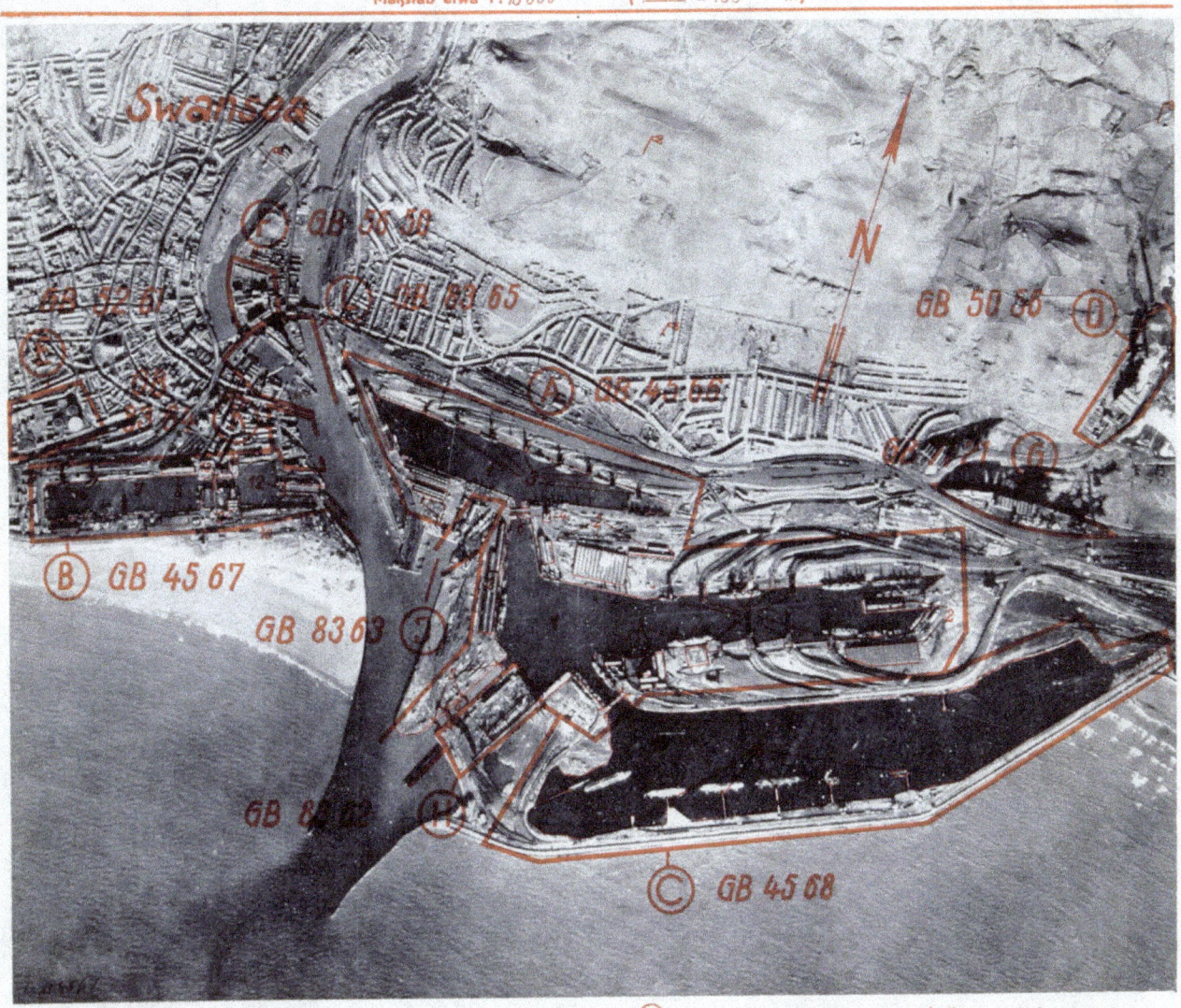

Ⓐ GB 45 66 Kings Dock und Prince of Wales Dock mit Schleusen
  1) 2 Hafenbecken
  2) Lagerhallen und Gebäude etwa 66 700 qm
  3) Kohleentladestationen mit Verladekränen
  4) Licht- und Kraftstation etwa 1 300 qm
  5) 3 Schleusentore
  6) 3 Eisenbahnbrücken
  bebaute Fläche insgesamt etwa 68 000 qm

Ⓑ GB 45 67 South Dock mit Schleuse
  7) Hafenbecken
  8) Lagergebäude etwa 6 000 qm
  9) 2 Kühlhäuser etwa 4 000 qm
  10) 1 Fischlagergebäude etwa 2 300 qm
  11) Kraftstation etwa 700 qm
  12) 1 Schleuse mit 2 Schleusentoren
  13) 1 Eisenbahnbrücke
  14) Kohlenentladestationen
  bebaute Fläche insgesamt etwa 13 000 qm

Ⓒ GB 45 68 Queens Dock (Ölhafen)
  15) Hafenbecken
  16) Ölentladestationen

Ⓓ GB 50 56 Großkraftwerk (Tir John North)
Ⓔ GB 52 61 Gaswerk
Ⓕ GB 56 50 Getreidemühle (Weavers Flour Mills)
Ⓖ GB 71 21 Magnesiumwerk
Ⓗ GB 83 62 Palmers Trockendock
Ⓙ GB 83 63 Prince of Wales Trockendock
Ⓚ GB 83 64 Commercial Trockendock Nr. 1 und 2
Ⓛ GB 83 65 Trockendock beim North Basin

Annexes

In these Annexes I have collected information that I get frequently asked, not least because some of the history is either obscure or confusing. I regularly get asked about a mythical U-boat visit to various beaches in Gower or whether local chip shops were targeted by bombers. Neither of these things is true and I know people get disappointed when I explain the reality of the facts to them.

Firstly U-boats. Although all navies had some form of underwater craft for warfare, the Germans took the weapon to their hearts, and eventually paid dearly with the lives of thousands of their finest young men. The German Navy 'U-boat' menace was a combination of some fine German propaganda and the memoirs of Winston Churchill who was keen to develop the 'victory myths' and cement his own place in history. The Germans had fifty-seven U-boats at the beginning of the war. Thirty of those were too small to be used for any meaningful tasks. The German Naval Command were very clear in 1939 when they said they needed at least three hundred boats to make any meaningful impact on the British Royal Navy and the equally large British merchant fleet. The rapid construction of new U-boats in the winter of 1939-40 was severely hindered by the extremely cold weather and prevented new boats being delivered. The U-boats the Germans used were at the time at the leading edge of technology with revolutionary magnetic mines and magnetic detonators in torpedoes. The rush to war meant that some of the new technologies were untested and resulted in failures. The potential success of magnetic mines against western harbours in 1939-40 was compromised by the Luftwaffe dropping mines in soft mud allowing British experts to dismantle them and understand how they worked and develop effective countermeasures. However the Bristol Channel was a particularly fine proving-ground for U-boat and magnetic mine technologies and became a popular hunting ground for U-boats in 1939 and again in 1944. We have one remarkable surviving record of a magnetic mining mission by U32 from December 1939 when the boat was part of a series of mining missions against Swansea and Cardiff. I've included the full records here with a translation. If you read the diary you will get an appreciation of the realities of early U-boat operations in the Bristol Channel.

The second Annex is a closer examination of the Luftwaffe record known as the *Zeilstammkarte* (Target Master Map). This type of record is central to understanding the air war as it was conducted by the Luftwaffe against British towns and cities. As mentioned briefly in the earlier chapters, understanding of the true nature of the air war has been understandably twisted by the histories of the victors and the demands of the film industry. Re-examining the *Zielstammkarte* helps remove some of the inaccurate and unhelpful assumptions about the air war. Particularly the air war against civilians. The Luftwaffe always knew less than we thought.

The final Annex is a closer look at the Magnetic Mine. The use of mines is always a source of confusion because of the nature of the weapon. An expensive air-dropped parachute mine of massive explosive potential often dropped on British civilians. Here is the technical background to what was a truly dreadful terror weapon. Eventually this type of bomb was used with great enthusiasm by the RAF in their terror raids on German cities...after the RAF understood the true benefits of deploying such horror on people's houses by examining the results of Luftwaffe attacks on Coventry, Cardiff and Swansea.

Left: Swansea's South Dock fish market in the early 1930s. This was part of Luftwaffe bomb target GB 45 67. Food (particularly frozen food) was a primary target in early 1941.

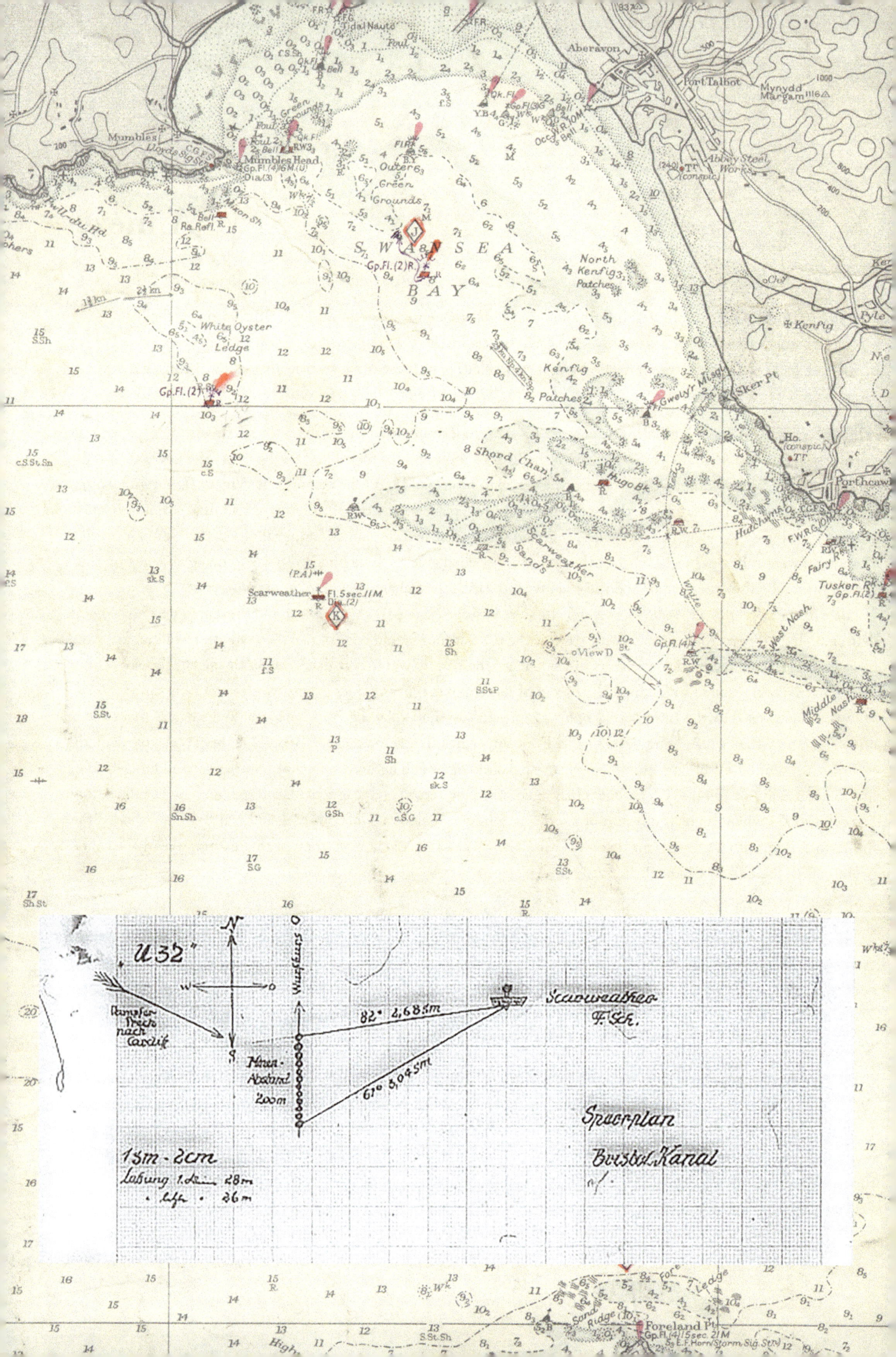

1. U32 Mining the Scarweather in 1939

U32 was an early Type VII U-boat, built in 1936. The boat played a prominent role in early attacks on the ports and trade around the British Isles. U32 had an operational career of nine patrols between August 1939 and October 1940. Under the command of *Kptlt*. Paul Büchel, the boat entered the Bristol Channel early in September 1939 with twelve TMB magnetic mines. The plan was to lay mines close to the Scarweather Lightship as it was on the main route up to Cardiff, Newport and Barry. The shoals and sandbanks around the Scarweather were the perfect depth conditions for the TMB mine. Her sister boat U28 would sail the same route and same mission in December 1939. The Bristol Channel was an ideal environment for this type of operation and mining the channels to Swansea and Cardiff became a regular practice for the German Navy and eventually the Luftwaffe. Very often, news blackouts prevented the Germans from learning about magnetic mine casualties and some mining missions were regarded as failures.

The *Kriegstagebuch* (War Diary) for the Scarweather mission survived the war, so you can read for yourself how Captain Büchel and his crew completed their mission. Unusually, Büchel s log contains a plot of where he dropped his mines. The mines claimed two victims, the SS Marwarri ()Br 8063 tons), and SS Lochgoil (Br 9462 tons). On its way back out of the Bristol Channel, U32 confronted the SS Kensington Court (Br 4863 tons) and eventually sunk her with gunfire. That incident is also recorded here.

In October 1940, U32 was acting as a meteorological observer for the Luftwaffe west of Ireland. However, the boat was eventually cornered by the destroyers HMS Highlander and HMS Harvester and after a long chase and many depth charges, U32 was forced to the surface and scuttled whilst most of the crew were picked up by the destroyers.

I have just given a straight translation of the war diary to give you an appreciation of what happened.

Left: The Admiralty chart of the Bristol Channel in the 1940s. The Scarweather Light is in the centre of the map, south of Swansea Bay, and (inset) the war diary sketch from U32 of the minelaying location.

Below: U32 looking weather worn from an early mission. The rigour of the missions meant that boats would often require weeks of repair and refurbishment after a mission,.

Datum und Uhrzeit	Angabe des Orts, Wind, Wetter, Seegang, Beleuchtung, Sichtigkeit der Luft, Mondschein usw.	Vorkommnisse
15.9.39 0800 Uhr	Gute Sicht, 30 sm südl. Irland.	Getaucht. Kurs auf Bristolkanal genommen.
1030 Uhr		Auf mitlaufendem Kurs (90°) amerikanischer Dampfer Bb. querab, E = 1000 m.
1830 Uhr		An Bb. englisches Kriegsschiff E = 15 - 20000 m mit wechselnden Kursen, umkreist von Flugzeugen, in Sicht. Obere Teil des Gef.Mastes und eines Schornsteines waren zu sehen. Wahrscheinlich Flugzeugträger "Hermes".
1930 Uhr		Kriegsschiff aus Sicht.
16.9.39 18-1900 Uhr		Weitermarsch unter Wasser wegen Flugzeuge. Bewacher in Sicht. (2 Fischdampfer, 1 Torp.-Boot). Dampfer in Sicht auslaufend Bristol-Kanal. Ich folgere daraus, daß keine Minen im Bristol-Kanal liegen.
17.9.39	N 2, in der Kimm dunstig, unmittelbar über Wasser schlechte Sicht. Günstig für U-Boot.	Nachts Anmarsch auf Position für Minen-Unternehmung, laufend beleuchteten und unbeleuchteten Fahrzeugen (Bewacher und Dampfer) ausgewichen. Der Bootsanstrich bewährt sich sehr gut. Diesmal und auch später von Bewachern nie gesehen, selbst bei Entfernung von 600 m.
0400 Uhr		Getaucht.
0405 Uhr		Beginn des Minenwerfens. Auf vorgesehener Position lag Bewacher, darum Sperre etwas westl. geworfen. In Gewässern, wo Tiden- und Drehstrom herrscht, wird die Zeit von 20 Min, nach der die Mine scharf wird, aus Sicherheitsgründen für das eigene Boot zu knapp, besonders dann, wenn man gezwungen ist, unter Wasser abzulaufen.
0425 Uhr		aufgetaucht. In 500 - 600 m abgeblendetes grosses Fahrzeug (Bewacher) in Sicht. Typ nicht auszumachen, sehr langes Heck. Diesem Bewacher und einem entgegenkommenden beleuchteten Dampfer über Wasser mit E-Maschine langsam aber sicher ausgewichen. Nicht gesehen! Bis zur Dämmerung über Wasser abgelaufen mit Kurs West. Beim Ablaufen ständig Dampfer gehorcht und gesichtet. Keine Angriffe wegen Geheimhaltung der Unternehmung.
2045 Uhr		
18.9.39 1238 Uhr	Gute Sicht, ca. 20-30 hm. NO 3. Sonnenschein.	Rauchfahne gesichtet, angesteuert, Dampfer ohne Flagge festgestellt. Beim Näherkommen versucht Dampfer mit hoher Fahrt und abdrehend zu entkommen. Bei E 90 hm Artl.Feuer eröffnet. Schüsse lagen links und rechts und

Date and Time	Information about the Location, Wind, Weather, Sea State, Visibility in the air, Moonlight etc.	Incidents
15. 9. 39 0800 Uhr	Good visibility, 30 nm south of Ireland.	Dived. Set course for the Bristol Channel.
1030 Uhr		On the same course (90°) American steamer port abeam, E = 1000 m.
1830 Uhr		At port, English warship E = 15 - 20000 m with changing courses, circled by aircraft, in sight. The upper part of the vessel's mast and a chimney were visible. Probably aircraft carrier "Hermes". Warship in sight. *Büchel*
1930 Uhr 16.9.39 18-1900 Uhr		Continuation of the travel under water because of airplanes. Patrol vessels in sight. (2 trawler, 1 torp boat). Steamer in view leaving Bristol Channel. I conclude that there are no mines in the Bristol Channel. *Büchel*
17. 9. 39	N 2, hazy on the horizon, poor visibility immediately above the water. Favourable for submarines.	Approaching position for mining operations at night, constantly avoiding illuminated and unilluminated vehicles (Patrol vessels and steamers). The boat paint works very well. This time and later never seen by patrols, even at distances of 600 m. F
0400 Uhr 0405 Uhr	F *The only telltale thing is the red faucet of the exhaust at 2 x HF. This was remedied by flooding diving cell 1 to bring the exhaust under water. Disadvantage of this measure Very strong source of noise*	Dived.. Mine laying begins. A patrol vessel was lying in the intended position, so the barrier was laid a little to the west. In waters where there are tidal and three-phase currents, the time of 20 minutes after which the mine becomes active is considered too short for safety reasons for your own boat, especially if you are forced to go underwater.
0425 Uhr		[(0425 hours)] surfaced. At 500 - 600 m, a dimmed large vehicle (guard) is in sight. Type cannot be identified, very long tail. Dodged this guard and an oncoming lighted steamer over water. Not seen !
2045 Uhr		(2045 hours) Sailed over water heading west until dusk. When sailing, the steamer was constantly heard and sighted. No attacks because of the secrecy of the undertaking.
	Good visibility, approx. 20-30 hm. NE 3. Sunshine.	*Büchel*
18. 9. 39 1238 Uhr		Smoke plume spotted, headed for, found steamer without flag. When approaching, the steamer tried to escape at high speed and turning away. At E 90 hm Artl (Gunfire). Fire opened. Shots were left and right and

Datum und Uhrzeit	Angabe des Ortes, Wind, Wetter, Seegang, Beleuchtung, Sichtigkeit der Luft, Mondschein usw.	Vorkommnisse
		vor dem Bug des Dampfers. Beim 13. Schuß E 9500 drehte der Dampfer bei. Artl.Feuer eingestellt. Signal für Stoppen und Nichtgebrauch der F.T. gesetzt. F.T. wurde trotzdem benutzt. (S.S.S. unter Angabe des Ortes und Name). Besatzung des Dampfers ging in die Boote. Um 1400 Uhr bei E = ca 14 hm auf Dampfer Torpedoschuß abgegeben. Torpedo traf Vorkante Brücke. Dampfer wurde langsam vorlastig und krängte nach St.B. Dampfer sank nach etwa 40 Min. Torpedo detonierte durch Aufschlagzündung. Torpedo machte beim Einsteuern ein Bajonett nach rechts von etwa 20 - 30 m., lief sonst aber normal. Vom Dampfer wurde auch nach dem Torpedo-Treffer mit F.T. weitergesendet. Längseit des Dampfers lag noch ein Rettungsboot. Es wird angenommen, daß es für den an Bord gebliebenen Funker bereitlag, der noch die F.T. weiter bediente. Das Rettungsboot kann auch von der Besatzung, da überflüssig, zurückgelassen sein, dann muß aber ein Maschinensender an Bord vermutet werden. Aus dem Morsespruch des Dampfers wurde der Name "Kennington" herausgehört. Als Ladung wird Erz vermutet. Im Lloyd-Register ist ein Dampfer solchen Namens nicht verzeichnet. Danach könnte es nur der Dampfer "Kensington" Court" (4863 t) gewesen sein. Auf F.T. "Kennington" sagte der Admiral von Devonport funkentelegrafisch Hilfe zu 1700 Uhr M.G.Z. zu. Sofort auf Gegenkurs abgedreht und mit G.F. abgelaufen, um einen anderen am Horizont gesichteten Dampfer anzusteuern. Dieser Dampfer gab ebenfalls Funksignale unter Angabe des Standortes von "U 32".
1422 Uhr	Stratusschicht am Himmel, Kimm dunstig, mittlere Sicht	Flugzeug gesichtet, getaucht, eine Stunde abgelaufen, aufgetaucht, sofort wieder getaucht, da Flugzeug wieder in Sicht.
1600 Uhr		Etwa 1600 Uhr wurden in der nächsten Nähe die Detonation von 3 Flugzeugbomben gehört. Das Boot fuhr auf Sehrohrtiefe von 14 m. Das Flugzeug muß das Boot unter Wasser erkannt haben. Sehrohr war zu dieser Zeit nicht gezeigt worden. Die letzte (3.) Bombe lag am nächsten. Das Boot erlitt keine Beschädigungen. Das Boot ging sofort auf 50 m. Die Tiefe war gerade erreicht worden, als auch die näherkommenden Schraubengeräusche zweier Fahrzeuge gehorcht wurden. Die Fahrzeuge müssen den ungefähren Standort des Bootes gewußt haben, denn "U 32" wurde genau angesteuert. Fahrzeuge stehen parallel zum Kurs mit Horchfahrt auf und ab. Müssen z.T. in großer Nähe gestanden haben. Schraubengeräusche wurden sogar im Turm gehört.
1945 Uhr		Schraubengeräusche entfernen sich langsam. Von einem Fahrzeug sind sie plötzlich nicht mehr zu

Date and Time	Information about the Location, Wind, Weather, Sea State, Visibility in the air, Moonlight etc.	Incidents
		in front of the steamer's bow. With the 13th shot of E 9500, the steamer turns over. Art. (Gun) Fire stopped. Signal for stop and non-use FT set. FT was still used. (SSS stating the location and name). The crew of the steamer went into the boats. At 1400 hours at E= approx. 1400 m a torpedo shot was fired at the steamer. Torpedo hit forward edge of bridge. Steamer slowly became overweight and heeled to starboard. Steamer sank after about 40 minutes. Torpedo detonated by impact ignition. Torpedo made a bayonet to the right of 20-30 m when steering, but otherwise ran normally.
		The steamer continued transmitting with FT even after the torpedo hit. There was another lifeboat alongside the steamer. It is assumed that it was ready for the radio operator who remained on board and continued to operate the FT.
		The lifeboat can also be left behind by the crew because it is superfluous, but then it must be assumed that there is a machine transmitter on board.
		The name "Kennington" was heard from the steamer's Morse code. Ore is suspected to be the cargo. There is no steamship with that name listed in the Lloyd Register. After that it could only have been the steamer "Kensington Court" (4863 t).
		On FT "Kennington" the Admiral of Devonport radioed for help at 1700 GMT.
		Immediately turned to the opposite course and ran at GF to head for another steamer spotted on the horizon. This steamer also gave radio signals indicating the location "U 32".
1422 Uhr	Stratus layer in the sky, horizon hazy, medium visibility.	Plane spotted, dived, an hour passed, surfaced, immediately dived again, the plane was in sight again.
1600 Uhr		At approximately 4:00 p.m., the detonation of 3 aircraft bombs were heard nearby. The boat was traveling at a periscope depth of 14 m. The aircraft must have recognized the boat under water. Periscope was not shown at that time. The last (3rd) bomb was the closest. The boat suffered no damage. The boat immediately went to 50 m. The depth had just been reached when the approaching sound of two vessels was heard. The vehicles must have known the approximate location of the boat, the "U 32" was headed precisely. Vehicles are parked parallel to the course with listening up and down. Some of them must have been very close. Screw noises were heard even in the tower.
1945 Uhr		Screw noises slowly fade away. Suddenly you can no longer hear them coming from a vehicle.

Datum und Uhrzeit	Angabe des Ortes, Wind, Wetter, Seegang, Beleuchtung, Sichtigkeit der Luft, Mondschein usw.	Vorkommnisse
		zu hören. Fahrzeug hat scheinbar gestoppt zum besseren Horchen, oder erwartet Auftauchen des Bootes bei Dunkelheit. Daher bis 2400 Uhr unter Wasser nach S.W. abgelaufen. Hierbei wurden noch Schraubengeräusche gleicher Art, anscheinend noch andere Bewacher, gehorcht. Gegen 2300 Uhr wurden 4 Bombendetonationen in großer Entfernung gehört. Aus der Art der Horchfahrt war zu erkennen, daß systematisch nach einem Prinzip verfahren wurde. Ich kann mir vorstellen, daß das Flugzeug die erste Sichtstelle des U-Bootes durch eine Boje gekennzeichnet hat, und von dieser aus sektorenmäßig die nächste Umgebung abgesucht wurde. Technisch können die Horchgeräte, mit denen anscheinend gehorcht worden ist, nicht sehr gut gewesen sein bezw. sie wurden schlecht bedient. Während der Horchfahrt wurde im eigenen Horchgerät in kurzen Abständen Geräusche gehört, die an das Aufschlagen eines Hammers auf Metall erinnerten. Ob dies das Arbeiten eines S-Gerätes gewesen ist, kann ich nicht beurteilen. Aus der ganzen Situation des Dampfer-Aufbringens in feindlicher Küstennähe kann gefolgert werden, daß immer mit feindlichen Flugzeugen zu rechnen ist, die das Boot unter Wasser drücken, die U-Abwehr heranholen und ein Dampfer-Aufbringen verhindern. Wenn man sich in der Nähe der feindlichen Küste aufhalten muß, ist damit zu rechnen, tagsüber unter Wasser zu fahren, und nur nachts über Wasser operieren zu können. Die Zeit des Operierens wird noch beeinträchtig durch das Aufladen der Batterie.
19.9.39 2400 Uhr	Sternenklar, gute Sicht. Gegen Morgen in der Kimm diesig werdend. Ost 3 - Seegang 2.	Aufgetaucht, Kurs 270°, Südgrenze Operationsgebiet abgelaufen.
0710 Uhr		Getaucht, Kurs 0°, um den Dampfertreffpunkten wieder näher zu kommen.
0840 Uhr		Kurzschluß in der St.B. Hilfsschalttafel der Zentrale. Feuer wurde gelöscht.
0845 Uhr		Boot muß auftauchen zum Durchlüften des Bootes und Herausdrücken der verspritzten Kohlensäure.
0850 Uhr		Kurs 270° zur Westkante Operationsgebiet. Entstandene Schäden sollten während der Überwasserfahrt ausgebessert werden.
0940 Uhr		Flugzeug voraus gesichtet. Getaucht. Boot wurde nicht gesehen. Während der Unterwasserfahrt Schäden ausgebessert.
1750 Uhr		Nördlich des eigenen Kurses nach Osten auswanderndes Geräusch, anscheinend unter Wasser fahrendes U-Boot. Durch Sehrohr nicht zu sehen.

Date and Time	Information about the Location, Wind, Weather, Sea State, Visibility in the air, Moonlight etc.	Incidents
		The vessel appears to have stopped to listen better, or is expecting the boat to appear in the dark. Therefore remained under water to the SW until 2400 hours. At this point, screwing noises of the same kind were heard, apparently from other patrol vessels. At around 2300 hours, 4 bomb detonations were heard at a great distance. From the nature of the listening log it was clear that the procedure was carried out systematically according to one principle. I can imagine that the aircraft marked the first point of view of the submarine with a buoy, and from this the immediate area was searched in sectors. Technically, the listening devices that were apparently used to listen could not have been very good. they were poorly served. During the listening log, noises were heard at short intervals in the listener's own listening device that were reminiscent of a hammer striking metal. I can't judge whether this was the work of an S device. {(echo-location, later known as SONAR)} { From the entire situation of the capture of steamers near the enemy's coast, it can be concluded that enemy aircraft must always be expected, which will push the boat under the water, bring in the anti-submarine warfare and prevent the capture of the steamship. If you have to stay close to the enemy coast, you can expect to be able to operate underwater during the day and only be able to operate above water at night. The operation time is further affected by the charging of the battery. *Büchel*

Secret!

Target master card (L)

Country: Location: Target=No
             (Nearby location)   Card sheet=No.
             Geogr. location   GB No.

1. Name of the Target
Compare with target-no

2. Significance

3. Description of the Target

a) Professional connections

b) Total dimensions

c) Type of systems and equipment, design, construction, vulnerability to air, risk of fire

d) Products

e) Production quantity per month

f) Workforce
Men, women, ethnicity, political attitudes, accommodation

g) Vital parts, water and power supply, cabotage

h) Raw material extraction

i) Storage

j) Miscellaneous

4. Active and passive air protection, local surveillance

5. Orientation points for target identification

6. Picture and map documents of the target and the target area
    a) Attached   b) Also available for the Target Area

7. Has target documents

2. The *Zielstammkarte* (Target Master) Document

The Zielstammkarte (Target Master Map) was the Luftwaffe's primary intelligence document for collating and exploiting information about areas classified as bombing targets.

The German intelligence organisation was a complex mix of Government, Nazi Party, Army, Navy and Air Force intelligence. It was unwieldy, uncommunicative and uncoordinated. The Luftwaffe had intelligence sources in the German security services, the radio intercept service, the Reich Air Ministry Press Group and a series of semi-official aerial survey enterprises. In 1935, the decision was made inside the Luftwaffe to begin collating information, processes, and structures into a usable form. This wasn't easy.

Targets for attack in potential enemy countries (at that time France and Poland) were listed and technical information was gathered in portfolios of information known as *'Zieldossiers'* (Target Dossiers). Information was arranged by military, industrial, communications, and transport themes. A target numbering system was devised to break down the massive amounts of data into usable categories to aid the classification. Groups of objectives were subdivided into *Zielkarten* (Objective Cards) using the system. Each target contained a portfolio of small-scale maps, large-scale maps, and an information sheet (the *Zielstammkarte*) with assessments of significance, importance for the enemy, political or economic significance, vulnerability to attack, air defences, and even social and political information. There was even provision for logging work patterns and work-shift timings.

The numbering system is the feature we often see on surviving photographs and sketch plans (*Bildskizzen*). The system was very comprehensive and ensured bombing priorities could be quickly understood or changed at short notice. Each Luftwaffe airbase had a library of potential targets listed in the target documents, which is why so many survived the mass destruction of documents in 1945. British targets began to be added to the Target Libraries in late 1938 due to the Munich Crisis. The research into the potential of Britain as a dangerous enemy, *Studie Blau* (Study Blue) added considerable amounts of target material to the library in 1939.

Luftwaffe Target categories covered Armed Forces, Administration, Power, Gas and Water Supply, Chemical Industries, Iron and Metal Industries, Agricultural Production, Transportation and Communication, and special targets such as convoy assembly points, radar stations, and urban area targets (for potential mass retaliation). Every target type was given a two-digit identifier for the nature of the target. So, for example, Target GB 52 61 was Swansea Gasworks ('GB' for Great Britain, '52' for Power, Gas or water supply and '61' identifying the individual target).

The Luftwaffe's developing attitudes are seen in the target description categories. Amongst the ten categories of information relating to the target description are sections on workforce information, including ethnicity, political attitudes, and homes and accommodation. The Luftwaffe would not need such information unless they (at some stage) planned to wage war on these things. There is a precedent for collecting such information. At the end of World War One, the social collapse in Germany was seen by many as the main reason for the defeat of the German army. The air war principles of 1920s air war theorist Giulio Douhet advocated air war against civilians as the most effective method of attack, so it is not surprising that the Luftwaffe made provision for collecting such social information in their bombing documents.

Here are the target category numbers from the original Luftwaffe records that I came across. There are many more across South Wales will cover army and air force bases, town halls and important bridges. But, mostly, these are the targets in and around the Welsh ports. The amount of information is huge and thankfully the Luftwaffe never had the time or resources to destroy these targets in the way they would have like, although the damage and loss of life was still severe across Wales.

Geheim	Ort: Felindre.	Ziel=Nr. G.B. 53 70.
Zielstammkarte (L)	(Nähere Lage): Südl. Becken: 10 km N Swansea (Mitte), 1,3 km NO Felindre, am Oberlauf d. Lliw-Flusses.	Kartenbl.-Nr.Engl.26/1:100000.
Land: Großbritannien (S) England (Glamorganshire).	Geogr. Werte: 51°42'45" N. 3°57'25" W.	E.B.Nr.Engl.101/1:63360.

1. **Bezeichnung des Zieles:** Wasserwerke Swansea (Reservoire Felindre).

Vgl. mit Ziel·Nr. G.B. 53 69 Wasserwerke Swansea (Reservoir Cray).

2. **Bedeutung:** Wichtige Sammelbecken für die Wasserversorgung von Swansea und Umgebung.
Die Wasserreservoire von Felindre und Cray decken 9/10 des Wasserbedarfs von Swansea.

3. **Beschreibung des Zieles:** Höhe über NN: etwa 200 m.
   a) **Verkehrsanschlüsse:** Kein Eisenbahnanschluß.
   Fahrweg zur Straße Felindre-Swansea.

   b) **Ausdehnung insgesamt:**   **Bebaute Fläche:**

   c) **Bauweise, Bauausführung, Luftempfindlichkeit, Brandgefahr:**
   1. **Lower Lliw Reservoir.**
      Langgestrecktes, schmales Talsperrenbecken (1,3 km NO Felindre)
      Nördliche Hälfte (in N-S=Richtung verlaufend) 500 m lang und 50 m breit,
      südliche Hälfte (in O-W=Richtung verlaufend) 500 m lang und 120 m breit.
      Am SW-Rand des Beckens der 200 m lange, geradlinige Staudamm in NW-SO=Richtung verlaufend.
      Baumaterial des Staudammes: Erdaufschüttung mit schmaler Tonschicht in der Mitte.
      Höhe des Dammes vom Flußbettgrund bis Dammkrone: 35 m,
      Stärke des Dammes an der Basis etwa 60 m, an der Krone etwa 5 m.

   2. **Upper Lliw Reservoir.**
      Fast rechteckiges, breites Talsperrenbecken (4 km NO Felindre) in N-S=Richtung verlaufend.
      N-S = 700 m, O-W = 250 m.
      Am S-Rand des Beckens ein 250 m langer, erdaufgeschütteter Staudamm.
      In der SW-Ecke des Beckens das Ventilschieberhaus.

   d) **Erzeugnisse:** Trink- und Nutzwasser für öffentliche, gewerbliche und industrielle Zwecke.

   Flughindernisse: Im O, W und N der Talsperrenbecken unmittelbar ansteigende Höhen bis 300 m.

   f) **Belegschaft:**
   Männer, Frauen, Volkszugehörigkeit,
   politische Einstellung, Unterbringung.

Secret

Target master card (L)

Country: Great Britain (s)
England
(Glamorganshire)

Location: Felindre
(Close location) Sudl. pool Swansea (centre)
Felindre on the upper reaches of the d. Lliw River
Geogr. location

Target=No G.B. 53 70

Card sheet=No.
Engl. 26/1: 1: 100 000

GB No. Engl. 101/1: 63 360

1. Name of the Target: Waterworks Swansea
(Felindre Reservoirs)

Compare with target=no G.B. 53 69 Swansea Waterworks (Cray Reservoir)

2. Significance:
Important collecting basins for the water supply of Swansea and the surrounding area.

The Felindre and Cray reservoirs provide 9/10 ths of Swansea's water needs

3. Description of the Target

a) Professional connections

b) Total dimensions

c) Type of systems and equipment, design, construction, vulnerability to air, risk of fire

1. Lower Lliw Reservoir

Elongated, narrow dam basin (1.3 km NE Felindre)
Northern half (running N-S direction) 500 m long and 50 m wide
southern half (running E-W) 500 m long and 120 m wide.
On the SW edge of the basin is the 200 m long, straight-line dam running in a NW-SE direction.
Construction material of the dam: earth fill with a narrow clay layer in the middle
Height of the dam from the bottom of the riverbed to the top of the dam: 35 m
Thickness of the dam at the base about 60 m, at the crown about 5 m

2. Upper Lliw Reservoir

Almost rectangular, wide dam basin (4 km NE Felindre) running in a N-S direction.
N-S = 700 m, E-W = 250 m
On the S edge of the pool is the valve house.

d) **Products:** Drinking and industrial water for public, commercial and industrial purposes.

Obstacles to flight: Immediately rising heights of up to 300 m in the E, W and N of the dam basin

e) Production quantity per month

Geheim   GB. 5370 c

Felindre
Wasserwerke Swansea
(Reservoire Felindre)

Länge (westl. Greenw.) 3°57'25", Breite 51°42'45"
Missweisung:- 12°19' (Mitte 1940)
1:63360   Bl. Nr. 101
1:100000 Bl. Nr. 26

① Ventilschieberhaus
② Staudamm
③ "   "

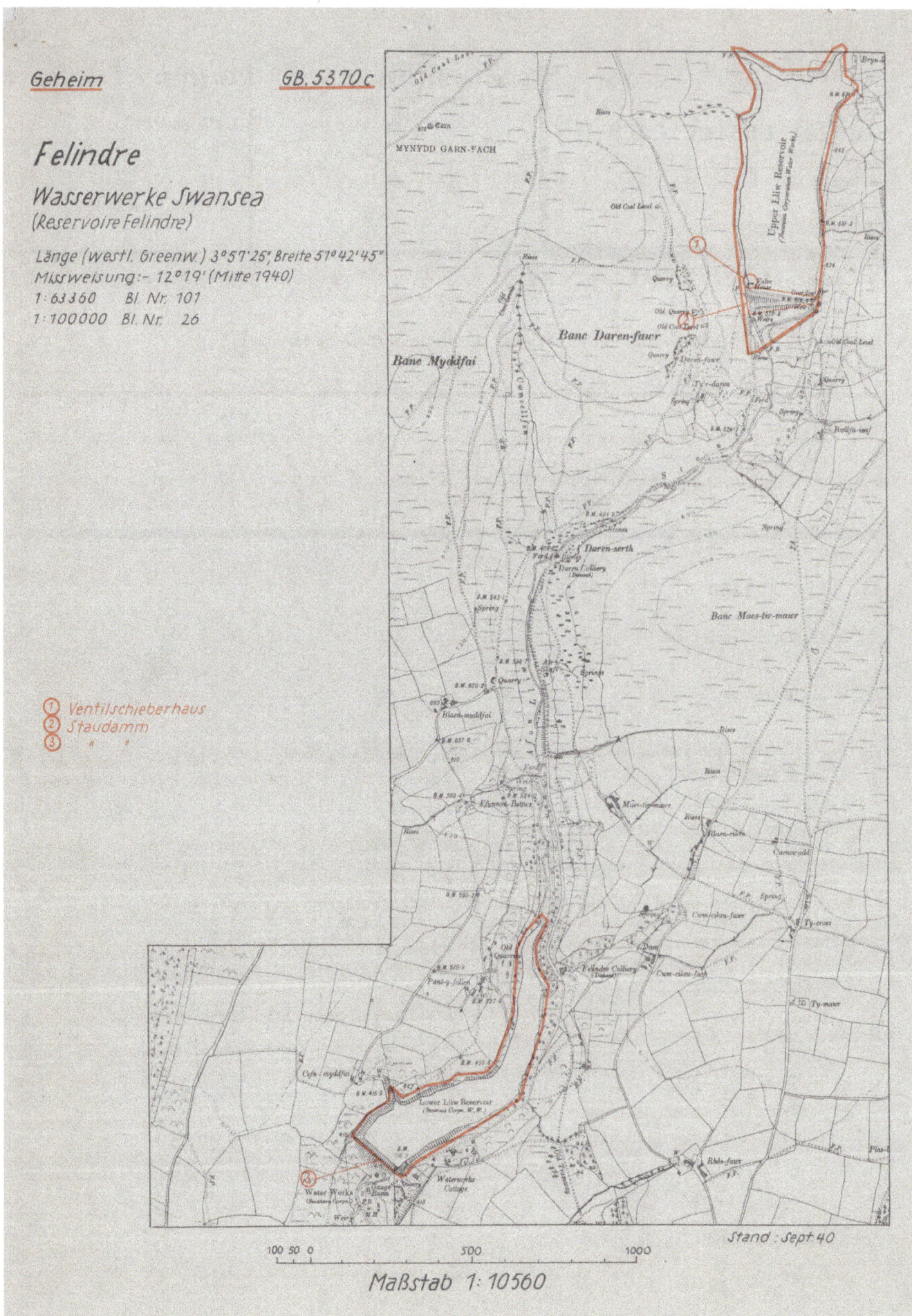

Stand: Sept. 40

Maßstab 1:10560

Target Type	Target Numbers	Welsh Examples
Military Installations	10. Airfields and ground services	1037 Cardiff, Airfield 10226 Swansea, Airfield 10294 Llandewi, Airfield
	11. Flak positions and barrage balloons	
	13. Barracks, schools	
	14. Military training areas	
	15. Military Radio stations	
	16. Fortifications and coastal fortifications	
	17. Radar	
	20. Supply bases for the air force	2021 Newport, Storage
	21. Fuel storage	2155 Cardiff, Ely Fuel storage 2156 Swansea, Tank farm Queen's Dock
	22. Ammunition store	2253 Swansea, Munitions
	23. Army/Navy administrative buildings	
	24. Arsenals and repair workshops	
Administration	30. Central Authority	
	31. Regional Administrative Authorities	
	33. Authorities of Civil Air Defence	
Transportation and communication	40. Railway Stations, loading ramps, workshops	
	41. Railways, bridges, tunnels, junctions	
	42. Railway lines	
	43. Streets, Bridges, Tunnels	
	44. Roads	

Left: The Luftwaffe *Bildskizzen* for the Felindre Reservoirs. The date at the foot of the sketch of September 1940 confirms this research was part of Study Blue. The Luftwaffe had specialised bombs and aircraft to attack these kinds of structures, however, luckily, their special units were busy attacking the naval bases of Portsmouth and Plymouth. This is a good example of the wider scope of economic warfare that the Luftwaffe wanted to conduct, but ultimately they never had the resources or the strategy. It is one of the enduring British myths that the RAF pioneered 'dam-busting' tactics.

Above and following pages: A summary of all of the targets and target numbers I have come across in researching targets across South Wales. There will be many more but records have not survived or have yet to come to light for historical analysis.

Target Type	Target Numbers	Welsh Examples
	45. Port Facilities	4557 Newport, South and North Docks 4561 Cardiff, Bute East Dock 4517 Cardiff, Roath Basin 4560 Cardiff, Roath Dock 4562 Cardiff, Bute West Dock 4559 Cardiff, Queen Alexandra Dock 45183 Penarth, Dock 4564 Barry, Docks 4565 Port Talbot, Harbour basin, lock and dry dock 45120 Briton Ferry, Dock 4567 Swansea, South Dock 4566 Swansea, King's and Prince of Wales Docks 4568 Swansea, Queen's Dock 45118 Llanelli, Dock 4570 Burry Port, Dock
	46. Inland waterways	
	47. Telephone and telegraph centres	
	48. Cables for telephone and telegraph	
	49. Radio stations	
Power, Gas, Water Supply	50. Power stations	5054 Newport Power Station 5055 Cardiff, Large power station 5056 Swansea, Power Station
	51. Electrical Installations	
	52. Gasworks and pipelines	5256 Newport, Crindau Gasworks 5257 Cardiff, Gasworks 5261 Swansea, Gas works 5257 Cardiff, Grangetown Gasworks
	53. Waterworks, pumping stations, reservoirs	5369 Cray, Reservoir for Swansea 5370 Felindre, Reservoirs for Swansea
	54. Drainage and sewage plants	
Chemical industry		
	60. Coal mines	
	61. Coking plants	
	62. Chemical industries	
	63. Explosives factories	
	64. Factories for pulp, paper, rayon, textiles	
	65. Petroleum industries	6551 Llandarcy, Oil refinery

Target Type	Target Numbers	Welsh Examples
	66. Smelting plants for calcium carbide, and ferro-alloys	
	67. Artificial materials and insulating materials	
	68. Gas protection products, nebulisers and plants	
Iron and Metal industries	70. Ore mills, blast furnaces, steel mills and rolling plants, rolling mills	7032 Cardiff Dowlais works 7067 Port Talbot, Blast furnaces and steelworks 7063 Port Talbot, Steelworks 7069 Swansea, Landore industrial complex 7070 Swansea, Landore industrial complex
	71. Non-ferrous metals, ore mines, metallurgical plants, rolling mills	7115 Newport, Aluminium works 7127 Swansea, Swansea, Industrial complex
	73. Factories for aircraft engines	
	76. Explosives and ammunition factories	7617 Cardiff, Munitions
	78. Arms factories	7811 Newport Arms Factory 7810 Newport, Lysaghts Iron
	83. Shipyards	8353 Newport, Graving docks 8354 Newport, Mountstuart Yards 8355 Newport, Tredegar Yards, Cruisers 8356 Cardiff, Dry dock 8357 Cardiff, Dry dock 8358 Cardiff, Mountstuart dry dock 8359 Barry, 3 Drydocks 8362 Swansea, Palmers Drydock 8363 Swansea, Prince of Wales Drydock 8365 Swansea, Drydock
	84. Electrical Engineering	
	85. Optics, precision factories	
Agricultural	56. Storage, warehouses, large mills, sugar factories	5622 Cardiff, Grain store 5643 Cardiff, Grain store 5642 Cardiff, Grain store 5648 Barry, Grain and Cold stores 5650 Swansea, Weavers Grain Mills

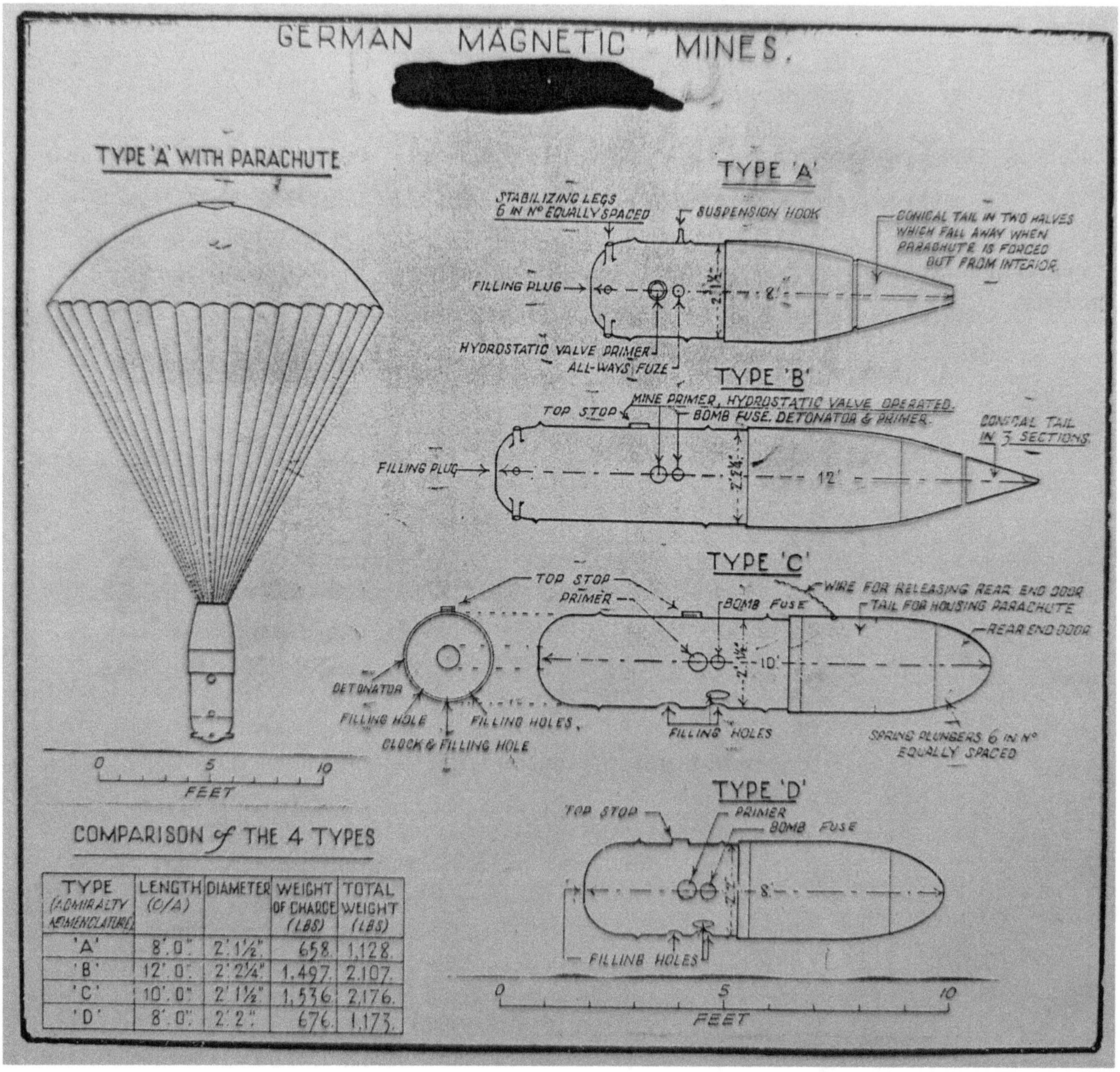

GERMAN MAGNETIC MINES

TYPE 'A' WITH PARACHUTE

TYPE 'A'
- Stabilizing legs 6 in N° equally spaced
- Suspension hook
- Filling plug
- Hydrostatic valve primer
- All-ways fuze
- Conical tail in two halves which fall away when parachute is forced out from interior.
- 8'
- 2'1½"

TYPE 'B'
- Mine primer, hydrostatic valve operated.
- Bomb fuse, detonator & primer.
- Top stop
- Filling plug
- Conical tail in 3 sections.
- 12'
- 2'2¼"

TYPE 'C'
- Top stop
- Primer
- Bomb fuse
- Wire for releasing rear end door
- Tail for housing parachute
- Rear end door
- Detonator
- Filling hole
- Filling holes
- Clock & filling hole
- Filling holes
- Spring plungers 6 in N° equally spaced
- 10'
- 2'1½"

TYPE 'D'
- Top stop
- Primer
- Bomb fuse
- Filling holes
- 8'

COMPARISON of THE 4 TYPES

TYPE (ADMIRALTY NOMENCLATURE)	LENGTH (O/A)	DIAMETER	WEIGHT OF CHARGE (LBS)	TOTAL WEIGHT (LBS)
'A'	8' 0"	2' 1½"	658	1,128
'B'	12' 0"	2' 2¼"	1,497	2,107
'C'	10' 0"	2' 1½"	1,536	2,176
'D'	8' 0"	2' 2"	676	1,173

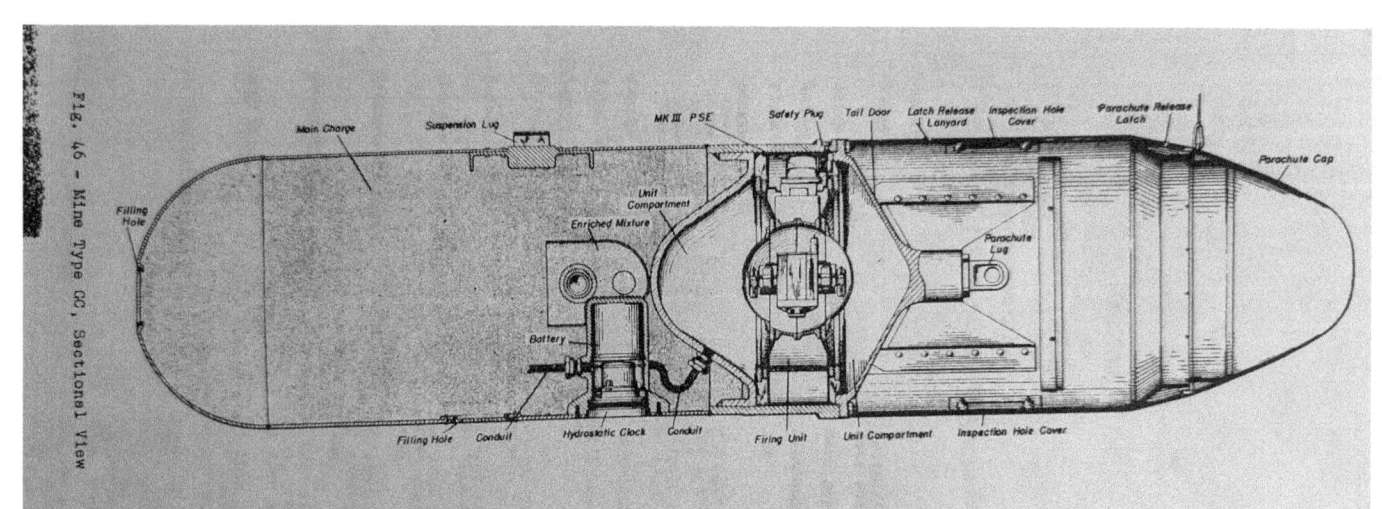

Fig. 46 - Mine Type GC, Sectional View

164

3. Air-dropped magnetic mines

The mine war in the Bristol Channel was discussed in an earlier chapter. However, the adaptation of the magnetic mine into a massive blast terror weapon was a dreadful development. All air forces entered the war with the belief that high explosive bombs were the best weapon to use against both armies and civilians. The Luftwaffe certainly had a growing view that this was not necessarily the case and that civilian areas and houses were better destroyed with incendiaries. However, in the early years of the war, the 'big bomb' argument was popular with both the Luftwaffe and the RAF. German and American firemen were increasingly vocal about the danger of fire attacks and the need for effective fire defences.

The Luftwaffe's perennial shortage of larger bombs not least because of Nazi government intervention in procurement policies) and the inadequacy of most Luftwaffe bombers in carrying large bombs meant that the Germans had limited capacity to drop big bombs on the ports.

The fact that the magnetic mine had a series of fuses designed to explode the bomb if it didn't land in water quickly led to the understanding of the huge devastation that could be caused by a mine landing (by mistake) on an urban area. Luftwaffe crews who had witnessed mines detonating over urban areas remarked on the massive flash and shock wave generated by these high-capacity explosive devices. The Luftwaffe never liked the parachute-retarded delivery of a mine as its tendency to drift in the wind made aiming impossible. But in a terror-bombing war, this didn't matter.

Magnetic mines as terror weapons were first dropped on London on 16 September 1940. That night, at least seventeen of the hugely expensive devices failed to detonate, providing the Royal Navy with opportunities to defuse and understand the mine. After this attack, mines were dropped on urban areas in addition to normal bomb attacks. The devastation created by the mine detonating at rooftop height was massive and far reaching and it was a point not lost on the RAF when they came to create massive blast bombs for use against German cities after 1943.

Swansea and Cardiff were both attacked with air-dropped mines as terror weapons. However, the Luftwaffe also regularly dropped mines as anti-ship weapons off Swansea and Cardiff and the wider Bristol Channel in the sea lanes, causing considerable chaos for ship movements.

Left: Extracts from official British records from 1941 illustrating the nature of aerial mines being dropped on towns and cities. As the mine was a naval weapon, it fell to the Royal Navy to lead defusing mines and devising countermeasures. The emergency fuses designed to detonate the mine if it fell on dry land often malfunctioned, leading to many examples of the mine eventually made available for British technical experts. All the Royal Navy had to do was defuse them in the first place. The history of bomb disposal records many incidents of extreme valour where naval officers worked to defuse bombs in incredibly difficult circumstances.

Index

A

Abadan in Persia (later Iran) 123
Air Ministry, British 12
apples, (Canadian) 12

B

Barcelona 8
Barrage Balloons, Barry 112
Barry 105
   Port improvements. See 105
Bildskizzen (sketch plans) 157
bomb aiming (difficulties) 24
   bombsight would cause considerable difficulties 32
   Schwerpunkt Swansea 1941 138
Bombing decoy sites
   Leckwith 99
Bombs
   Advanced electrical fuses 33
   bomb packages 33
   characteristics 34
   SC-250 31
Bristol/Avonmouth 42
British radar service 10
Büchel, Kptlt. Paul 149

C

Cardiff
   Dowlais steelworks 88
   first mentioned as a target 42
   Leckwith dummy bomb site 99
   Port improvements. See 88
Coal
   Coal exports 41
   pitwood and mining timber 42
   pitwood and mining timber pond, Barry 106
   strategic campaign against the timber trade 83

D

Deutsch Lufthansa 10
diversion of shipping, 1917 13
Docks
   Alexandra Docks (North and South), Newport 75
   Briton Ferry 127
   Bute East Dock, Cardiff 87
   Bute West Dock, Cardiff 87
   Channel Dry Dock, Cardiff 91
   Dock No. 1, Barry 105
   Dock No. 2, Barry 105
   growth of road haulage 54
   King's Dock, Swansea 131
   marshalling yards, junctions and working routines 54
   No. 9 Transit Shed, Newport 76
   North Dock-Half-Tide Basin, Swansea 139
   North Dock, Swansea 131
   Palmer's Dry Dock, Swansea 61
   Penarth Dock 101
   Prince of Wales Dock, Swansea 131
   Queen Alexandra Dock, Cardiff 27, 87
      grain mills 50
      in Stadtplan 51
   Queen's Dock, Swansea 46, 136
   Roath Dock, cardiff 44
   Roath Dock, Cardiff 87
   South Dock, Swansea 131
   Supply Reserve Depot (SRD), Barry 106
   Tredegar and Eastern No. 2, Newport 76
Douhet, Giulio 7, 157
Dowlais, Cardiff steelworks 18
   background and images 96
   Dowlais works rebuilt 56
   photo 20, 50

F

'familiarity bias' 5
Fear of terror bombing 7
Felmy, Helmut Air Fleet Two 12
   initial battle plans 15
   lack of preparation 15
firestorm in Paris in 1918 7
Food
   cold storage 42
      refrigerated meat wagons 90
   grain mills and silos 42
   increase in frozen meat trade 54
   Live cattle imports into Cardiff 87
   Rank grain mill, Barry 106
   Spillers Mills (grain), Cardiff 87
   Weaver's Grain Mills, Swansea 131, 139
French airbases and airfields 32
'Fritz-X' (radio-controlled glide bombs.) 16

G

Generalstab des Heeres Abteilung für Kriegskarten und Vermessungswesen 42
German intelligence services

chaotic state 15
German Navy 18
Glamorganshire Canal 87
Graf Zeppelin (airship) 26
Grangemouth on the Forth estuary 123
Great Western Railway Company (GWR) 41
   Welsh ports in the Bristol Channel 41

H

Hansard 28
Haushofer, Karl 8
Headlam Committee, 13

I

incendiary bomb (Elektron') 29
   (Brandgefahr) 90
   firestorms 29
Intelligence gathering 8
Intelligence myths 5
Intelligence services in Nazi Germany 10

J

Jeschonnek
   and Studie Blau 27
Jeschonnek, Hans 22

K

Karlsruhe Monographs 6
Kesselring, Albert 30
Knauss, Robert 8

L

Langdon-Davies, John 8
Liverpool 42
Llandarcy (oil storage) 24
   Anglo-Persian storage 46
   as a target 42
Llandarcy (Swansea) 123
Lower Swansea Valley. 140
Luftwaffe
   destroying documentaion in 1945 6
   Fernaufklärungsgruppe 123 (Aufkl.Gr.(F)123 67
     Buc Airfield 72
     first reconnaissance flights 68
   Fliegerausgabe (Aviation Edition) 67
   Flight maps 48
   III/KG 30 63
   Karlsruhe monographs 6
   KGr 126 63
   map libraries 34
   nine types of 'missions.' 33
     Mission Type Five: Combat action against enemy resources 33
     Mission Type Seven: Disruption of enemy food supplies 33
     Mission Type Six: Action to prevent enemy import traffic 33
   priority targets 33
   radio intercept services 26
     constructs RAF order of Battle 28

M

Militärgeographische Angaben. 42
Militärgeographische Angaben (Military Geographic Details) 42
Militärgeographische Einzelangabe 16
Mines, magnetic 7, 147, 165
   aerial mines as blast bombs 36
   British diagram 58
   degaussing of ships 56
   HMS Vernon 62
   limitations in use 58
   Rheinmetall-Borsig 58
   Shoeburyness. 62
   submarine-launched 58
   TMB mine 58
   TMC mine 59
mine war
   air dropping mines 62
   Bristol Channel 59
   German developments 56
   war gamed 27
Ministry of Transport, (Britain) 14
Monmouthshire and Brecon Canal 75
Mountstuart shipyards Cardiff 50
   photo 54
Munich 1938 10
   For the British 11
   For the Germans 14
   Munich Agreement 18

N

Newport
   Alexandra Docks (North and South) 75
   Aluminium manufacturing 85
   Crindau Gasworks 48
   Neptune Works 75
   Port improvements 77
   Railway timber 54
   Stadtplan 75

O

Oil
   introducing oil refining into South Wales 41
   Llandarcy 42, 123
Open-source intelligence 28
   Cardiff example 94
Ordnance Survey maps 15

P

parachute flares 20
Paris, firestorm attacks 1918 35
Penarth Docks 101
poor moral fibre of British citizens, 6
Port, primary functions 49
   general cargo 49
   heavy-lift cranes 49
Port Talbot
   Port improvements. See 117

Q

Queen Alexandra Dock, Cardiff
   unloading grain 27

R

radar service (British) 10

radar networks 26
RAF Middle Wallop 73
Reich Defence Committee, 1934 10
Royal Air Force Air Historical Branch 6

S

Scarweather Lightship 149
Schmid, Joseph 'Beppo' 15
Schwerpunkt (main emphasis) of any bombing. 90
Severn Tunnel 112
   moving goods through 14
Severn Tunnel, critical link 54
Ship repair crisis, January 1941 56
Ships
   Loch Goil 59
   Protesilaus
     photo 70
   Protesilaus, 59
     The British steamer cut in half 61
South Wales road map 54
Spanish Civil War 7
Stadtpläne (town plans)
   Cardiff Bay 87
   Central Swansea. See 130
   Newport 75
   Port Talbot. See 116
   Queen Alexandra and Roath Docks 94
   Swansea's Royal Docks. See 132
Steinmann, Heinrich 16
   background 24
   target classification system 30
stereoscopic photography 5
Studie Blau (Study Blue) 16
   and Studie Blau 27
   conclusions 30
   reconstructed, 1950s 26
   research team 27
   scope 26
   Studie Blau begins 18
   Studie Blau details 20
   the three pre-requisites 30
   transportation and communication 28
Supply Reserve Depot (SRD), Barry 106, 112
Swansea
   Blitz attack February 1941 29
   Cambrian Spelter works, 140
   Clyne Valley 70
   first mentioned as a target. 42
   impact of incendiaries 35, 70
   Kilvey Hill 138
   Lower Swansea Valley. 140
   Singleton Abbey 71
   Singleton Park 137
   Townhill estate 71
   White Rock and Middle Bank 140

T

Taff Vale Rail Company 101
target classification system 24
   Target numbers in the ports 34
telecommunication network (Wales) 22
'terror-bombing 8
   terror bombing to achieve a quick capitulation of defences 33

Tir John North, Swansea (power station) 16
transit shed, importance 49
   D Shed, Swansea 136
Trenchard, Hugh 8

U

U-boats
   U28 58
     off Ilfracombe 59
     Swansea mission 59
   U29 58
   U32 58, 147
   U33 58

V

victory' bias 5
von Clausewitz, Karl 32
von Rohden, Hans Detlef Herhudt 8

W

Weimar Republic 28
Welsh main electricity network 16

Z

Zeppelin airships against London 6
Zielstammkarten (Target Dossiers) 7, 24, 157
Zielstammkarte (Target Master Map) 16, 147
   Briton Ferry, Target GB 45 120. See 129
   Cardiff Queen Alexandra Dock (Target GB 45 59) 90
   llandarcy Oil Refinery 124
   Lliw Reservoirs, Swansea, Target GB 53 70. See 159
   Newport Target GB 45 67 79
   Penarth, Target GB 45 183 102, 124
   Port Talbot, Target GB 45 65 118
   South Dock, Swansea, Target GB 45 67 144
   Swansea (Weavers) grain mills, Target GB 56 50. See 142

www.ingramcontent.com/pod-product-compliance
Lightning Source LLC
Chambersburg PA
CBHW080902230426
43663CB00013B/2603